S0-BDM-144

The
ADA
Programming
Language

A GUIDE FOR PROGRAMMERS

I.C. PYLE
Department of Computer Science
University of York, England

Prentice Hall **PHI** **International**

ENGLEWOOD CLIFFS, NEW JERSEY   LONDON   NEW DELHI
SINGAPORE   SIDNEY   TOKYO   TORONTO   WELLINGTON

British Library Cataloguing in Publication Data

Pyle, Ian C
 The Ada programming language.
 1. Ada (Computer program language).
 I. Title
 001.6'42 QA76.73.A35
 ISBN 0-13-003921-7

Library of Congress Cataloguing in Publication Data

Pyle, Ian C 1934-
 The Ada Programming Language
 1. Ada (Computer program language)
 I. Title.
 QA76.73.A35P94 001.64'24 80-25034
 ISBN 0-13-003921-7 (pbk)

© 1981 by PRENTICE-HALL INTERNATIONAL INC.

All rights reserved. No part of this publication may be reproduced,
stored in a retrieval system, or transmitted, in any form or by any
means, electronic, mechanical, photocopying, recording or otherwise,
without the prior permission of Prentice-Hall International Inc.
London.

ISBN 0-13-003921-7

PRENTICE-HALL INTERNATIONAL, INC. *London*
PRENTICE-HALL OF AUSTRALIA PTY. LTD., *Sydney*
PRENTICE-HALL OF CANADA, LTD., *Toronto*
PRENTICE-HALL OF INDIA PRIVATE LIMITED, *New Delhi*
PRENTICE-HALL OF JAPAN, INC., *Tokyo*
PRENTICE-HALL OF SOUTHEAST ASIA PTE., LTD. *Singapore*
PRENTICE-HALL INC., *Englewood Cliffs, New Jersey*
WHITEHALL BOOKS LIMITED, *Wellington, New Zealand*

10 9 8 7 6 5 4 3 2 1

Printed in the United States of America

Contents

Chapter 11   INPUT/OUTPUT AND REPRESENTATIONS   138

Chapter 12   MORE ON TYPES   163

Chapter 13   MORE ON TASKING   200

APPENDICES

To Margaret

Preface

Ada is a new programming language, sponsored by the United States Department of Defense, designed under the leadership of Jean D. Ichbiah. The language is a major advance in programming technology, bringing together the best ideas on the subject in a coherent way designed to meet the real needs of practical programmers. It is the first result of a substantial effort to identify the requirements for programming and satisfy them effectively.

This book is written primarily for practicing programmers of embedded computer systems, giving a full presentation of the power of Ada to those whose working environment will be greatly changed by it during the next few years. Other readers will include programmers of non-embedded systems, for whom most of the facilities will be relevant, and teachers of programming who will benefit from the breadth and coherence of Ada's facilities. In addition, the book should be of value to managers of programming projects, since Ada strongly assists the development of large programs.

In keeping with the primary aim of the book, the style of presentation presumes a knowledge of programming. Topics are introduced in the context of embedded computer systems, in an order which reflects the normal pattern used in programming. This is not necessarily the best order for introductory teaching of the skill of programming itself.

Chapters 1 to 5 cover the basic features of Ada, which any programmer needs to know. The subsequent chapters deal with more advanced features, which should only be studied after the basic features are thoroughly understood. Chapters 6 to 8 deal with particular programming concepts in Ada which will probably be new to most programmers. Chapters 9 and 10 cover the issues of program structure, which take traditional ideas as the start, but make significant extensions. Chapter 11 deals with machine specific issues, and shows how they can be expressed in a machine independent language. Chapters 12 and 13 give an advanced treatment and more details on topics introduced previously. The appendices contain certain notes and definitions of various particular items in Ada.

The official definition of Ada is the Language Reference Manual and Formal Definition, not this book. It is possible that the language may be changed in the light of experience and discovered problems; also, it is to be submitted for formal standardization, and this may require changes at some time in the future. This book differs from an official definition in that the official definition of a language must satisfy both programmers and compiler-writers, two very different kinds of reader. Unfortunately, this usually means that the definition goes barely far enough to satisfy the compiler-writers, and tends to have complications of notation and formality which make it unsatisfactory for programmers. This book is intended to explain the language to programmers who wish to learn Ada without having to become compiler specialists.

Most of the chapters finish with some programming exercises, which readers may use to test their understanding of the ideas presented. The solutions to these exercises are given elsewhere in the book, as examples of other aspects of Ada programs.

As most readers will know, the language is named after a real person, Augusta Ada, Countess of Lovelace, who first programmed a computer, before either computers or programming had been recognized as such.

I wish to thank the many people who have helped me during the course of preparing this book, particularly Ian Wand and Brian Wichmann. The syntax diagrams were produced by a program written by Colin Runciman and David Keeffe. Most of the typing was done by Val Fry.

Most of all, I thank my family for their encouragement and support while Ada has been living with us.

March 1981   I.C.P.

CHAPTER 1

Introduction

Ada is for programming embedded computer systems - that is, systems in
which a computer is directly connected to some apparatus or plant which
it monitors and/or controls. This means that Ada can be used for
conventional programming (which actually accounts for the majority of
embedded computer system programming) and also for the special technical
requirements concerning input/output, timing relationships, contingency
programming to cope with errors, and long-term maintenance.

Embedded computer systems range from intelligent terminals and smart
instrumentation to air traffic control or factory automation, via
laboratory data monitoring, numerically controlled machine tools,
navigation and guidance systems, stored program controlled telephone
exchanges, batch and continuous production control, environmental
monitoring, and future domestic products containing microcomputers. The
computer involved may be large or small, single or a collection of many
processors, or part of a computer network.

It is expected, however, that the program concerned in each system
would have a lifetime of several years, and consequently that people
other than the original programmers would be involved in maintaining it.
This concern for maintenance underlies much of the style of Ada.

Ada gives special attention to the ease of reading and understanding
programs - it is based on the realisation that it is more important to
be able to read a program and understand it clearly than to be able to
write it quickly or briefly. We therefore tend to use fairly long names
and identifiers in an Ada program, and state the assumptions which the
design of the program implies. The reason for this is that the writer
of the program does his job once, but maintainers of the program may
have to read the program many times throughout its life.

1

1.1   An Ada program

Programs in Ada specify not only the actions inside computers, but also
the interactions between the computers and the environment in which they
are embedded. Since the interactions with the environment can be quite
tricky to program, it is usual to design separate pieces of program to
deal with the various kinds of input/output devices, and the resulting
pieces of program are kept in libraries. For a simple Ada program, we
use an existing library package to handle the input/output, and specify
the particular actions we want by calling on facilities made available
by the package.

   In this first example we show a trivial program in Ada. The program
is written as a procedure, which specifies the actions to be carried
out. In an Ada development environment, many procedures will be held in
a library, where they are available for use in other programs. In
practice, all programs are likely to refer to the library for units
defining many commonly required actions such as input/output and
mathematical functions. A package called STANDARD is always available;
it is specified in Appendix A. For this example, we use a library
package called TEXT_IO. (Its definition is also given in Appendix A.
It is significant that the package specification is itself written in
Ada.) A program must begin by listing the units it needs; these will be
extracted from the library by the translator.

```
with TEXT_IO; use TEXT_IO;
procedure EX_1 is
  pragma MAIN;
begin
  NEW_LINE;
  PUT ("Hello");
end EX_1;
```


   The program is written using special key-words such as **with**,
procedure, **begin** and **end**, together with other words such as TEXT_IO,
PUT. The keywords are fixed for all Ada programs, and show the structure
of the program. The other words are called identifiers, and are invented
by the programmers to denote the particular entities concerned in the
program.

   This program needs the unit TEXT_IO (and no other), which defines the
procedures NEW_LINE and PUT (among others), and sets up input/output
files on suitable devices. The program prints the message

   Hello

on a new line on the output device. Notice that the program has a name
EX_1 which is given at the beginning and end, so that the body of the
program is clearly delimited.

1.2   Another program

This is a slightly more complicated program, but still very trivial and
unrealistic. It adds together two simple integers.

```
with TEXT_IO; use TEXT_IO;
procedure EX_2 is
  pragma MAIN;
  A, B : INTEGER range 0 .. 999;
begin
  GET (A); GET (B);
  NEW_LINE;
  PUT ("The sum of");
  PUT (A); PUT ("and"); PUT (B);
  PUT ("is"); PUT (A + B);
end EX_2;
```

Notice that the names A and B are used to hold the values which are read
in by the procedure GET (also defined in TEXT_IO). In order that the
program can know what to expect for the values before they are used, the
type and range for each must be declared at the head of the program.
The package STANDARD includes the definition of INTEGER and "+". This
package is automatically available for every program unit.

1.3   A real program

Any program for a genuine embedded computer system will be quite large,
and may be written as a collection of separate units in order that it
can be maintained effectively. Here is one unit of a program to control
a filtration plant (see figure 1a). River water is pumped through a
filter and clean water is delivered. After a time, the filter gets
clogged with debris and has to be cleaned by blowing air through and
draining out the sump; filtering can then resume. Occasionally a fault
in the valves may make it necessary to close down the whole plant.

```
with MAJOR_PHASES; use MAJOR_PHASES;
procedure SINGLE_FILTER is
begin
  START_UP;
```

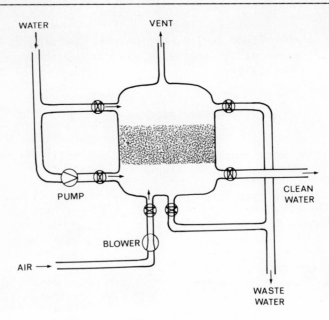

Figure 1a: Filtration Unit

```
loop
   DELIVER_WATER;
   CLEAN_FILTER;
end loop;

exception
   when others =>        -- FAULT or other trouble
      CLOSE_DOWN;
end SINGLE_FILTER;
```

Further details of the filtration unit are given in later examples.

Notice that this program unit shows how the action of SINGLE_FILTER is achieved in terms of application-specific procedures. These would be expressed in a separate unit that contains the specifications of the other procedures etc.:

```
package MAJOR_PHASES is
   procedure START_UP;
   procedure DELIVER_WATER;
   procedure CLEAN_FILTER;
   procedure CLOSE_DOWN;
   FAULT : exception;
end MAJOR_PHASES;
```

The details (bodies) of the procedures such as START_UP are written in a corresponding package body.

1.4   Form of an Ada program

The text of the Ada program consists mainly of two kinds of words and various punctuation marks. Words like **procedure**, **is**, **separate**, **end** (conventionally written in small letters) are reserved for special uses in Ada, and determine the main structure of the program. These are known as keywords. The other words, like SINGLE_FILTER, START_UP, FAULT, CLOSE_DOWN (conventially written in capital letters) are invented by the programmer, to denote the various entities in the program; these words are technically called identifiers. They must always be different from the Ada keywords.

As well as the main text of the program, whose structure is prescribed by the Ada language, there may be comments on any line, introduced by a double hyphen. Comments may contain any characters without restriction, for the rest of the line. They are used by the programmer to give additional information to the reader of the program, but this is not checked in any way by the compiler.

Another special construct in an Ada program is called a **pragma**: this is a phrase used to give information to the compiler about translating the program. A main program is written in Ada as a procedure, but marked:

   pragma MAIN;

Pragmas do not affect the meaning of a program, but may affect the way it is implemented (e.g. choice of optimisation). The possible pragmas in Ada are listed Appendix D.

1.5   Identifiers and naming

Identifiers are the fundamental creation of the programmer: they name the entities which are needed for the particular program he is designing. An identifier is made up using letters and digits (linked by underline characters) - which must be different from the Ada key words, disregarding the case of the letters. Identifiers may not contain spaces, and may not spread over from one line to another.

The words used to make an identifier should be carefully chosen to be a suitable name for the entity concerned: for example a verb (or verb clause) for a procedure (which denotes an action), and a noun (or a noun clause) for a data object (variable or constant). A type may be named by a suitable abstract noun. Choosing appropriate names is an important aspect of programming. These suggestions are of course not enforced by Ada, and do not constrain the creativity of the programmer. Examples of names are given throughout the book, as we introduce the various kinds of entity that can occur in an Ada program.

1.6   The environment of Ada programs

Ada programs are intended for execution in embedded computer systems – implying significant differences from the usage of conventional programming languages. The differences concern the way Ada programs are developed, and their operational environment. The main consequence is that Ada programs are usually cross-compiled on a host computer, distinct from the target computer for operational use; another important consequence is that an Ada program is likely to be the only program in a computer, with complete responsibility for its activities, not sharing facilities or implying an "operating system" of the conventional kind. The Ada programmer may specify how the various parts of the program interact with one another and with the equipment connected to it.

Some specific differences between Ada and other programming languages are noted in Appendices B (Fortran) and C (Pascal). The translation of an Ada program into its executable form is more than traditional compilation. It includes also the operations of linkage-editing and library module incorporation (which are done separately with other languages), and the provision of run-time facilities to implement the various semantic features of the language such as inter-task communication and dynamic storage allocation.

1.6.1   Ada Programming Support Environment

For the development of Ada programs, an Ada Programming Support Environment is planned. At the time of writing (1980), the requirements and main outline of this environment have been specified, but the actual details have not yet been settled.

Translation of an Ada program involves compilation of the separate units, with cross-checking of interfaces and provision of other required units from a library. The environment includes all the necessary utility programs and the data-base to contain the compiled units. This of course implies backing store equipment and peripherals for programmers to use - completely different from the target environment of the embedded computer system.

In order that Ada programs can be tested, it is expected that the support system would include facilities for simulating features of the target environment. These, and the other programs in the support environment, would also be written in Ada.

1.6.2   Ada Run-time Environment

Ada programs are executed in one or more computers embedded in a target environment. The run-time environment comprises hardware and software which together implement the semantics of Ada. How the run-time facilities are split between hardware and software is not prescribed by Ada; different computers require different run-time software to implement Ada on them.

An Ada program may be run on a single-computer system; this is the common way to presume its implementation. However, Ada does not require there to be only one computer, and a program with suitable restrictions (corresponding to the lack of direct communication between the processor in one computer and the store in a different computer) may be implemented in a multi-computer system. No details have yet been established for the restrictions necessary for multi-computer implementation of an Ada program.

A computer running an Ada program is dedicated to a specific task - controlling the system in which it is embedded. Consequently the Ada program in it is presumed to be the only program in the computer - not sharing facilities with others. (The Ada program may involve units written in other languages, provided that their interfaces and overall structure are consistent with Ada.) Thus Ada implies a single program but not necessarily a single computer.

Exercises

1. By analogy with A and B in EX_2, declare YEAR to be an integer between 1901 and 2099 inclusive.
    (See Appendix A, package CALENDAR, type TIME.)

2. Invent suitable names for the valves in the filtration unit in figure 1a.

(See section 2.1)

3. Cleaning the filter requires a blast of air and flushing with water
    (twice), then draining the sump.   Invent names for the actions,
    presume they are specified as in MAJOR_PHASES, and write the
    statements for the body of CLEAN_FILTER.
    (See section 5.2)

CHAPTER 2

Types and Values

In any program we are concerned with many different values of different
kinds. A fundamental idea in Ada is that every data item has a
particular type, which determines the possibilities for the values it
may have. For example, an integer has a value such as 1, 23, -54 or
7215802; a character has a value such as ´A´, ´x´, ´5´, ´%´. In common
with other `strongly-typed´ programming languages, Ada requires the
programmer to specify the type for every data item concerned in the
program, so that its usage can be checked. Most checking is done when
the program in Ada is compiled, and does not imply any run-time
overhead. Ada includes some predefined types; but most of the types in a
program will be invented by the programmer, suitable for the particular
application involved.

A type, then, gives the set of possibilities for a data item -
specifying not so much what its value currently happens to be, but what
it might ever legitimately be. This is of great importance in program
checking and maintenance: compilers make sure that the usage of every
data item is consistent with its set of possibilities, and when a
programmer needs to change a program, the type helps him to understand
the purpose of a data item.

2.1   Scalar Types

The simplest types are called scalars, and include numbers (integers and
real), characters (ASCII, or any other specified character set), truth
values (TRUE and FALSE) and enumeration types (in which the possible
values are listed explicitly).

9

An enumeration type is written

type DAY_NAME **is** (MONDAY, TUESDAY, WEDNESDAY,
                       THURSDAY, FRIDAY, SATURDAY, SUNDAY);

This allows data items of type DAY_NAME to have values which are one of
the given words. The notation DAY_NAME´FIRST means MONDAY and
DAY_NAME´LAST means SUNDAY. Enumeration types are a powerful way of
showing a set of possibilities:

    type VALVE_STATUS **is** (OPEN, CLOSED);

    type VALVE **is** (WATER_INLET,
        AIR_INLET, FLUSH_WATER, AIR_EXHAUST, SUMP_WATER,
        CLEAN_WATER, DIRTY_WATER);

    type PRESSURE **is** (THIN, LOW, MEDIUM, HIGH);

    Truth values record whether or not a condition is true. Ada has the
predefined type BOOLEAN for this purpose. It is actually an enumeration
type, with only two possible values, TRUE and FALSE.

    Numbers must always be given with a range, so that the lowest and
highest possible values are stated. For integers, this is sufficient to
define the type:

    type CENTS **is range** 0 .. 99;
    type BYTE **is range** 0 .. 255;
    type PROC_NO **is range** 0 .. 255;
    type BIG **is range** 1 .. 20000;

(This means that any attempt in a program to take such a data item
outside the range would be detected as an error, usually at run time).
The lowest and highest values need not be given explicitly, but may be
written as expressions (see chapter 3). Each implementation of Ada has
a predefined type INTEGER which covers the whole range of values
expressable in a machine word, also SHORT_INTEGER and LONG_INTEGER for
implementation-determined ranges shorter and longer than a machine word.
Ada allows the programmer to write machine-independent programs by
stating the range explicitly (as above), or when the situation demands
it, to go for machine dependence with consequent loss of portability by
use of a predefined implementation-dependent type.

    For characters, there is a predefined character set CHARACTER (see
Appendix A).   Other character sets may be introduced as enumeration

types; for example

    type HEXDIGIT **is** (´0´, ´1´, ´2´, ´3´, ´4´,
                    ´5´, ´6´, ´7´, ´8´, ´9´,
                    ´A´, ´B´, ´C´, ´D´, ´E´,
                    ´F´);

Notice that single characters may be given as possible enumeration values, enclosed in single quotes. An enumeration type containing characters may also contain other literal values given as identifiers, for non-printable characters (e.g. NUL, ENQ, CR, LF in the predefined character set).

All the types introduced above refer to discrete data items. They are collectively called discrete types.

The final group of scalar types refer to continuous quantities, although the values are of course still actually discrete. They are for approximate calculations – either floating point with a particular number of significant digits, or fixed point with a particular absolute accuracy (called delta).

    type DISTANCE **is digits** 6 **range** 0.0 .. 20000.0;
    type HEIGHT **is digits** 10 **range** 0.0 .. 1.0E5;   -- 1.0E5 = 100000.0
    type ANGLE **is digits** 4 **range** 0.0 .. 90.0;
    type FLOATING_POINT **is digits** 10 **range** -1.0E38..1.0E38;

    type FINE **is delta** 0.1 **range** 0.0 .. 1.0;
    type VERY_FINE **is delta** 0.001 **range** 0.0 .. 1.0;
    type FRAC **is delta** 0.001 **range** 0.0 .. 1.0;
    type VOLTS **is delta** 0.001 **range** 0.0 .. 5.0;

(meaning VOLTS are accurate to one millivolt, up to five volts.) Each implementation of Ada has a predefined type FLOAT, which covers the whole range of values expressable in a machine floating-point word, also SHORT_FLOAT and LONG_FLOAT for implementation determined floating point values shorter and longer than a machine word. Further details on real types are given in chapter 12.

2.2   Subtypes

There are many cases where the programmer expects a data value to take a subset of the values possible for a particular type, and it is more convenient to regard this as a constrained form of the base type rather than a completely separate type. If we have

subtype WEEK_DAY **is** DAY_NAME **range** MONDAY .. FRIDAY;

then any variable declared as a WEEK_DAY is of the type DAY_NAME but its values are constrained to be in the range MONDAY to FRIDAY. Any assignment to such a variable may require a run_time check to ensure that the constraint applies. Similarly,

subtype LOW_PRESSURE **is** PRESSURE **range** THIN .. MEDIUM;

allows objects to be declared which are type-compatible with PRESSURE, but constrained to the stated range.

A particularly important subtype is predefined:

subtype NATURAL **is** INTEGER **range** 1 .. INTEGER´LAST;

indicating definitely positive integral values up to the maximum of the implementation. We also use

subtype NON_NEGATIVE **is** INTEGER **range** 0 .. INTEGER´LAST;
subtype UP_TO_ONE **is** FLOAT **range** −1.0 .. 1.0;
subtype POSITIVE_FLOAT **is** FLOAT **range** 0.0 .. FLOAT´LAST;
subtype LOWER_CASE **is** CHARACTER **range** ´a´ .. ´z´

The idea of subtypes and constraints is to allow the programmer to state the intended set of values which might arise, both as an aid to his own thinking when writing the program, and to assist subsequent maintenance programmers who may have to change it. Subtypes are constructed by specifying an existing type by name, and, if required, giving a further constraint.   There are several different kinds of constraint, which are explained in chapter 12.

2.3   Records

Almost all useful data values are more complicated than scalars: typically they include a number of distinct components, each with its own type.

type SECTOR **is**
  record
    RADIUS : LENGTH;
    WIDTH : ANGLE;
  end record;

This defines a compound data type SECTOR consisting of two components — one called RADIUS which is of type LENGTH, the second called WIDTH, of type ANGLE. If there is a variable S of type SECTOR, its components are written S.RADIUS and S.WIDTH respectively.

A value of type SECTOR could be

(RADIUS => 1.0, WIDTH => 90.0)

or

(RADIUS => 2.1E5, WIDTH => 11.25)

or with expressions (of the right kind) where we show numbers. These compound values (called aggregates) may also be written with just the composed values in the correct order, thus

(1.0, 90.0)

or

(2.1E5, 11.25)

respectively. A record can have any number of components, of the same or different types:

```
type CABLE is
  record
    REDWIRE : BOOLEAN;
    BLUEWIRE : BOOLEAN;
  end record;

type VALVE_PARAMETERS is
  record
    TRANSITION : DURATION;
    CONDITION : VALVE_STATUS;
    CHANNEL : NATURAL;
  end record;
```

and adjacent components of the same type may be written together:

```
type TIME_OF_DAY is
  record
    HR   :  INTEGER range 0 .. 24;
    MIN, SEC : INTEGER range 0 .. 59;
  end record;
```

```
type SECTOR_3D is
  record
    R: LENGTH;
    THETA, PHI: ANGLE;
  end record;

type POSITION is
  record
    EAST, NORTH : LENGTH;
    HEADING : ANGLE;
  end record;
```

A POSITION consists of three components of which EAST and NORTH are both
of type LENGTH, and HEADING is of type ANGLE. A possible data value for
a variable of type POSITION is

    (EAST => 23.7, NORTH => -62.0, HEADING => 180.0)

A possible value of type TIME_OF_DAY is

    (HR => 7, MIN => 45, SEC => 0)

The components in a record may be of any named type or subtype (but
not the outer record type, or any type containing it). A constraint on
the type or subtype may be given explicitly, as shown in TIME_OF_DAY
above. The type of a record component may be given as a named
enumeration type, as in

```
type WIND_LAYER is
  record
    SPEED, HEIGHT : NON_NEGATIVE;
    AIR     : PRESSURE;
  end record;
```

The components of a record may themselves be records (with the
obvious restriction that they can not contain themselves):

```
type TRACK is
  record
    HERE : POSITION;
    NOW  : TIME_OF_DAY;
  end record;
```

The components of a variable of type TRACK themselves have components:
with the variable T, of type TRACK, we have components

```
T.HERE   -- of type POSITION
T.NOW    -- of type TIME_OF_DAY
```

and also subsidiary components such as

```
T.HERE.EAST   -- of type LENGTH
T.NOW.HR      -- of type INTEGER, constrained to range 0..24
```

Records may have variants (see section 12.3)

2.4   Arrays

Frequently data values include a number of distinct components all of
the same type; the individual components are distinguished by an index
which is a discrete type, an integer or enumeration type (including
Boolean and character).

```
    type COL_VEC is array (1 .. 4) of FLOAT;
    type SECTOR_LIST is array (1 .. 5) of SECTOR;
```

Any data value of type SECTOR_LIST consists of five components all of
type SECTOR. Thus, if SL is of type SECTOR_LIST, it has components
SL(1), SL(2), SL(3), SL(4), and SL(5), all of type SECTOR; consequently

```
    SL(3).WIDTH
```

is the WIDTH of the third component of SL, and is of type ANGLE.

A possible value of SL is

```
    (1 => (RADIUS => 10.0, WIDTH  => 360.0),
     2 => (RADIUS => 20.0, WIDTH  => 180.0),
     3 => (RADIUS => 40.0, WIDTH  =>  90.0),
     4 => (RADIUS => 80.0, WIDTH  =>  45.0),
     5 => (RADIUS => 160.0, WIDTH =>  22.5))
```

If several components have the same value, they may be written   together
as

```
    (1    => (RADIUS => 50.0,   WIDTH => 360.0),
     2|3 => (RADIUS => 150.0,  WIDTH => 120.0),
     4|5 => (RADIUS => 0.7,    WIDTH => 5.0))
```

or

```
(1     => (RADIUS => 50.0,    WIDTH => 360.0),
 2..4 => (RADIUS => 0.5,     WIDTH => 7.0),
 5     => (RADIUS => 0.7,     WIDTH => 5.0))
```

or

```
(1|3    => (RADIUS => 0.5, WIDTH => 7.0),
 others => (RADIUS => 0.7, WIDTH => 5.0))
```

The elements of an array may be of any named type. If the elements are required to be records, the element-type must be first declared and given a name. (It is not allowed to give the element-type-definition within the array definition.) The element-type may be constrained, either by an intermediate subtype declaration or by attaching a constraint to the element type in the array definition. Thus we may write

```
type VALVE_CONTROL is
  record
    OPERATE : CHANNEL;
    CHECK   : CHANNEL;
  end record;

type VALVE_CHANNELS is
  record
    CONTROL : array (VALVE_STATUS) of VALVE_CONTROL;
    LAMP    : CHANNEL;
  end record;
```

The components of an array may be records, and the components of a record may be arrays.

If a component of a record is an array, then the array definition may be given explicitly in the record definition, without needing a distinct type declaration:

```
record
  DAY : DAY_NAME;
  LEVELS : array (1 .. 5) of PRESSURE;
end record;
```

For any other kind of component (enumeration, inner record, derived type), the type must be declared explicitly in a type declaration, and the type name used in the component of the record.

The index of an array may be of an enumeration type:

type LED_CODE **is array** (HEX_DIGIT) **of** BYTE;

for which a possible data value is

(´0´ => 16#5F#, ´1´ => 16#18#, ´2´ => 16#6D#,
´3´ => 16#79#, ´4´ => 16#3A#, ´5´ => 16#73#,
´6´ => 16#76#, ´7´ => 16#19#, ´8´ => 16#7F#,
´9´ => 16#3B#,
´A´ => 16#1F#, ´B´ => 16#7D#, ´C´ => 16#43#,
´D´ => 16#5D#, ´E´ => 16#67#, ´F´ => 16#27#)

corresponding to use of a seven-segment LED display as shown in figure 2. (Notice that hexadecimal numbers are introduced by 16; similarly octal numbers are written 8#...#.)

An array whose index is an enumeration type, and whose components are BOOLEAN, represents a set (in the mathematical sense) of the elements of the enumeration type. Thus

type DAY_SET **is array** (DAY_NAME) **of** BOOLEAN;

gives us a set of possible days – for example

(SATURDAY| SUNDAY => FALSE, **others** => TRUE)

Similarly

type STATUS_SET **is array** (STATUS) **of** BOOLEAN;

introduces a type with data values such as

(SUCCESS| NO_IPM_BUFFER .. NO_NET_BUFF => TRUE,
  others => FALSE)

Note that all the components of the array must have their values specified (TRUE or FALSE). The keyword **others** stands for all index values not previously mentioned.

Arrays may have multiple indices, each of a stated type:

type MATRIX **is array** (1 .. 4, 1 .. 4) **of** FLOAT;
type GRID **is array** (1 .. 100, 1 .. 100) **of** BOOLEAN;

so that a data item of type GRID, say G, has components (all of type BOOLEAN) such as

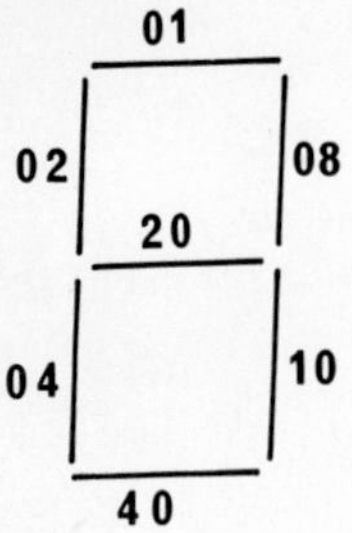

Figure 2a: Seven-segment LED

0	5F	01011111
1	18	00011000
2	6D	01101101
3	79	01111001
4	3A	00111010
5	73	01110011
6	77	01110111
7	1B	00011011
8	7F	01111111
9	7B	01111011
A	3F	00111111
B	76	01110110
C	47	01000111
D	7C	01111100
E	67	01100111
F	27	00100111

Figure 2b: LED characters

$$G(=,=)$$
$$G(1,1), \; G(15,25), \; G(99,1), \; G(1\tfrac{1}{4}\tfrac{1}{4}$$
$$G(1,1), \; G(15,25), \; G(99,1), \; G(100,100)$$

and the whole array G has a possible value

$$(\text{others} \tfrac{3}{8}$$
$$(\text{others} == \text{ FALSE})$$

The indices may have different types:

type RATE **is array** (DAY_NAME, 0 .. 23) **of** FLOAT;

A data item of type RATE would have a component for each possible day name with each integer from 0 to 23. All the components are floating point.

The component-type of an array must always be named. Frequently it is a record, in which case the record definition must be made in a distinct type declaration.

2.5   Strings

A particularly useful kind of array is one where components are characters (and with one index, of type integer, subtype NATURAL). This is called a string. The number of characters in the string must be fixed for an individual data item (in other words, the number of components in the array must be static).

Formally, STRING is defined (see Appendix A) as a type in which the string length is not specified, but only its subtype (NATURAL). When the programmer introduces any data item as a string, he must specify the number of characters it is to contain, either by giving the initial value or the particular range for the index, thus:

MESSAGE : STRING (1 .. 5);

This introduces MESSAGE as a string of exactly five characters, so its possible values include "HELP!", "ENTER", "*****", "12345" and "   " (five spaces). String values are given by enclosing the appropriate sequence of characters in double quotes; if the double quote character itself is required, it must be written twice. To avoid mistakes, the string may not spread over more than one line.

Control characters such as carriage return, line feed, form-feed and bell are written using the appropriate identifiers: LF, FF, BEL (see appendix A). The same method is used for denoting characters available on the target system which may not be available for use in the source program - for example if the target can output lower case letters but the program has to be written all in capitals, the identifier LC_C denotes the lower case letter C.

Strings (and identifiers denoting strings) can be concatenated by using the operator &, so that the value of "ABC" & "DE" is the same as

"ABCDE", and other values for MESSAGE include "?" & CR & LF & BEL & "?".

2.6   Data items

Every data item (variable or constant) in a program has a particular
type, which is specified when it is introduced. A data item for a
particular part of the program (block or unit body) is introduced by an
object declaration which gives its name, type or subtype, and optionally
an initial value. An object is taken as a variable unless it is
explicitly stated to be a constant.

```
D : DISTANCE;
ANGLE_OF_ATTACK : ANGLE;
CLEARANCE  : SECURITY_CLASSIFICATION;
THETA      : ANGLE;
REVOLUTION : constant ANGLE := 360.0;
LED_3      : HEX_DIGIT;
IS_CLEARED : BOOLEAN := FALSE;
MAX_SIZE   : constant INTEGER := 132;
WD         : WEEK_DAY;
H          : HEIGHT;
PI         : constant FLOAT := 3.14159;
S          : SECTOR;
FRED       : FINE;
NOW        : TIME_OF_DAY;
ORIGIN     : POSITION;
C : CHARACTER := "?";  -- initial value
```

Several similar variables may be introduced together;

```
X, Y, Z    : FLOAT;
I, J, K    : INTEGER;
U, F, T : FLOAT := 0.0;  -- all initialised
A_COUNT, B_COUNT : NATURAL;
TODAY, TOMORROW : DAY_NAME;
P,Q  : PRESSURE := LOW;  -- both initialised
L,M,N  : FRAC;
RADIUS, R1, R2 : FLOAT;
HARD, SHINY, WET : BOOLEAN;
HERE, THERE : POSITION;
```

For arrays, the type definition may be stated directly in the object
declaration (avoiding the need to declare and name the type separately).
Constraints may also be stated directly, corresponding to a subtype
declaration.

```
VALVE_DATA  : array (VALVE) of VALVE_CHANNELS;
ALTIMETER   : array (1 .. 5) of CABLE;
IMAGE       : array (1 .. MAXSIZE) of CHARACTER;
C1, C2      : INTEGER range 0 .. 99;
R,RR        : FLOAT range 0.0 .. 3.0E8;
NAME        : STRING (1 .. 30);
```

Other types (enumeration, record or derived types) must be declared in a type declaration, and the type name used in the object declaration.

To refer to a particular element we use indexing for an array and a selector for a record:

```
VALVE_DATA (WATER_INLET)                   -- of type VALVE_CHANNELS
VALVE_DATA(DIRTY_WATER) . CONTROL          -- an array
VALVE_DATA(FLUSH_WATER).CONTROL (OPEN)     -- of type VALVE_CONTROL
VALVE_DATA(SUMP_WATER).CONTROL(CLOSED) . OPERATE -- of type CHANNEL
VALVE_DATA(AIR_INLET).LAMP                 -- also of type CHANNEL
```

2.7   Strong Typing

Ada is a strongly typed language, which means that the types of all data values used in the program are checked for consistency with their usage. Keeping types distinct has been found to be a very powerful means of detecting logical mistakes when a program is written and to give valuable assistance whenever the program is being subsequently maintained.   In Ada, every type definition introduces a new type (even if it looks the same as another). Checks for type consistency are strictly applied. Thus

```
type OUNCE is range 0 .. 15;
type HEX   is range 0 .. 15;
```

allow values of both types to cover the same numbers, yet to be guaranteed distinct in use: any data value of type OUNCE is always distinguished from data values of type HEX.

The type consistency rule means that in any assignment

```
X := EXPRESSION;
```

the types of X and the expression must be the same: if they are different, the program gets a diagnostic message from the compiler. This has some surprising consequences: if X is of type FLOAT, then you cannot

write X := 0; because 0 is a literal denoting an integer value. Instead
you must write a literal denoting a real value, such as

    X := 0.0;

    Similarly, if I is of type INTEGER, you cannot write X := I; because
the types of X and I are different. You must write

    X := FLOAT(I);

where the expression on the right is called a type conversion: it
converts the value given to the stated type (see chapter 3)

    In general in Ada, it is good practice to have many different types,
because the compiler can then ensure they are kept separate. You should
only use the same types for values which can in principle be equally
meaningful in the sense that the same operations can be applied to them.

    Another way of interpreting the "strong typing" rule is in terms of
the abstract values which can occur. Each type defines a set of abstract
values, and any object of that type can only take values from that set.
Strong typing means that the abstract values for any type are absolutely
distinct from those of any other type (even though their representations
may be handled by the computer similarly). This means that any overlap
between one type and another is logically impossible.

2.8   Names and Objects

In a simple program each object has a single name and each name denotes
a single object. In a more complicated program names and objects may be
related in other ways. The same object may have several names (known as
aliases) or no name at all. Each name is valid in a particular part of
the program (over which it is said to be visible), and in distinct parts
of the program it is possible for the same name to be used without
confusion for completely different purposes.

    Names are used to denote many kinds of entity in Ada: not only data
objects (variables and constants) but also types, modules, subprograms,
entries and exceptions. When the entity is introduced in the program, it
is given an identifier (or possibly a character string in the case of a
function subprogram, to overload an operator). This identifier is the
local name for the entity, which can be used wherever the declaration is
directly visible: principally the statements which follow the
declaration. In other parts of the program, it is still possible that

the entity can be referred to, but in this case a fuller name would have to be used, to establish which part of the program contains the required declaration.

Names (other than simple identifiers) are formed by using existing names followed by indexes, selectors or qualifiers. The way in which a name is used does of course depend on the kind of entity it denotes. A name which denotes an array, for instance, may take an index, and this forms the name of a component of the array. A name which denotes a record may take a selector, and this forms the name of a component of the record. Names of all kinds may take qualifiers, the particular qualifier depending on the kind of entity the name denotes. These give the predefined attributes of the entity (see Appendix E).

Thus in the context of the declarations

```
type L_V is
     record
        LENGTH : NATURAL;
        VALUE : INTEGER;
     end record;
KEY_TABLE : array (SYMBOL_SET) of L_V;

SYMBOL : SYMBOL_SET;
```

the identifier KEY_TABLE is the name of the whole array, and accordingly may be indexed. We can therefore construct names such as

```
KEY_TABLE(SYMBOL);
```

to denote a component of the array. Because this component is itself a record, we can attach a selector to it to choose a particular field from the record. Thus

```
KEY_TABLE(SYMBOL).LENGTH
```

is the name of a component of the record, which is a scalar of type NATURAL. We can have qualified names related to all of these, for example

```
SYMBOL_SET´FIRST
```

(the first value of the enumeration type);

```
KEY_TABLE´LENGTH
```

(the number of elementary records in the array), or

    KEY_TABLE (SYMBOL)´SIZE

(the number of bits used to represent this elementary record in the array). Similarly

    SYMBOL_SET´SUCC

is the name of a function with formal part

    (X : **in** SYMBOL_SET) **return** SYMBOL_SET;

When this function is applied to an actual argument (which must be a value of type SYMBOL_SET), it returns another value in SYMBOL_SET: the value which succeeds X, if any; it raises the exception RANGE_ERROR if X has the value SYMBOL_SET´LAST.

Names may be formed by attaching indexes, selectors or qualifiers like this without limit, depending only on the nature of the entity (not on the name itself). If an array is multidimensional, then the appropriate number of index values must be given.

A local name may be introduced for an existing object by renaming it, thus:

    L : NATURAL **renames** KEY_TABLE (SYMBOL).LENGTH;

The object which this declaration refers to is fixed when the declaration is met in the program. Thus the particular value of any index (SYMBOL here) at that time determines which object is to be known as L, even though SYMBOL might be subsequently changed.

Exercises
(Possible answers to these will be found in other examples in the book).

1. Messages are sent with precedence ROUTINE, PRIORITY or FLASH. Define the appropriate type.

2. Measurements are in feet and inches (with no fractions). Define the type for such measurements (not to exceed one mile).

3. Dates are given by year (from 1900 to 2099), month (using three letter abbreviation for the name) and day in month. Neglecting the fact that some months are actually shorter than 31 days, define a

suitable type. Write down some values of this type, including some which are formally legal although not sensible dates because of the simplifying assumption.

4. To check that dates are sensible, we need to know the number of days in each month. Declare an object of a suitable type to express this, and state its value for a leap year.

5. Define a type suitable for PDP-11 output devices, in which there is a control and status register (one word) and a buffer register (one character).

6. Define a type suitable for holding an operation code, for which the possibilities are: modify, open, close, reset link, reset initial call, restart.

7. Define a type suitable for associating a key with an item, having a status indication to show whether the association is valid, deleted or empty.

CHAPTER 3

Expressions

An expression is a formula for calculating a value. The type of the
value calculated, and the types of all constituents in the expression,
are determined at compile time   to   give   strong   checking   for
inconsistencies.   In this chapter we explain the rules for writing
expressions in Ada, first for particular types of data then in general.

   Expressions are mainly used for numeric types (section 3.1) but are
also used to calculate truth values from logical expressions (section
3.2). Other types which may arise in expressions are discussed in
section 3.3.

   The general rules concerning expressions (section 3.4) distinguish
operators and operands.   The various operators are explained in section
3.5, and operands in section 3.6.

3.1   Numeric Expressions

Ada includes standard facilities for dealing with data values of the
numeric types explained in section 2.1, so that expressions of integers
or approximate quantities can be written in the normal way.   The strict
type matching rules are applied in expressions, so a ´mixed´ expression
containing quantities of different types (e.g. an integer and a floating
value, or two distinct derived types) must usually be written with
explicit type conversions.

3.1.1   Integer Expressions

The operators + - * / have their usual meanings (division giving an
integer, formed by truncating the real result towards zero). The
operators **rem** and **mod** give the remainder on integer division, differing
only in the sign convention:

```
    I rem J   -- has the sign of I;
    I mod J   -- has the sign of J.
```

The exponentiation operator ** raises an integer to a power. To ensure
that the result is also an integer, the power must be non negative
(otherwise the exception CONSTRAINT_ERROR is raised). The function ABS
gives the absolute value.

   In the following expressions, we assume that the variables I and J
have values 13 and 5 respectively.

```
    + I               --  13
    I - 3             --  10
    I / 2             --   6
    I / J             --   2
    I rem J           --   3
    J mod (-2)        --  -1
    J ** 3            -- 125
    ABS (J - I)       --   6
    2 * J + 4         --  14  =  (2 * J) + 4
    2 * (J + 4)       --  18
```

An integer expression whose mathematical value is outside the
implemented range causes the NUMERIC_ERROR exception to be raised.
This includes the case of division by zero.

3.1.2   Floating Point Expressions

The operators + - * / have their usual meanings.   The exponentiation
operator ** raises a floating point value to an integer power, so that
the result is still a real value.   The function ABS gives the absolute
value.

   In the following expressions, we assume that the variables X and Y
have values 25.2 and 3.0E8 respectively.

```
    - X               --  -25.2
```

```
X + 5.2            --    30.4
0.25 * X           --    6.3
X / Y              --    8.4E-8
Y ** 2             --    9.0E16
X / 10.0 + 0.06    --    2.58
```

A floating point expression is evaluated approximately, depending on the precision of the constituents: the number of digits specified. (There is a full mathematical model of the approximate numbers and operators on them, which gives the error bounds on the result.) If the mathematical value of an expression is outside the implemented range, the NUMERIC_ERROR exception is raised. This includes the case of division by zero.

3.1.3   Fixed Point Expressions

The operators + and - have their usual meanings. For multiplication and division, fixed point values may be combined with integers. A fixed point value multiplied by an integer (or vice versa) produces a value of the same fixed point type. A fixed point value divided by an integer also produces a value of the same fixed point type.   (Note that this does not apply to an integer divided by a fixed point value.)

Two fixed point values (not necessarily of the same type) may be multiplied or divided together, but in this case the required type for the result must be stated explicitly: it must be a fixed point type, but need not be the same as the types of the constituents. The function ABS gives the absolute value in the same type as its argument. Exponentiation is not defined for fixed point types.

In the following expressions, we assume that the variables E and F have the same fixed point type and values 0.1 and 0.6 respectively

```
F - E              --    0.5 approximately
4 * E              --    0.4
F / 2              --    0.3
FRAC (0.5 * F)     --    0.3
ABS (E - F / 2)    --    0.2
```

If the mathematical value of the expression is outside the implemented range, the NUMERIC_ERROR exception is raised.

3.2   Logical Expressions

Expressions in Ada may deal with truth values (of type BOOLEAN), testing the truth of relations or conformance with constraints. (The types of the values in the expression are checked at compile time, depending on the operators used, but constraints may need run-time checking.) Logical expressions are used in situations where a truth value is required (such as in if statements) as well as in expressions generally.

3.2.1   Relations

Any two values of the same scalar type may be compared, and the results taken as a truth value. The comparison is written using one of the six relational operators. Certain non-scalar values may also be compared.

The following examples assume the same values for variables as the section above, and variables P, C with values LOW, ´?´ respectively:

```
J /= 0                  --   TRUE because 5 /= 0
I < J                   --   FALSE
I - 3 = 2 * J           --   TRUE, since both sides equal 10.
X > Y                   --   FALSE
ABS (X + 5.2) > 40.0    --   TRUE
E <= F/2                --   TRUE
P = LOW                 --   TRUE
C /= ´?´                --   FALSE
```

(Note that /= means not equal, <= means less than or equal to, and >= means greater than or equal to.) Any two values of the same type (not necessarily scalar) may be tested for equality unless they have been declared to be **limited** (see section 12.2).

```
SL(1) /= SL(2)      --   comparing sectors in list (see 2.4)
```

For arrays or records this means testing whether all components are equal. (Any different components make the compound values unequal.)

Two one-dimensional arrays may be compared if the elements are of a discrete type, to determine their relative position in dictionary order.

```
"Ada"        <    "Adam"     --   TRUE
"Augusta"    <    "Byron"    --   TRUE
```

Note that the array lengths need not be the same.

3.2.2   Conformance

We can test whether a value of a scalar type satisfies a range
constraint. The constraint may be stated explicitly or as a subtype.

```
I in range 1 .. 10         --  FALSE as I = 13
J in NATURAL               --  TRUE as J = 5, in 1 .. INTEGER´LAST
C not in LOWER_CASE        --  TRUE
1.0 / X in UP_TO_ONE       --  TRUE
Y not in POSITIVE_FLOAT    -- FALSE
```

(The same notation may be used with other constraints and corresponding
values. Accuracy constraints are always taken to be satisfied.)

3.2.3   Boolean Expressions

Truth values may be combined using the operators not, and, or, xor with
their usual meanings. (xor means exclusive or, which is the same as
not-equivalence.) In addition, there are ´short circuit´ operators:
and then and or else. These avoid the evaluation of the operand on the
right when that is unnecessary.

```
not J = 0                        --  TRUE
I > 10 and J < 10                --  TRUE
I > 20  or J < 20                --  TRUE because J < 20
X < Y xor Y > 1000.0             --  FALSE because both hold.
C in LOWER_CASE and then J /= 0  --  FALSE, without testing J
```

The short circuit forms are useful for checking conformance to a
constraint before using the value:

```
J /= 0 or else I rem J /= 0       -- TRUE, and safe if J = 0.
C in HEX_DIGIT and then LED(C) /= 0  -- FALSE.
```

Note in the last example that the short circuiting skips evaluation of
the second term, so does not use an illegal index.

3.3   Other kinds of expression

There are some standard facilities for working with enumeration types
and one-dimensional arrays.   Other types (including array and record
types) are permissible components in expressions, and may be combined
using functions or programmer-defined operators.

3.3.1   Enumeration Expressions

The values in an enumeration type are written in order when the type is
declared, and for any given value the previous or following value may be
determined, using the qualifer PRED or SUCC with the type name.

        CHARACTER´SUCC(C)   -- ´ ´ as the value after ´?´
        PRESSURE´PRED(P)   -- THIN, the value before LOW

If the expression tries to calculate the successor of the last value in
the type, or the predecessor of the first value, the exception
CONSTRAINT_ERROR is raised.

3.3.2   Array Expressions

The Boolean operators may be applied to arrays of the same type, if the
element type is BOOLEAN; the result is another array of the same type,
whose value is formed by applying the operator to the constituents
element by element. The operator & concatenates two one-dimensional
arrays whose element types are the same; it produces a longer array
containing the same element values.   Concatenation also joins a single
element to an array of elements of the same type

        G or GG   -- assuming both of thpe GRID (see 2.4)
        "AB & "CD"   --   "ABCD"
        SL(1) & SL(2)   -- of type array(1 .. 10) of SECTOR

3.3.3   Expressions of programmer-defined types

A type which is declared as a derived type (see section 12.1)
automatically has all the properties of the base type, including
whatever operators are appropriate. A type that is declared as a private

type (see section 7.5) automatically has the equality comparison operators (= and /=) unless it is limited.

In addition to the operators automatically available (or instead of them if necessary), explicit operator declarations may be given to allow operators to apply to other types. Operator declarations are explained later (section 5.1).

The types of the values in an expression must match the types expected and produced by the operators. Any inconsistency is detected at compile time.

3.4   Expressions in general

Expressions are formed from operands and operators. An expression can consist of a literal value or the name of a variable or constant as special cases; in general it is one or more operands connected by operators. There is no limit in Ada to the size of an expression, but most programmers find that expressions longer than one line are hard to read and understand.

An expression is evaluated by evaluating the operands and combining them according to the operators, in an order defined by certain rules of precedence. The rules have been chosen to reflect common practice in mathematics and the conventions that have been established in other programming languages.

3.5   Operands

The operands within an expression can be of the following kinds:

a. Literals, giving values of scalar objects; these may be numbers

```
    12              -- integer (decimal value)
    273.0           -- real number (with decimal point)
    9.81E2          -- real number (with exponent)
    1E5             -- integer (with exponent)
    16#F000#        -- based integer (base 16)
    16#F#E3         -- same as 16#F000#
    8#0.37777#      -- real number (base 8)
```

or enumeration literals

```
MONDAY            -- of type DAY_NAME
EXPRESS           -- of type PRI_CODE
THIN              -- of type PRESSURE
´?´               -- of type CHARACTER
```

b. Aggregates, giving values of compound objects (records or arrays). The values of the components are given by innner expressions, either in the natural order or with the corresponding field names of index values.

```
(RADIUS => 1.0E1, WIDTH => 360.0)  -- SECTOR
(1.0E1, 360.0)          --  same value, if SECTOR
(1.0, 2.0, 3.0, 4.0) --  possible value for COL_VEC
```

Where the array elements are characters, the aggregate may be written as a sequence of characters in double quotes:

```
"A string"      --  all on one line
""              --  null string
```

To get a value containing a double quote character, write it twice. To get a value longer than one line, or containing control characters, use concatenation (see below: the & operator).

c. Names of objects (variables or constants). An object may be scalar or compound.

```
REVOLUTION          --  constant ANGLE
FRED                --  of type FINE
S                   --  of type SECTOR
IMAGE               --  array of CHARACTER
ALTIMETER(4)        --  of type CABLE
KEY_TABLE(SYMBOL).LENGTH --  of type NATURAL
```

The name may involve indexes, selectors or qualifiers as explained in section 2.8. An index value is given by an inner expression, whose value must be of the right type and range.

d. Allocators, in which a value of an access type is obtained, denoting a newly created base object with a given value or constraint:

```
new MESSAGE_ITEM (5, IMAGE, null)
```

Further details are given in chapter 12.

e. Function calls, in which a value is calculated in a subprogram (see chapter 5). The value may be scalar or compound, and the function may have parameters which are given as variables or inner expressions.

```
SIN (PI * X)              -- of type FLOAT
ASK ("Need help?")        -- of type BOOLEAN
ATAN2 (X, Y)              -- of type ANGLE
STRAIGHT (HERE)           -- of type POSITION
```

f. Type conversions, whereby a value in one type is converted to the appropriate value in a closely related type. This is the way Ada combines the advantages of strong type checking with the flexibility of mixed expressions: the programmer has to state the type conversions explicitly.

```
FLOAT (I + 4)        -- numeric type conversion
CENTS (X / 3.0)      -- rounds and checks range
FINE (PI)            -- conversion to fixed point
WEIGHT (19.32 * FLOAT (L1*L2*L3) )
```

The last example above shows conversion to and from derived types: L1, L2, L3 are assumed to be of a type derived from FLOAT, and WEIGHT is also derived from FLOAT. An array value can be type converted to another array of the same size and shape, if the component types are the same.

g. Qualified expressions, for resolving possible ambiguities and ensuring that constraints are met. If it is required to specify the type of a literal (or aggregate), this notation is used.

```
LENGTH´(3.4)          -- of type LENGTH
WEIGHT´(3.4)          -- of type WEIGHT
MONTH_NAME´(OCT)      -- resolves ambiguity
NUMBER_BASE´(OCT)     -- resolves ambiguity
WEEKDATE´(TODAY)      --- checks range
SECTOR´(1.0,90.0)     -- with aggregate
```

h. Subexpressions, that is inner expressions enclosed in parentheses (round brackets)

```
(X + 1.0)
(2.0 * PI * (R + RR))
```

The second example shows a nested inner subexpression. There is no limit to the number of levels of nesting that can be used in an expression, but for ease of comprehension it is preferable to keep within five levels. The compiler checks that the parentheses are in nested pairs.

3.6   Operators

The operators which can be used to compose expressions are as follows:

```
**                      --  exponentiation

* / mod rem             --  multiplying and dividing

+ - not                 --  unary

+ -                     --  adding and subtracting
&                       --  concatenation

= /= <= < > >=          --  relational
in      not in          --  membership

and    or    xor        --  logical
and then                --  short circuit
or else                 --  short circuit
```

Note that there are three unary operators; the rest are binary. The operators + and - may be unary or binary, depending on their position in an expression.

```
J ** 2
PI / 0.5
K rem B_COUNT
- 5                     --  unary -
not WET                 --  unary not
MAXSIZE - 1             --  binary -
MESSAGE & NAME
THETA <= REVOLUTION
Q in LOW_PRESSURE       --  special operand on right
HARD or SHINY
```

The membership operators in and not in take a special kind of right operand: a type or a subtype rather than a data value. Otherwise all the operands are data values, and the result of every operator is a data value.

In conformity with the ´strong typing´ rule, the operators refer to particular types of operand, and combine them to form results of known types. These operators are defined in Ada for particular predefined types (see Appendix A: the definition of package STANDARD), and may be extended by explicit programming if required for other types (see section 5.1 on overloading opertors).

3.7   Evaluating Expressions

An expression comprises one or more operands (as in section 3.5) linked
by operators (as in section 3.6), possibly preceded by a unary operator.

   The table of operators in section 3.6 shows the order of precedence,
highest at the top. The adding and concatenating operators have the
same precedence; the relational and membership operators have the same
precedence; the logical and short circuit operators have the same
precedence.

   The rules for evaluation are as follows:
a. Where an operand has operators on both sides of it, and the
    operators are of different precedence, the operator of the higher
    precedence is applied first. Where the operators are of the same
    precedence, the operator on the left is applied first.
b. A binary operator has operands on both sides. Unless the operator
    is a short circuit operator, both operands are evaluated (in either
    order) before the operator is applied. When the operator is a
    short circuit operator, the operand on the left is evaluated before
    the operator is applied; if necessary, the operand on the right is
    then evaluated.
c. A unary operator is applied to the resulting operand on its right,
    taking account of rule a.

   The expression may be evaluated in any order consistent with these
rules (to allow compilers to optimise the order, which may be different
on different computers). Note that many of the forms of an operand may
include inner expressions, so finding an operand may involve evaluating
the inner expression first.

   The rules of precedence can be visualised by using parentheses to
show the subexpressions:

   - Y ** Z < 4.0 + 0.5 * X **and** WET

has its constituents evaluated as though it had been written

   ((- (Y**Z)) < (4.0 + (0.5 * X))) **and** WET

Note that the unary operators have lower precedence than multiplying and
exponentiating operators, so are applied after them. It is wise to play
for safety in cases like this, and use parentheses explicitly in the

program to make the intended order of evaluation absolutely clear.

Exercises

1. Given

        INX : INTEGER **range** 1 .. SIZE;

   write an expression which increments INX by 1 if it is in the range, but wraps around from SIZE to 1.

2. Write an expression to calculate one plus alpha squared minus sigma squared, all over two sigma, where the variables are both floating point and non-zero.

3. Given

        subtype INDEX **is** INTEGER **range** 1 .. 10;
        A : **array** (INDEX) **of** FLOAT;
        I : INTEGER;

   write a logical expression to check that two consecutive elements of the array (at index values I and I+1) exist and are definitely positive.

4. Given

        T : POSITION;
        V : LENGTH;
        function SIN (X : ANGLE) **return** UP_TO_ONE;
        function COS (X : ANGLE) **return** UP_TO_ONE;

   calculate the value of type POSITION a total distance V in a straight course from T.

CHAPTER 4

Statements

The actions to be carried out in the program are specified by writing a
series of statements, in the order they are to be executed.

    Ada prescribes the basic form of statements, and how they can be
combined to form more complicated actions.   At any position in the
program, it is likely that the programmer will need to use some of these
basic statements but also (as shown in section 1.3) some application-
specific statements that call for the performance of actions whose
details are stated elsewhere.   Such statements are procedure calls;
they are introduced here, but the details are given in chapter 5.

    The basic statements include assignments of values to variables,
selection of actions according to particular criteria, and repetition of
actions. There are also statements for more advanced facilities,
explained in chapters 6 and 7.

4.1   Sequences of statements

Each statement specifies an action to be carried out; a sequence of
statements specifies a series of actions to be carried out, one after
the other, in the order written. Statements are classified as either
simple or compound : compound statements contain internal sequences of
statements (which may in turn be simple or compound).

    Any statement, whether simple or compound, may be labelled, to give
it a name. The label is put in front of the statement, enclosed in
double angle brackets:

    <<LABEL>> STATEMENT;

Some compound statements (loop and declare) may be given a local name using a colon:

```
OUTER : loop
-- sequence of statements
end loop OUTER;
```

This name is available only in the internal sequence of statements. Every statement is written with a final semicolon.

A simple statement is either sequential or branching. Sequential statements are executed in their order of occurrence; after a sequential statement has been executed, the statement which follows it in the sequence (if any) is executed. A branching statement is normally the last of a sequence of statements: when it has been completely executed, the statement executed next is determined not by its position, but by some other rule, dependent on the particular statement type. A compound statement may have either characteristic, depending on the simple statements of which it is composed.

If a compound statement contains another compound statement, they are said to be nested. Ada does not limit the depth of nesting, but it can be difficult for the human reader to be sure of his context in a deeply nested structure. It is good practice therefore to write programs using the layout to show the nesting : within each sequence, write the statements (whether simple or compound) underneath one another, starting each at the same left margin. Where there is a compound statement, write the statements which form each internal sequence similarly, but with an indented left margin. (In due course there will be Ada support tools which lay out programs automatically.)

Using this indented style of writing, the left margin of the program text shows the structure of the program, and there is a natural limit to the depth of nesting - do not let the indented left margins creep right across the page! If your program seems to be developing in this direction, give a particular compound statement a name and make it into a procedure (as explained in chapter 5).

The compound statements in Ada are bracketed by keywords, giving a clear indication of the start and finish of each sequence of statements. They include statements in which the actions to be carried out are selected according to particular criteria (if and case statements), or are repeated as required (loop statements), or have local declarations (declare statements); these are all described here. In addition, there are accept statements and select statements which are described in chapter 7.

4.2   Assignment

A variable is a data item whose value may be changed. A new value is
given to a variable by an assignment statement. The previous value of
the variable (which might be involved in calculating the new value) is
then completely lost. The variable may be of any type (including a
record or an array as a complete entity); the new value given to it must
of course be of the right type, and consistent with any constraints.
(The following examples use data items introduced in chapter 2).

```
  I := 0;
  X := Y * Z;
  S := (RADIUS => 1.0, WIDTH => 90.0);
  P.HEADING := P.HEADING + 60.0;
  SL(2) := S;
```

Note that the assignment gives the variable a complete new value. If it
is of a compound type, all the components get new values. If the
programmer wants to change some of the components of a record or array
and leave others unchanged, he must write the series of assignments for
the components to be changed in the order required.

4.3   Alternatives

Different actions may be required in different circumstances.   Each of
the different actions is written as a separate sequence of statements,
introduced by the appropriate clause which shows when those statements
are required to be executed.

    There are two basic methods of choosing from the possible actions:
either by testing conditions, or according to the value of a suitable
variable. Different kinds of statements are used for these: if to test
conditions, case to select by data value.

4.3.1   Selection by condition

In an if statement, the programmer states the condition to be tested,
then the sequence of statements to be executed if the condition is true.
If the condition is false, there may be other actions to be carried out,
which may include testing further conditions. Thus the basic idea is to
have a series of conditions to be tested in order, with corresponding
actions to be taken on finding the first condition which is true, and

finally actions to be carried out if none of the conditions are true.

```
if I < 0 then
  I := 0;
end if;

if COUNT < 100 then
  COUNT := COUNT + 1;
else
  XS_COUNT := XS_COUNT + 1;
  COUNT:=0;
end if;

if C /= ASCII("$") then
  D := A_TO_E(C);
else
  D := EBCDIC(" ");
end if;

if TODAY in MONDAY .. FRIDAY then
  WEEKDAY_PROC;
elsif TODAY = SATURDAY then
  SAT_PROC;
elsif TODAY = SUNDAY then
  SUN_PROC;
end if;
```

(Note the redundant test in this example, anticipating possible changes
in the future life of the program).

An if statement in general consists of a number of conditions to be
investigated in the given order; the first which is found to be true
determines which sequence of statements is executed. If none of the
conditions are true, a further sequence of statements may be executed.
The keywords used to identify these parts of the statement are if at the
beginning, before the first condition, elsif before each subsequent
condition (zero or more times); each condition is followed by then and a
sequence of statements; if actions are needed when no condition is true,
write else and the sequence of statements. The whole of the statement is
always terminated by end if;

4.3.2   Selection by discriminant value

In a case statement, the program gives an expression, whose value (which
must be of a discrete type, i.e. integer or enumeration) determines

which actions are required. The programmer states the possible expected
value (or values) as choices for the discriminating expression, then the
series of statements to be executed if the expression has that value.
Several values may be given for each choice, but the values given for
the different choices must of course be distinct.

```
    case TODAY is
      when MONDAY|WEDNESDAY|FRIDAY =>
        I:=9; J:=17;
      when TUESDAY|THURSDAY =>
        I:=8; J:=15;
      when SATURDAY|SUNDAY =>
        I:=10; J:=16;
    end case;

    case CMND is
      when CLOSE_DOWN =>
        STOP;
      when START_UP =>
        SET_GOING;
        PRINT_MESSAGE ("STARTED");
      when others =>
        PRINT_MESSAGE("DONT " &
          "UNDERSTAND");
    end case;
```

The choice **others** means any possible values of the discriminant which
are not given previously. It may only be given as the last choice.

   The basic difference between **if** and **case** is that in an **if** statement
the conditions are tested one after the other, whereas in a **case**
statement the expression´s value determines one of the various
possibilities directly.

4.4   Repetition

An action may need to be repeated, for example to carry out some
operations regularly to a series of items, or to iterate some improving
operation.   The unit of repetition is written as a sequence of
statements, forming the body of the loop, introduced by a suitable
phrase which may show a condition for stopping the repetitions.

   The basic loop simply groups the statements to be repeated, without
implying any termination; this is frequently needed in large program
structures, for example where the computer is continuously monitoring or

controlling something:

```
loop
   DELIVER WATER;
   CLEAN WATER;
end loop;
```

The repetitions of a loop may be controlled by either counting or testing a condition; these are expressed by the iteration specification at the start of the basic loop. Independently, during the course of execution of the loop, a condition might arise requiring exit from the loop.

Control by a condition is expressed by a **while** clause:

```
while NEXT /= HEAD loop
   SUM := SUM + NEXT.VALUE;
   NEXT := NEXT.SUCC;
end loop;

I := 0;
while A(I) >= 0 loop
   I := I + 1;
end loop;  -- get index error
           -- if no elements of A
           -- are negative
```

The condition is tested before starting each repetition: it may indicate that the body of the loop is not to be executed at all.

Control by counting is expressed by a **for** clause:

```
for DAY in DAY_NAME loop
   ADJUST_RATE (DAY);
end loop;

for LETTER in HEXDIGIT range ´A´ .. ´F´ loop
   MY_LED (LETTER)  := 0;
end loop;

for M in 1 .. MAX_SIZE loop
   if MORE_CHARS then
      IMAGE (M) := NEXT_CHAR;
   else
      IMAGE (M) := " ";
```

```
   end if;
end loop;
```

The loop parameter M is automatically declared by the **for** clause, with the appropriate type and range. It applies to all of the loop body. The limits of the range need not be constants: any expression may be given for each limit. Unless otherwise specified the loop parameter counts forwards through the range. However, if the keyword **reverse** is put in, the loop parameter counts backwards through the range.

```
for M in reverse 1 .. MAX_SIZE loop
   exit when IMAGE(M) /= " ";
end loop;
```

The **exit** statement is explained in section 4.7.1.

4.5   Call Statement

Higher order actions are constructed out of more elementary ones, and made available as procedures (or entries) either from libraries which have already been written, or by the programmers writing the current program. In this section we describe the simple features of call statements to execute these higher order actions, which serve most ordinary purposes. The full details covering the less usual features are explained in chapter 5 (for procedure calls) and chapter 8 (for entry calls).

Procedures and entries can have parameters, and each time one is called to carry out its action, appropriate values and variables must be specified for its parameters. Every procedure and every entry has a specification that states exactly what kinds of parameters it needs, if any.

The call statement gives the name of the procedure or entry to be executed, followed by the actual parameter values and/or variables to be used. To call a procedure or entry with no parameters, just write its name:

```
PRINT_HELP_FILE;
INITIALIZE;
```

To call a procedure or entry which requires parameters, put the required values or variables in parentheses after the name:

```
DRAW2(X1, Y1 + 1.0E0);
```

```
          -- parameters are two values of type FLOAT

     CLOSE(MY_FILE);
          -- parameter is a variable of type IN_FILE

     SIMPLE_BUFFER.READ (IMAGE(M));
          -- entry : see 8.1.2.
```

Note that a value can be given as a suitable expression. The rules for parameters are quite complicated (to allow for the variety of usage in actual programs), but they follow a logical pattern.

The same notation is used to call procedures and entries, because from the point of view of the caller they both carry out some action and then return. The difference is in the way they may interact with the rest of the program: a procedure in Ada is reentrable, so may be also executed in parallel by several tasks concurrently; an entry is not reentrable, and may only be accepted by one task at a time to carry out its action. These details are explained in chapters 5 and 8.

4.6   Declare statement

A declare statement is a compound statement containing a sequence of statements, optionally preceded by local declarations and optionally followed by local exception handlers (see chapter 6). This is also called a block. The local declarations apply within the block but not outside it in the rest of the program.

A declare statement may be given a local name, in which case the same identifier must also be given at the end of the statement:

```
     LOCAL_BLOCK: declare
       -- local declarations
     begin
       -- internal statements
     end LOCAL_BLOCK;
```

The declare statement is introduced by the keyword **declare** if there are any local declarations, which would be the normal case. (If there are no declarations, omit the word **declare**.) After the local declarations, the start of the sequence of statements is marked by the keyword **begin**. If any exception handlers are required they are written after the main statements, introduced by the keyword **exception** (see chapter 6).

4.7   Branching Statements

These are statements whose successor in execution is not necessarily
that which follows it in sequence, but some other, determined by the
particular statement type. The statements concerned are exit, return,
raise and goto.

4.7.1   Exit statement

An exit statement specifies explicit termination of a loop. Within a
loop, whether or not there is an iteration specification given by a **for**
or **while** clause, the repetitions may be stopped by execution of an exit
statement; the whole of the loop statement is then deemed complete.

```
    for J in 0 .. 100 loop
      if A(J) < 0 then
        I := J;
        exit;
      end if;
    end loop;   -- value of I is unchanged
                -- if no element of A
                -- is negative

    for MTH in MONTH_NAME loop
      if MTH = TODAY.MONTH then
        exit;
      end if;
      D := D + DAYS(MTH);
    end loop;
```


Note that **exit** usually occurs in an if statement; a special short
notation is available for this common and simple case:

```
    exit when MTH = TODAY.MONTH;
```

A loop statement may of course be one of the statements in the body of
another loop, and so on. The loops are said to be nested. If an exit
statement is written simply (as shown above), then it terminates
repetition of the smallest loop enclosing it; however, any required loop
of the nest may be terminated by giving the loop a local name and
writing that name in the exit statement:

```
    OUTER: loop
```

```
     -- outer body
   loop
     -- inner body
     exit OUTER when REQUIRED;
   end loop;
     -- more outer statements
 end loop OUTER;
```

4.7.2   Return statement

A return statement specifies the end of execution of a subprogram body, and indicates completion of the corresponding subprogram call.

If the subprogram is a function, then the return statement must specify the value to be delivered by the subprogram; it must be of the right type as determined by the subprogram specification (see section 5.1).   Thus a subprogram which returns an integer can contain the statement

```
   return COUNT;
```

where COUNT may be any integer expression. The statement may be in the body of an inner condition, loop or declare statement - if so it automatically terminates the inner statements by terminating the subprogram body.

A procedure which does not return a value may contain a return statement with no value attached - just

```
   return;
```

but in this case the return statement is not essential: reaching the normal end of the sequence of statements in the body equally indicates completion of the corresponding procedure call statement.

4.7.3   Raise statement

A raise statement specifies that an exception situation has been detected, so that normal sequential execution of statements cannot continue. The full details of exceptions are explained in chapter 6, including the description of how an exception handler is executed instead of the rest of the sequence of statements in which the raise statement occurs. The exceptional situations which might arise within a piece of program are given names in the usual way, introduced like this:

  MUST_CLOSE_NOW, OPERATOR_ERROR : **exception**;

(Note that this declaration, although it looks like an object declaration, merely states that the identifiers denote exceptional situations; no objects are associated with exceptions.)

   A raise statement usually occurs with an exception name, indicating which particular exception has been detected:

  raise MUST_CLOSE_NOW;

  raise OPERATOR_ERROR;

In the special context of an exception handler, it is permissible to give a raise statement with no name, to indicate that the present handler is incomplete. An example is given in section 6.4 when describing exception handlers.

4.7.4   Goto statement

A goto statement specifies its successor statement explicitly, by giving a statement label:

  goto TAIL;

   It is particularly difficult to debug programs containg goto statements, and they should be avoided if possible. If you cannot find a way of using the other kinds of statement to achieve the sequence of execution necessary, the potential future problems may be alleviated by giving the **goto** statement itself a label, and putting a "come from" comment with the destination statement, thus:

  <<HEAD>> **goto** TAIL;
  -- intermediate statements
  <<TAIL>> -- come from HEAD
  -- statement

The pair of statements connected by a goto and a label must be fairly close together in an Ada program. Specifically, they must both be in the same unit body, that is the same subprogram, package body (initialisation) or task body.

Within that body, if one is in an accept statement the other must also be in the same accept statement; if one is an exception handler the other must also be in the same exception handler.

The goto statement must be in a sequence of statements (usually at the end of the sequence), and this sequence will usually be in a compound statement which is part of an enclosing sequence of statements. The corresponding labelled statement must be one of the statements in a sequence containing or enclosing the goto statement.

4.8   Other normal statements

The normal rules of sequencing apply to delay and null statements which are described in the following sections. They also apply to abort statements, which are described in chapter 13, and to code statements, which are described in chapter 11.

4.8.1   Delay statement

The statements in a sequence are normally executed as rapidly as possible: as soon as each statement has been completed, the next statement in the sequence may be started. If you want to insert a timed delay in the sequence, use a delay statement:

delay 5.0 ;

The amount of the delay required must be given in seconds; it can be a constant, a variable or an expression. (A negative value is treated as zero.) The effect of such a statement is to delay starting execution of the next statement in the sequence for at least the specified duration. (Other parts of the program may be executed during that period, corresponding to other tasks - see chapter 8). Note that a delay statement gives a minimum time: it does not imply any upper limit to the interval before the next statement is started. (A different technique, timeout, explained in chapters 8 and 13 is used for this.) Note also that a delay is for a particular period of time (which may of course have been calculated in advance). A different method, rendezvous, explained in chapter 8, is used to cause a delay until a particular event happens or some other part of the program is ready.

The delay statement is the ordinary method of achieving timed sequential control, for example opening and closing a set of valves in the proper order.

```
   with TIME_SCALES; use TIME_SCALES;
   procedure AIR_FLUSH is
     begin
       FAN(ON); delay FAN_RESPONSE;
       AIR_VALVE(OPEN); delay BLOW_TIME;;
       AIR_VALVE(CLOSED); delay AIR_CLOSE;
       FAN(OFF);
     end AIR_FLUSH;
```

4.8.2   Null Statement

Sometimes the program structure requires you to write a sequence of
statements even if nothing has to be done - for example in an arm of a
case statement. The null statement is a positive indication that no
action is required. It is used to avoid the error of accidentally
omitting a sequence of statements that should be there.

```
   case DAY of
     when MONDAY| WEDNESDAY| FRIDAY  =>
       FULL_DAY;
     when TUESDAY| THURSDAY  =>
       PART_DAY;
     when others =>
       null;
   end case;
```

Exercises

1. Write assignment statements to double the radius and halve the width
    of sector S.

2. Write statements to increase a variable of type TIME_OF_DAY by one
    second on a 24-hour clock, in particular advancing from (23, 59, 59)
    to (24, 0, 0) and from (24, 59, 59) to (1, 0, 0).

3. Write statements to increase a variable of type DATE by one day,
    taking account of the different number of days in each month as
    given in array (MONTH_NAME) of NATURAL; when advancing from December
    31 to January 1, call procedure NEW_YEAR;

4. With an **array** (1 .. 100) **of** TRACK, write statements to call

    procedure OBSERVATION (T: **in out** TRACK);

    on the I-th element of the array, and then use

    function SPEED (T1, T2: TRACK) **return** FLOAT;

    on the old and new values. Test whether the resulting value is less
    than 3.0E8. If it is larger, call

    procedure IMPOSSIBLE (T: **in out** TRACK);

    (Note that it will be necessary to save a copy of the old value of
    the track before calling OBSERVATION in order to have it available
    for SPEED.)

CHAPTER 5

Subprograms

A subprogram is a program unit for describing an action. There are
three important aspects of subprograms: how to specify their interfaces
(section 5.1); how to describe in detail the action concerned (section
5.2); and how to call for that action to be carried out (section 5.3,
following from 4.5).

Subprograms include procedures and functions; in many ways they are
also similar to entries (which are explained in chapter 8). Procedures
are actions to achieve a particular effect; functions are actions to
calculate a value (usually with no other effect on their environment).
A function may be called either as a named function or by an operator in
an expression.

Each subprogram has a specification (which gives its signature, see
subsection h below) and a body (which also includes the specification,
and gives details of how the action of the subprogram is to be
achieved). In most cases it is not necessary to give the specification
apart from the body (section 5.2 below explains).

5.1   Subprogram specification

An important feature in Ada is the emphasis given to the specifications.
In the case of a subprogram, the specification tells you exactly what
kinds of parameters the subprogram needs, and what kind of effect it
has.

The specification gives the name of the subprogram and all the
necessary information about its parameters. It is written like this:

---

procedure CLOSE(FILE : **in out** IN_FILE);

This procedure has a single parameter (FILE) which is of type IN_FILE; a value is brought in at the beginning of the procedure from the actual parameter, given when the procedure is called, and a possible different value is sent out to that parameter at the end of the procedure. We might call this procedure by a statement such as

CLOSE (MY_FILE);

where MY_FILE is a variable of type IN_FILE.

Here is another subprogram specification:

procedure ADVANCE (C: INTEGER **range** 1 .. 99;
                    D: INTEGER :=0);

There are two parameters here, both of type integer. On any call of this procedure, the first parameter (corresponding to C) must have a value in the range 1 to 99. The second parameter (corresponding to D) is optional — this is shown by the value given in the specification, which provides a default value for the parameter.

function ASK (QUESTION : STRING) **return** BOOLEAN;

Here we see the specification of a function called ASK which has a single parameter named QUESTION, of type STRING. It returns a value of type BOOLEAN. Because it is a function, it may be called in an expression or where a BOOLEAN value is appropriate.

The specification

function ATAN2 (X,Y:FLOAT) **return** ANGLE;

indicates a function of two parameters of type FLOAT returning a result of type ANGLE. The various properties of the interface given in a subprogram specification are as follows.

a. Nature of subprogram

A subprogram may be specified as a function or a procedure; this indicates the intention of the subprogram: a procedure is intended to achieve an effect, a function is intended to calculate a value. There are special rules concerning a subprogram specified to be a function — any parameters it has must all be of mode **in**, and it must deliver a result; its effect on its environment must be solely determined by its parameters. (This permits expressions containing functions to be optimised).

b. Name of subprogram

In most cases the name of a subprogram is an identifier. However, it is possible to introduce an additional meaning for an operator by defining a function with the operator symbol (as a character string) given as its name. This is called overloading the operator. Subprograms named by an identifier may have any number of parameters (including zero). Subprograms named by an operator symbol must be functions and must have the number of parameters appropriate for that operator symbol (one or two).

c. Parameters

A subprogram may have parameters, each of which is specified with an identifier, mode, type and possibly a default value. For example the specification

   procedure PRINT_HELP_FILE;

tells us that PRINT_HELP_FILE is a procedure which has no parameters. If there are any parameters, each has a particular identifier: the formal parameter name. The specification

   procedure DRAW2(X, Y : FLOAT);

tells us that DRAW2 is a procedure which takes in two parameters, named X and Y. On each occasion this procedure is called, two values must be given for these parameters.

d. Mode

In most cases, a parameter stands for a value which the calling program provides to the subprogram. The direction in which the value is passed is called the mode of the parameter, and is written **in**, **out**, or **in out**. Mode **in** is implied if none is stated explicitly: the calling program passes a value **in** to the procedure parameter. For a parameter of mode **in**, the corresponding call must provide a value (of the correct type) which is given as an expression, including a variable or a constant. For a parameter of mode **in out**, the value is passed **in** at the begining, and out at the end of the subprogram. The mode **out** means that the procedure passes a value out to the parameter (but does not use its previous value).

For a parameter of mode **out** or **in out**, the corresponding call must provide a variable (of the correct type) which may be a simple variable or a component of a record or array.

In the specification:

> **procedure** CHECK_VAL (READING : **in** INTEGER;
>   OK : **out** BOOLEAN);

there are two (formal) parameters: READING bringing a value **in** to the procedure, of type INTEGER and no default value; and OK taking a value **out** of the procedure, of type BOOLEAN.

e. Parameter Association

The values and variables given as actual parameters when a subprogram is called must match those specified. The correspondence between the actual parameters given and the formal paramters required may be established either by the order in which they are written or by using the formal parameter names. For association by position, the first actual parameter given corresponds to the first formal parameter required and so on. For association by name, the actual parameter is given with the name of the formal parameter it matches, with different parameters given in any order.

f. Default parameters

A subprogram can be specified with defaultable parameters. A subprogram call need not then give the corresponding actual parameter, and the default from the specification will be used. Thus the specification

> **procedure** PRINT_LINES(FILE : IN FILE ;
>   START_LINE : NATURAL :=1);

has a default value of 1 for the START_LINE parameter. It may be called with the parameter explicitly

> PRINT_LINES(MY_FILE, 100);

or with nothing given for START_LINE (not even the separating comma)

> PRINT_LINES(HELP_FILE);

which is exactly equivalent to

    PRINT_LINES(HELP_FILE, 1);

The default value may be an expression, which is evaluated when
the subprogram specification is met in the program. Defaults
may only be used with **in** mode parameters.

g. Result

A subprogram can calculate a value for use in an expression.
Such a subprogram is a function. The specification

    function SIN(X : ANGLE) **return** FLOAT:

shows that the subprogram produces a result of type FLOAT.

    function GRID-COUNT (RADIUS : FLOAT) **return** NATURAL;

returns a count (subtype NATURAL), which might be the number of
grid points within a given radius of the origin.

A function may be called during evaluation of an expression,
where a value of the appropriate type is required.

    ACROSS := R * SIN(PHI);

and

    if ASK("NEED HELP?") then
      PRINT_HELP_FILE;
    end if;

h. Overloading

In Ada, there can be several subprograms with the same name
which are distinguished by the properties of their parameters.
Using the same name for distinct meanings in the same context
is called overloading. This is useful when substantially the
same action can be applied to objects of different types. Thus
it is necessary to be able to close files of all types -
IN_FILE, OUT_FILE, INOUT_FILE.

While the details of what must be done (e.g. on closing down
buffers) may be different in the three cases, the effect is the
same as far as the user is concerned. So the user writes

```
      CLOSE(MY_FILE);
```

whichever file type it has, but there are actually three procedures specified

```
      procedure CLOSE(FILE : in out IN_FILE);
      procedure CLOSE(FILE : in out OUT_FILE);
      procedure CLOSE(FILE : in out INOUT_FILE);
```

to cover the different cases. The choice of the procedure called is made by the compiler based on type matching. There is no overhead at run-time to select the correct procedure.

The properties of the parameters which distinguish different subprograms with the same name are their order, names, modes and types, together with the type of the result. All of this information, together with the subprogram name, is know as its signature.

The same principles apply to procedures, entries, functions and operators. In the case of operators, the existing operator symbols (+, *, <=, not etc.) can be overloaded to apply to other types; however, the action they carry out on objects of that type should be of the same kind as the ordinary meaning of the operator. It is the programmer's responsibility to ensure this: remember that the subsequent reader of the program will assume ordinary properties (associativity, commutativity) when he sees an operator. As an example:

```
      function "*" (X : MATRIX; Y : COL_VEC)
                  return COL_VEC is
                    C : COL_VEC;
                    XY : FLOAT;
      begin
        for I in COL_VEC'FIRST..COL_VEC'LAST loop
          XY := OEO;
          for J in COL_VEC'FIRST..COL_VEC'LAST loop
            XY := XY + X(I, J) * Y(J);
          end loop;
          C(I) := XY;
        end loop;
        return C;
      end "*";
```

5.2   Subprogram bodies

The body of a subprogram gives the details of what is to be done whenever the subprogram is called. The body begins with the specification of the subprogram; it may then have local declarations (introducing entities which are valid for the subprogram body but nowhere else in the program. The main part consists of a **begin** block which gives the sequence of statements to be executed, and optionally an exception handler.

Here is a subprogram body (with a prefix that gives its context for separate compilation):

```
with FILTER_OPERATIONS; use FILTER_OPERATIONS;
procedure CLEAN_FILTER is

begin
   CHANGE_TO_CLEANING;
   WATER_FLUSH(1);
   AIR_FLUSH;
   WATER_FLUSH(2);
   DRAIN_SUMP;
   CHANGE_TO_NORMAL;
 end CLEAN_FILTER;
```

Here is another subprogram body:

```
function ASK(QUESTION : STRING) return BOOLEAN is
     -- output message QUESTION and check for Y/N reply
   REPLY : CHARACTER;
begin
   loop
     PUT(QUESTION);
     GET(REPLY);
     SKIP_LINE;
     if REPLY = 'Y' then
       return TRUE;
     else if REPLY = 'N' then
       return FALSE;
     else
       PUT("Please reply Y or N");
     end if;
   end loop;
end ASK;
```

This has a local variable REPLY which is used in the body, and a series
of statements to be executed according to the normal rules until a
return statement is reached; **return** marks the logical end of execution
of the subprogram (see section 4.7.2). When the specification includes
a **return** part, the statement gives the particular value to be delivered
as the result of the function. In the above example the values returned
are constants but in general they could be any expressions of the
specified type. For example

```
    function STRAIGHT (P : POSITION; L : LENGTH) return POSTION is
    begin
      return POSITION´
        (NORTH => P.NORTH + L * COS (P.HEADING),
        EAST => P.EAST + L * SIN (P.HEADING),
        HEADING => P.HEADING);
    end STRAIGHT;
```

This calculates a new position on a straight course.

A subprogram body is very similar to a block (see section 4.6),
except that it starts with the specification instead of the word
declare. After the specification there may be local declarations, and
there always is an executable part introduced by the word **begin** which
may be defended by exception handlers.

The declarations may be of any kind, including subprograms and other
program units. However, since the program tends to be difficult to see
clearly if too much text is included here, it is preferable to declare
bodies of inner units as **separate** (see chapter 10), unless they are very
small.

The formal parameters in the specification, together with the local
declarations, establish entities for the subprogram body. Formal
parameters have the force of object declarations with the specified type
or subtype; those with mode **in** or **in out** are effectively initialised to
the value of the corresponding actual parameter or default value (and
those with mode **out** have no significant value initially). Parameters
with mode **in out** or **out** have significant final values - the value of the
parameter at the end of the subprogram is assigned to the variable in
the caller stated as the corresponding actual parameter.

Within the executable part of the subprogram body, the main sequence
of statements expresses how the action of the subprogram is to be
carried out.

For a function, the specification contains a **return** part, and the
statements in the body must include a **return** statement with an

expression of the type specified, to define the result of the
subprogram. For a procedure, the specification does not contain a
return part, but a **return** statement may be used (without an expression)
to mark the end of execution of the body.

A subprogram body occurs either in the declarative part of some
larger program unit or on its own as a separate compilation unit (see
chapter 10). If it is in a declarative part of a subprogram or block,
the specification given with the body is usually sufficient and does not
have to be repeated. However, there are two cases where a specification
must be given by itself early in the declarative part, and also again
with the body late in the declarative part. The cases are

a. When two or more subprograms include calls of one
    another: a specification must be given before any call
    of the subprogram.

b. When a subprogram is defined as part of a package (see
    section 7.3): the specification must be given in the
    visible part of the package.

Other than these two case, it is sufficient to give the specification
at the beginning of the body of a subprogram.

5.3   Subprogram calls

The action that a subprogram carries out may depend on parameters which
are provided for each call : thus at different places in the program the
action may be carried out using different values or variables. On each
call of a subprogram, the right kinds of parameters must be used – for
example, if the procedure expects to receive a value of a particular
type, then the call must provide a value of that type.

Essentially the subprogram call must specify information to match the
parameters in the specification. Every parameter has a name, mode, type,
and possible default value.

The actual parameters to be used in a subprogram call are given
either in the proper order, or with the proper names, as stated in the
subprogram specification.

In the context of the specifications in section 5.1, a procedure call

```
CHECK_VAL (5, IS_CLEARED);
```

would be executed with the value 5 matching the first parameter
(READING), and the variable IS_CLEARED matching the second parameter
(OK). The actual parameters are in the same order as in the
specification, so names are not necessary. If a procedure has many
parameters, it is clearer to use the names for the parameters
(particularly if there is a sequence of parameters of the same type). We
could express the same call as

```
CHECK_VAL (READING => 5, OK => IS_CLEARED);
```

or

```
CHECK_VAL (OK => IS_CLEARED, READING => 5);
```

Notice that the linking symbol => is used to associate the formal
parameter name with the required value or variable, like the notation
for an aggregate. The mode indicates the direction the data value
passes between the procedure call statement and the corresponding
procedure body: in, out or both.

If the mode is in, the parameters in the procedure call statement
must give a value of the right type. If the mode is out, the parameter
must be a variable capable of receiving a value of the stated type. If
the mode is in out, the parameter must be a variable and its existing
value may be used by the procedure.

If the procedure specification includes a default value for an in
parameter, then there is no need for the procedure call to give any
corresponding actual parameter. Consequently the number of actual
parameters may be less than the number of formal parameters, and if any
subsequent parameters are needed they must be identified by their names.
For example,

```
procedure ADVANCE (C: in INTEGER range 1 .. 99;
                   D: in INTEGER := 0);
```

can be called with one or two parameters:

```
ADVANCE (5);
```

calls the procedure with value 5 for C and the default value 0 for D.

```
ADVANCE (7,2);
```

calls it with 7 for C and 2 for D, as also does

    ADVANCE (D => 2, C => 7);

The values for an **in** parameter may of course be given as an expression
of any complexity, and an **out** or **in** parameter may similarly be a
variable of any complexity (such as a record or array).

    ADVANCE (MAX_SIZE - L1);
    CHECK_VAL (J - K, GRID (J,K));

Since a variable is a particular case of an expression, it may be used
for any mode of parameter - but the difference in context is important,
and the mode determines whether the original value of the variable may
be used in the procedure body, a new value may be assigned to it, or
both. The following table shows the relationship:

    mode   -- effect with variable

    in   -- used
    out   -- assigned
    in out   -- used and assigned

There is no difference in meaning between giving the parameters by
position or by name: it is simply a matter of convenience in writing and
reading. If there are many parameters, say more than five, it would
probably be preferable to use names, to emphasise their distinctiveness,
particularly if many of them could take the same value. It is permitted
to use name parameters with functions but not with operators; however,
this is not likely to be common or as useful.

Exercises

1. Write the specification for a procedure called SA which two
    parameters, of types CAMAC_ADDRESS and F_OP1 respectively.

2. Write the body for a procedure READLN which inputs characters up to
    the next LF character.

3. Write a sequence of statements to operate the valves AIR_INLET and
    DIRTY_WATER, with an interval of at least 5 seconds between them,
    then after a further 2 seconds check both values, using the
    procedure MOVE_VALVE (V : VALVE); and procedure CHECK_VALVE (V :

VALVE);

4. Write the specification for a procedure to carry out the processing
    in section 4.3.1. example 4, using TODAY as a parameter.

5. Write a call of procedure TEXT_IO.SET_LINE_LENGTH with the FILE
    parameter being the variable F1 and the N parameter having the value
    80.

CHAPTER 6

Exceptions

Ada is designed to permit defensive, or fault-tolerant programming. This is in contrast with traditional styles of programming, in which there is an implicit assumption that everything is correct – the program, the translator, and the computer hardware (with only some concessionary provision for faults in peripherals or operator behaviour).

Notwithstanding the emphasis on verification and testing of Ada programs, it must be acknowledged that there will be occasions when unexpected situations arise and the system must be programmed to deal with them in whatever way is best in order to allow normal operation to continue. Such situations are called exceptions; in general they indicate conditions not intended to arise, which make further normal processing impossible.

Any action might fail. To keep a real-time system in continuous operation, the designer must be able to specify a recovery action to be taken as the effective replacement for the remainder of the action which was not successfully completed. This is a form of software redundancy.

There are a number of exceptions predefined in Ada, for situations which are logically possible in the language. For example, with an array, the expression given for an index may have a value out of bounds: IMAGE (I + J) might have I + J not in range 1 .. MAXSIZE, in which case there is no such component of the array. The language-defined exceptions are explained in section 6.6 below. In addition to the predefined exceptions, any number of further exceptions may be declared, for particular exceptional situations relevant to the program. Programmer-declared exceptions are explained in section 6.1.

The action of indicating that there is an exceptional situation is called raising the exception. Some constructs in a program may implicitly raise an exception (IMAGE (I + J) is an example); the program may also contain explicit statements to raise exceptions.

For each exception, whether predefined or explicitly declared in the program, the programmer may declare handlers to carry out whatever recovery action is necessary and then to resume the normal sequence of execution of the program. The place in the program where normal execution is resumed depends on the position of the corresponding exception handler – the handler always comes at the end of a block and completion of the handler has the same effect as normal completion of the block.

Exceptions are dealt with according to the dynamic block structure of a program. As each statement is executed, it may involve the execution of statements elsewhere in the program (by subprogram calls); in this sense all the blocks of a program are dynamically nested during execution. When an exception arises, the dynamic block structure is "unwound" in the course of recovery and resumption of normal processing, from the smallest block enclosing the offending statement to the first dynamically enclosing block containing a handler for the relevant exception.

In this chapter we explain exceptions in sequential programs. (There are some special properties of exceptions in the context of tasks, which are discussed in chapter 13).

6.1   Declaring exceptions

Each exception is denoted by an identifier, which must be introduced by a suitable declaration:

    STICKY_VALVE : **exception**;
    REACTOR_CRITICAL : **exception**;
    TAPE_DRIVE_FAULTY, BAD_TAPE_BLOCK : **exception**;

A number of identifiers may be introduced in the one declaration; this has no special significance – they are all introduced as exception names. As with all declarations, the identifiers so introduced apply throughout the current context: they may be used in the subsequent declarations and executable statements. Exception declarations may occur in the visible part of a package specification (where most kinds of declaration are allowed), but since they are not data objects they may not occur as procedure parameters.

A local name may be introduced for an existing exception, thus

TRANSFORM_ERROR : **exception renames**
                TRANSFORM_PACKAGE.MATRIX_SINGULAR;

This presumes that there is a package called TRANSFORM_PACKAGE which contains the declaration of MATRIX_SINGULAR, and introduces the name TRANSFORM_ERROR locally for it. Renaming does not hide the old name for an exception, but can be used to introduce a suitable local name.

The predefined exceptions of Ada are listed in section 6.6. The situations they refer to are programming faults that cannot be detected at compile-time. The identifiers introduced there are automatically available in any compilation unit. In contrast, any identifiers introduced by the programmer are available in other compilation units only if they have a suitable **with** clause (see chapter 9). Apart from this difference relating to visibility, there is no difference between the predefined and user-defined exceptions.

6.2   Raising exceptions

An exception, whether predefined or user-defined, may be raised anywhere in the scope of its declaration by a **raise** statement (see section 4.7.3). For example, in the procedure which changes a valve setting and checks that it has moved, if the program detects that the value has not reached the proper position in a reasonable time it could execute

    raise STICKY_VALVE;

which would indicate the failure to the rest of the program. This would normally occur in some conditional part of the program, for the case when the exceptional condition has been detected. There may of course be any number of **raise** statements for any exception. Within an exception handler, the raise statement can be given without an exception name, thus

    raise;

The effect of this statement is to reraise the exception which caused the handler to be entered (even if that exception cannot be named). It implies a further raise of the exception which is currently being handled. This technique allows a particular part of the program to give a specified partial handler for an exception, which is executed first, before passing on to a general handler for it.

A predefined exception is raised implicitly if the corresponding
fault is detected in the program. An exception, whether predefined or
user-defined, may also be raised implicitly by a call of a subprogram
(procedure, function or operation). This happens if an exception arises
during execution of the subprogram body and there is no handler for it
within the subprogram. (The exception is then said to be propagated
:see section 6.4).

Although exceptions can only be explicitly raised in the scope of
their declarations, the implicit raising of exceptions can occur in
situations outside that scope, as a result of propagation.

Whenever an exception is raised, the current block is executed no
further, and a handler is executed instead.

6.3   Handling exceptions

A handler for an exception, to carry out the specific recovery action
after it has arisen and before normal processing can continue, may be
written in any block in the scope of the declaration for the exception.
Exception handlers are always written at the end of a block: the word
exception is put after the last normally executable statement, and
introduces the exception part of the block. This consists of a series of
handlers, written like alternatives in a **case** statement, with exception
names as the selectors. There can be several handlers for one
exception, in different blocks.

Each particular handler is introduced by a **when** clause giving the
relevant exception name (possibly several exception names if the same
recovery action is to serve for more than one exception), then after the
=> sign, a sequence of statements forming the body of the handler.

Elsewhere in the program containing STICKY_VALVE, where it calculates
the required valve setting and calls the procedure to make the change,
there could be

```
exception
when STICKY_VALVE =>
    -- statements to warn operator
    -- log fault
    -- and change parameters
    -- for related valves
end;
```

The last handler in a block may be introduced by **when others,** in which case it applies to any exception detected in the block which is not named in the previous handlers - including any exception which cannot be named in the current context.

For example, suppose we had an undefended **declare** statement,

```
declare
  A : FLOAT;
begin
  A := X * X;
  Y := A * EXP(A);
end;
```

and we wish to defend it against the possible exception NUMERIC_ERROR (which could arrive implicitly during either * operation or the EXP function). We can add an exception part in which Y is given the largest floating-point value if this situation is detected:

```
declare
  A : FLOAT;
begin
  A := X * X;
  Y := A * EXP(A);
exception
  when NUMERIC_ERROR =>
    Y := FLOAT'LAST;
end;
```

The sequence of statements in a handler may be any statements allowed in the current block. In particular, if the block forms the body of a subprogram, the statements may refer to the parameters of the subprogram, and would normally contain a **return** statement. Further, if the subprogram returns a value (as in a function or operator) then each handler should finish with a **return** statement giving a value of the correct type. If an exception arises during execution of an exception handler, the action is as though the exception had arisen in the associated main block without the current handler.

While the several handlers in the exception part of a single block must of course refer to distinct exceptions, it is possible for there to be different handlers for the same exception in different blocks (whether disjoint or nested). This allows the programmer to adapt the recovery action to the broad context in which each exception may arise. In this case, the handler which is used on each occasion is that of the smallest block which dynamically encloses the statement being executed

when the exception is raised. Depending on the position at which the
programmer puts the handler, the recover action would be small-scale or
large-scale: on completion of the statements in the handler, the whole
of that program unit is deemed to be complete, and normal processing
continues.

Thus a handler may contain statements for dealing locally with an
exception, and either permit normal processing to continue from the end
of the current block, or call for further handling in the dynamically
enclosing block, for the same exception name by

    raise;

or a named exception EX by

    raise EX;

6.4   Propagating exceptions

Whenever an exception arises, whether it is a user-defined exception,
the subject of a **raise** statement, or one of the predefined exceptions,
the normal course of execution of the program ceases and a handler is
sought for the exception: one with the exception name in its **when**
clause, or one introduced by **when others**. As soon as a matching handler
is found, its sequence of statements is executed instead of the
remainder of the block containing it.

In the first instance a matching handler is sought in the block
currently being executed. If there is none (particularly if the block
has no exception part), or if the handler itself detects an exception,
then the exception is raised implicitly in the dynamically enclosing
block. This is called propagating the exception. If the handler raises
another exception (by an explicit raise statement or any statement which
implicitly raises an exception) then <u>this</u> exception is propagated to the
dynamically enclosing block.

Propagation is automatic through a compound statement to the
enclosing sequence of statements (i.e. from part of an **if, case, loop,
accept, select** statement or block to the sequence of which that
statement is part). In the case of propagation through an **accept**
statement, an exception is also raised in the associated task (see
chapter 10). This continues through nested statements until a matching
handler is found or the sequence of statements is that of a main program
or task.

The application of the general rule on propagation leads to the following cases, where the effect may not be immediately obvious. If the exception arises (directly or by propagation) in the sequence of statements which form a subprogram body, then the dynamically enclosing block is that containing the current call of that subprogram – either a procedure call statement or a function call or operator call in an expression. Note that the possibility of exceptions in the evaluation of an expression means that the exception could arise when dealing with the declarations of a block (from the calculation of a default value or an initial value which turns out to be impossible for the declared object).

If an exception arises in a declaration, it is propagated back from the block containing the declaration to the statement or declaration that called it, until a statement is reached; a handler is then sought in the block containing that statement.

If the exception arises in the initialisation part of a package (and there is no local handler), then the unhandled exception is considered to have arisen in the package declaration, so is propagated to the enclosing block.

If the package is a separately compiled main unit, this prevents execution of the whole program: the initialisation cannot be carried out. If the package is a subunit, then the exception is propagated to the unit containing the corresponding stub

package body P **is separate;**

from which it is propagated as from a declaration. If the exception arises (directly or by propagation) in the sequence of statements which are the substance of an **accept** statement, then in addition to propagating the exception to the block of which the **accept** statement is part, an exception is also raised in the task which is currently in rendezvous through the corresponding **entry** declaration. This is at the point of the statement in the task which calls the entry.

If the exception arises in the body of a task, then an unhandled exception is not propagated: it is deemed to be **null.** The task is terminated and no further action taken.

There is inevitably a certain amount of overhead associated with exception handling, particularly to propagate an exception. The aim in Ada is to have no overhead in normal execution (in particular no overhead on entering a program unit containing exception handlers) but to tolerate some overhead after an exception has arisen. This ensures that performance is only lost when it is necessary to achieve safety.

6.5   How to use exceptions

A simple use of exceptions is to check for consistency as the program
runs, by the use of assertions.

   As the actions of a program are carried out, the state of the system
changes; however relationships between variables in the system may have
to remain true while their individual values change. A useful way of
checking that the program is running correctly is to test such
relationships at appropriate stages. This can be done by declaring:

```
ASSERT_ERROR : exception;
procedure ASSERT (CONDITION: BOOLEAN) is
begin
   if not CONDITION then
      raise ASSERT_ERROR;
   end if;
end ASSERT
```

An assertion gives a condition which is supposed to apply at that point
in execution.

```
ASSERT (AREA > 0);
```

```
ASSERT (X * Y < Z);
```

The decision on placing assertions in a program is an essential part of
the program design, as it involves consideration of the trade-off
between the risk and the time taken to carry out the run-time check.

   The most common places for assertions are on entry to subprograms, to
check that the values provided for in parameters are suitable, on
completion of loops, and after a set of alternatives (to state
properties which should now hold). If the assertion is found during
execution to be false, the sequence of statements containing it is not
executed further, and the exception ASSERT_ERROR is raised. Assertions
may also be useful on exit from a procedure, to confirm that the results
satisfy required relationships.

   Exceptions allow one to program for survival after a catastrophe.
The general technique for making programs fault-tolerant (with respect
to faults in both the control software itself and the devices which it
controls) can be summarised thus:

   a. At each stage in the design process, consider that any action
       might fail; assess the seriousness of such a failure. Identify

the conditions which could prevent completion of a significant action.

b. Review methods of protective redundancy which would allow the system to recover to a normal condition after a fault. Choose alternative actions within appropriate cost and performance constraints.

c. Identify what tests are needed to detect the fault. Write **raise** statements within the chosen tests.

As with assertions, the difficult balance is that between the cost of frequent testing for faults, and the risk of damage because of consequences from a fault before it is detected. One way is to work backwards from each output action, and put a positive check as early as possible before it. A recovery action may be to retry the action during which the fault was detected (hoping it was transient), to carry out a less satisfactory but nevertheless acceptable substitute, or to report the trouble and call for outside help.

This approach leads to a program in which there can be recoverable procedure bodies, such that alongside the ordinary procedure body there is a recovery section, activated on detection of an appropriate fault during execution of the ordinary body. The recovery section might be entered at any stage while executing the body (not necessarily between actions), and must bring the whole action to a well defined finish.

It is a good practice to plan a program so that the exception handlers can cope with a situation which might have been detected at any time within the defended block. Remember that the raising of the exception indicates only the symptom, not the cause, of the trouble.

Remember also that the exception handler for **others** will catch any exception not explicitly mentioned in the current exception part; as a consequence it can be entered in obscure circumstances. It should only be used for the most extreme cases, and make miminal assumptions about the state of the system on entry.

6.6   Predefined exceptions

The following exceptions are defined in the standard language environment (see Appendix C)

CONSTRAINT_ERROR -- The current value is inconsistent with the current requirement. This exception is raised whenever an assignment is attempted with a value out of range for the variable, an array component is referenced with an index value out of range, a record component is referenced with a field selector for the wrong variant, an access type object is referenced with an access value of null or similar situations (for example when matching subprogram parameters).

NUMERIC_ERROR -- The current value is not within the implemented range. This exception is raised if the result of a calculation is toolarge or mathematically infinite. The actual limits for detecting this situation depend on the implementation, and there is no guarantee that the exception will be raised anyway.

SELECT_ERROR -- Execution is blocked by a select statement. This exception is raised if a select wait statement is met (see section), with all its select alternatives closed, and no else part. Such a statement can never complete its execution.

STORAGE_ERROR -- Storage is needed which cannot be provided. This exception is raised if the program requires more storage space than is available, by execution of an allocator or use of dynamic storage in a task.

TASKING_ERROR -- Communication with the required task cannot occur. This exception is raised if an entry call is met, and the task containing the corresponding accept statement is terminated before it can accept the entry.

In addition to the above, which are in effect declared at the outermost level of the program, each task has a special exception which is automatically available as a predefined attrivbute of the task. For task T, there is an implied declaration

T´FAILURE : **exception;**

and the task may contain handlers for T´FAILURE. Any other task can cause the exception condition to be raised in T by the statement

raise T´FAILURE;

provided that the task name T is visible. The other task continues executing normally after raising T´FAILURE. (A task may raise this exception for itsel, when of course the normal execution is abandoned.)

Exercises

1. Given

    ```
    subtype SHORT is range 1..5;
    function PEX(I : NATURAL) return SHORT is
      S : SHORT := I;
    begin
      return 6 - S;
    end;
    ```

    check that PEX(4) returns the value 2 and PEX(7) raises an
    exception. (Note that the exception would have been raised slightly
    differently if S had been declared of type NATURAL). Modify the
    body of PEX to defend it against the possibility of a parameter
    value outside the range for which 6 - I is of subtype SHORT, so that
    it raises the exception BAD_PARAMETER in that case.

2. Write a procedure to read an item from a table, given a key, using
    an inner call (EXAMINE) that provides an out parameter to indicate
    whether the keyed item is present; make the procedure raise an
    exception if the requested item does not exist in the table.

CHAPTER 7

Packages

The facilities described in the previous chapters allow you to write a
simple program in Ada, relying on a previously written library to
provide all the further information needed. For a program of any
complexity (more than 50 statements, say) you need to be able to split
it into manageable units which can be individually designed and checked.
Most programming languages allow you to write subprograms, which have
been described for Ada in chapter 5, as program units for describing
actions. This chapter deals with packages, which are the second of the
three kinds of program unit in Ada. (The third kind of program unit, a
task, is explained in chapter 8).

A program in Ada is written as a number of logical pieces, each of
which covers one aspect of the problem. A package is the general form of
one such logical piece; it defines a set of facilities which the rest of
the program may use. These might either be specially designed for the
program currently being written, or already in existence because a
similar problem has arisen previously. The fundamental idea is to
separate the use of a facility from its provision. In this way a
program can be arranged to show what is meant to happen without a
clutter of detailed implementation.

7.1   Packages of data

Several parts of the program may need to refer to the same common data.
The declarations for these variables and constants logically belong
together, and such a collection is one form of a package. Any part of
the program that needs to refer to this data can then do so, without
having to repeat all the declarations.

Thus we may have a collection of objects associated with a graphical display:

```
package VIEW_POINT is
    XP, YP, ZP: FLOAT; -- viewer position
    XC, YC, ZC: FLOAT; -- centre of view
    FIELD : FLOAT;      -- field of vision
    AXES : BOOLEAN;     -- whether axes wanted
end VIEW_POINT;
```

and this specifies a package. The objects may be constants or variables, and they can be given initial values if needed. Elsewhere in the program (wherever the declaration of this package is visible), the objects in the package may be referred to, by names such as

```
VIEW_POINT.XP
VIEW_POINT.AXES
```

(or in a shorter notation explained below). The entities in the package may be used in any way consistent with their declaration: in this case, as variables, either to be assigned new values or to have their current values used. Here are some more package declarations (actually derived from a program in another language : see appendix C).

```
package STORE is
    SCALE  : FLOAT;
    K      : INTEGER;
    JUMP   : INTEGER := 11;
    A      : FLOAT;
    SM     : FLOAT;
    INPUT  : INTEGER;
    IFM    : INTEGER;
    ALAT   : FLOAT;
    ALONG  : FLOAT;
    EORW   : CHARACTER;  -- not INTEGER
    NORS   : CHARACTER;  -- not INTEGER
    CHANGE : BOOLEAN := FALSE;
    FRACT  : BOOLEAN := FALSE;
    SIG    : BOOLEAN := FALSE;
    VAL    : BOOLEAN;
    LEG    : BOOLEAN;
end STORE;

package NSEW is
    N      : CHARACTER := ´N´;
    S      : CHARACTER := ´S´;
    E      : CHARACTER := ´E´;
```

```
   W       : CHARACTER := ´W´;
end NSEW;

package UNHIO is
   KIN     : constant INTEGER := 1;
   KOUT    : constant INTEGER := 3;
   K7      : constant INTEGER := 7;
   K8      : constant INTEGER := 8;
   ISCR1   : constant INTEGER := 21;
   ISCR2   : constant INTEGER := 22;
   ISCR3   : constant INTEGER := 23;
   ISCR4   : constant INTEGER := 24;
end UNHIO;

package BTP is
   BIGTHT : FLOAT;
   BIGPHI : FLOAT;
end BTP;

package RFUNC is
   CSP     : FLOAT;
   TSP     : FLOAT;
   SP      : FLOAT;
end RFUNC;

package FORMAT
   FMT     : STRING(1..80) := "(2(F9.0,A1),T1,F5.0)"
                             & (others => " ");
end FORMAT;
```

A package may be given among the declarations within the program (when
it applies like other declarations), or compiled separately as a library
unit (see chapter 10). In the latter case, any other compilation unit
may refer to the library unit by giving its name in a context
specification, written:

```
with STORE;
--- heading of unit using STORE
STORE.SCALE
STORE.LEG
```

Note that it is not necessary to repeat the contents of the package.

A shorthand notation is available for referring to entities in a
package without prefixing the package name, if no confusion can arise.
The declaration

use STORE;

may be used wherever the package STORE is visible, and allows the names
within STORE to be used directly unless an identical name is already
visible or is made visible similarly from another package. (Remember
that the names in one package need not be all different from those in
another: they might have been written by different people.) Thus by
writing

with STORE; **use** STORE;

the objects in the package may be referred to by their simple names

SCALE
LEG

(provided that the names are not otherwise used in this context.) If it
happens that these names are in use already, or are repeated in
different packages, the **use** declaration is ineffective and the longhand
name must be written.

7.2   Reference to packaged entities

The entities declared in any package can be used elsewhere in the
program after they have been declared, as determined by the following
rules:

- a. If the package specification is in the declarative part of some
  program unit, then its scope extends throughout that program
  unit, after the specification. (If the package needs a body,
  then that or the stub must also be in the same declarative
  part.)
- b. If the package specification is reduced to a stub in the
  declarative part of some program unit, with the specification
  expanded as a separate compilation unit (which in this case is a
  subunit), then its scope extends throughout the program unit
  containing the specification stub, after the stub.
- c. If the package specification is a separate compilation main
  unit, (i.e. not having a specification stub within another unit)
  then its scope extends over all other compilation units that
  specify the package name in their context specification (i.e.
  state that they must be compiled with the given package): e.g.

with VIEW_POINT;

The entities declared in the package can be used in ordinary statements and declarations, with names like components of a record:

```
VIEW_POINT.XP := 100.0;
if VIEW_POINT.AXES then
    DRAW_AXES;
end if;
```

This notation is used for packaged objects and anything else declared in a package. There is a short-hand notation to allow the names of packaged entities to be given more briefly. You may put

```
use STORE, UNHIO;
```

before a series of declarations, to open the context to that of the specified unit or units. Having done so, you may use just the entity name without the package name as a prefix. You can put several package names in a use-list; the corresponding entity names are then all available. This short-hand applies only to names that are not declared in more than one place among the specified units or local context, in order to prevent ambiguity. Further details are given in section 9.4.

7.3   Packages with defined types

A package is also a good way to connect the definition of an application-dependent type with the objects of that type which the program can use, for example

```
package VALVE_DETAILS is
  type VALVE is (WATER_INLET,
    AIR_INLET, FLUSH_WATER, AIR_EXHAUST, SUMP_WATER,
    CLEAN_WATER, DIRTY_WATER);
  type VALVE_STATUS is (OPEN, CLOSED);
  type VALVE_PARAMETERS is record
     TRANSITION : DURATION;
     CONDITION : VALVE_STATUS;
     CHANNEL : NATURAL;
   end record;
  CONTROL_VALVE : array (VALVE)
    of VALVE_PARAMETERS;
end VALVE_DETAILS;
```

The rules for using this package are exactly as described in section 7.2. We can use the types and objects declared here in ordinary declarations and statements, with names formed as explained above. For example we can if necessary declare as working variables other objects of type VALVE_DETAILS.VALVE or VALVE_DETAILS.VALVE_STATUS . In another program unit starting

     with VALVE_DETAILS;

we could refer to these either using their full names or by putting

     use VALVE_DETAILS;

and the simple identifiers. Thus we could declare

     SUSPECT_VALVE : VALVE;

and have statements like

     SUSPECT_VALVE := AIR_INLET;

     CONTROL_VALVE(FLUSH_WATER).CONDITION := OPEN;

to manipulate and use the packaged objects.

7.4   Packages with subprograms

We frequently have a set of subprograms which are closely associated; there might also be some data or special types which they use. In this case the package is written in two pieces – a specification and a body. The purpose of this is to show clearly what information the user of the package needs to know, without burdening him with implementation details that may be irrelevant. The specifications of the subprograms give all the information needed to call them (explained in sections 5.1 and 5.3). The package body contains all the corresponding subprogram bodies. We could for example declare another package :

```
  with VALVE_DETAILS;  use VALVE_DETAILS;
  package VALVE_MOVEMENT is
    procedure MOVE_VALVE(V : VALVE);
    procedure CHECK_VALVE (V : VALVE);
    procedure MOVE_AND_CHECK_VALVE (V : VALVE);
  end VALVE_MOVEMENT;
```

The programmer can then write another part of the program, headed by

    with VALVE_DETAILS, VALVE_MOVEMENT ;

to refer to the types and objects in package VALVE_DETAILS and the procedures in VALVE_MOVEMENT. Using full names we might have

    VALVE_MOVEMENT.MOVE_VALVE (SUSPECT_VALVE);
     -- call with full procedure name

or in the shorthand notation,

    use VALVE_DETAILS, VALVE_MOVEMENT;

followed by statements such as

    MOVE_VALVE(SUSPECT_VALVE);

By defining the procedures with parameters of the type VALVE, the programmer has arranged that they can only be used with properly declared objects. For any package containing subprograms, there must be a package body (see section 7.6).

7.5   Packages with private types

There are some circumstances when we want a special type for the problem, and subprograms to work with values of that type, with a means of ensuring that no other operations are applied to the corresponding objects. This might be for example with control blocks where some internal checks or private details are stored on behalf of the user. Such types are called abstract data types, and are discussed further in section 12.4.

    In this case we have the package specification and package body as in section 7.3, but the package specification is itself split, into a visible part and a private part. The purpose is again to show clearly the information needed by the user of the package; the visible part contains the declaration of the special type and the subprogram specifications, while the private part gives details of the type and values for any constants needed, together with any representation specifications (see section 11.6). Several private types may be declared in the same package.

    package PDP_11_INTERRUPT_CONTROL is
       type CSR is private;

```
      procedure ENABLE(DEVICE : CSR);
      procedure DISABLE (DEVICE : CSR);
   private
      type CSR is array(0..15) of BOOLEAN;
   end PDP_11_INTERRUPT_CONTROL;
```

This introduces a special type, so that in another part of the program suitable objects can be declared. For example, after with and use clauses for PDP_11_INTERRUPT_CONTROL,

```
   LA36 : CSR;
```

introduces an object of this private type, for which the possible operations are

```
   ENABLE(LA36);
```

and

```
   DISABLE(LA36);
```

Values of a private type can be assigned and compared with one another but none of their internal details can be used outside the package body.

Sometimes the values of the special type must be kept unique, so that at most one object has any given value (such as a file control block). We can prevent assignments between objects of the type by declaring

```
   type CHANNEL is limited private;
```

The word **limited** in this declaration makes any objects of the given type eligible only for use as parameters to subprograms which work with that type.

7.6   Package specification in general

A package specification can occur either among the declarations in a program unit or as a separate compilation unit (see chapter 10). It makes a collection of entities available for other parts of the program to use.

The main part of a package specification is its visible part, which gives the public information about the entities it contains. A package specification may also contain a private part, which gives further details about types and constants. (The private information is needed by the translator, but not by the programmer using the package).

All kinds of program entity can be declared in a package: constants, variables, types, subprograms, exceptions, tasks and inner packages (for more closely associated entities).

If a subprogram in a package may detect an exception which should be handled by its caller, the package specification should say so:

```
package TIMED_VALVE_MOVEMENT is
  procedure MOVE_VALVE(V : VALVE);
  VALVE_TIME_OUT : exception;
end TIMED_VALVE_MOVEMENT;
```

As a package is a program unit, it may contain smaller program units and be itself contained in a larger program unit, corresponding to the logical structure of the problem. This can be seen in the predefined package definition TEXT_IO (see Appendix A).

7.7   Package bodies

A package body is distinct from a package specification; every package needs a specification, but sometimes a body is not necessary. If the package provides any subprogram, task, or inner package, their specifications must be collected in the package specification, and their corresponding bodies written in the package body. If the package contains any variables whose initial values must be calculated by executing statements, the initialisation must be written in the package body.

A package body need not occur immediately after its specification - it may even be written as a separate compilation unit (see chapter 10). The body of a package consists of a declarative part and an optional executable part.   The declarative part contains the bodies of all subprograms specified, and also any other declarations they need : local variables or procedures, etc. Anything declared in the body which was not in the specification part is entirely restricted to the body: it cannot be used in any other part of the program.

```
package body VALVE_MOVEMENT is

  function SENSE_VALVE(C : NATURAL) return VALVE_STATUS is
  begin
```

```
        -- discover status by I/O on channel C
  end SENSE_VALVE;

  procedure EFFECT_VALVE(C : NATURAL, S : VALVE_STATUS) is
  begin
        -- set status by I/O on channel C
  end EFFECT_VALVE;

  procedure MOVE_VALVE(V : VALVE) is
     VP : VALVE_PARAMETERS renames CONTROL_VALVE(V);
     S : VALVE_STATUS;
  begin
     S := SENSE_VALVE(VP.CHANNEL);
     if S /= VP.CONDITION then
       EFFECT_VALVE(VP.CHANNEL, VP.CONDITION);
     end if;
  end MOVE_VALVE;

  procedure MOVE_AND_CHECK_VALVE(V : VALVE) is
     VP : VALVE_PARAMETERS renames CONTROL_VALVE(V);
  begin
     while SENSE_VALVE(VP.CHANNEL) /= VP.CONDITION loop
       EFFECT_VALVE(VP.CHANNEL, VP.CONDITION);
       delay VP.TRANSITION;  -- see section 4.9.3.
     end loop;
  end MOVE_AND_CHECK_VALVE;
end VALVE_MOVEMENT;
```

Subprograms in the body may be used to implement tricky aspects of the package - without risk of misuse or interference by other parts of the program. In the above package body (corresponding to the specification in section 7.3), the subprograms SENSE_VALVE and EFFECT_VALVE may be used in the rest of the package body but not outside it. In this way, special or privileged actions may be confined to restricted sections of the program. This feature of Ada makes it possible to ensure safe use of potentially dangerous facilities, for example in library packages.

Variables declared in a package specification or body retain their values through-out the lifetime of the package - their values are not lost between calls of subprograms in the package. These are sometimes called "own" variables (of the package). Those in the body are available for communication between one of the subprograms and another.

The executable part of the package body is executed when the package declaration is elaborated, and is used to initialise objects in the package (whether declared in the specification or the body). The body may also contain exception handlers, in case an exception during initialisation; such a handler does not apply after initialisation of the package.

Exercises

1. In the same compilation unit as the packages specified in section 7.1, there is a subsequent program unit which uses ALAT, ALONG, KIN, and KOUT. What must be written at head of this unit?

2. Write the package specification for the objects and types concerned with time, tracks and sectors in chapter 2.

3. Specify a package for a collection of procedures SA operating on a CAMAC address (consisting of a crate number up to 63, a station number up to 31, and a subaddress up to 15) and a function code (up to 31); if the function code is less than 8, the procedure produces a data word; if the function code is between 16 and 23 the procedure absorbs a data word.

CHAPTER 8

Parallel Programming

A program for an embedded computer system is usually dealing with many activities that are happening at the same time. An effective way of designing such a program is to identify the several strands of activity, each sequential, that have to be running together. Ada recognises this style of programming, and permits a program to be written as a number of quasi-independent sequences of statements, arranged so that each sequence is executed in its own order, without any prescribed ordering between one sequence and another. These are called tasks.

The several tasks may run on separate processors in a multi-computer system, or in a single processor by sharing its computing time among them, resulting in interleaved execution. Of course, if the program can be run on a single processor then the several tasks could, in principle, be merged into a single sequence of statements, fixing the way the tasks interleave. This does not allow for the variety of timing that may arise in practice, and the resulting program would be obscure, convoluted, and hard to maintain. Writing the program in distinct tasks for the parallel strands is usually more convenient and shows a clearer solution to the problem.

The idea of multi-tasking is of course not unique to Ada, although there are not many high-level languages with multi-tasking facilities. In other languages the parallel strands of activity may be called processes or activities.

It is inherent to Ada that the tasks are expected to cooperate, being aware of one another´s existence, and being designed to work with one another to solve an overall problem. If several tasks have to share to resource, they are expected to be programmed to use the resource responsibly; in particular, if any task acquires a resource that other tasks would need, it should release it in a reasonable time. Failure

to do this would be a fault in the program, to be detected and put right
before operational use.

This chapter deals with the basic properties of tasks - how they are
declared, and how they are executed (section 8.1); it also covers the
basic facilities for communication between one task and another, called
a rendezvous (section 8.2). The concept of a rendezvous in Ada is new;
its implication on task structure is discussed in section 8.3, giving
rise to a distinction between active and passive tasks. The few
special facilities for active tasks are described in section 8.4
(leaving passive tasks to Chapter 13). In the final section, we
describe how tasks are used in Ada for dealing with input/output and
interrupt handling (section 8.5).

There are a number of more advanced features of tasks which are
explained in chapter 13.

8.1   Tasks and their relationships

Every task in Ada is written in the declarative part of some enclosing
program unit, which is called its parent. The execution of the parent
determines the overall start and finish of execution of the task. If
several tasks are written in the same declarative part, they are
executed in parallel with one another (and in parallel with the body of
the parent unit). We call these sibling tasks. The parent unit may be
a subprogram, a declare block, a package or another task.

Whenever the parent unit comes to be executed, all the tasks in is
declarative part are started, and each is executed in its own sequential
order, independent of the order of the others (unless there are explicit
statements to relate them). Each task may came to the end of its
statements and thus finish its execution, or it may be brought to an end
by the influence of other tasks. Only when all the tasks declared in
the parent unit have finished (and the parent itself has reached its
end) is the parent deemed to have finished its execution. Thus the
exectuion of tasks in Ada is fully nested.

The normal structure of a multi-task program is to write the several
tasks that do the actions required, and declare them as siblings in the
same parent; the body of the parent is responsible for overall control,
in particular to ensure that the tasks are running properly, and to
close them down when necessary.

It is useful to distinguish two kinds of tasks among the siblings,
which we call active and passive. Passive tasks provide some service

to the others, such as buffering messages between two active taks.
Each passive task may provide a set of services (with appropriate
names), and the active tasks call for these services as they need to use
them.

8.1.1   Declaring a task

A task is written with a specification and a distinct body (like a
package),

```
    PARENT:
    declare      -- parent unit
      P: constant PRESSURE := CURRENT_PRESSURE;

      task ALERT;   -- specification

      task body ALERT is   -- body
      begin
       if P = LOW then
          NEW_LINE;
          PUT (ASCII.BEL);
       end if;
      end ALERT;

      begin    -- execution of parent
      --    statements for parent
      end PARENT;
```

This simple task ALERT would begin execution within its parent (which
has an intialised constant P, of type PRESSURE). The body of the task
tests the value of P and gives the warning if it is LOW, in parallel
with the execution of the parent and any other sibling tasks.

     A simple task is declared in this way; another way of declaring a
task (as one of several similar tasks) is explained in chapter 13.

     The specification gives the task name and lists any services it
provides. Services are specified like procedures, but introduced by the
word entry. Sibling tasks (or the parent body) may call for these
services. The body gives local declarations and the sequence of
statements to implement the services provided by the task, when it
accepts a call to one of its entries.

8.1.2   Interaction between tasks

To be effective, tasks must be able to communicate with one another. In accordance with the normal visibility rules of Ada, the statements (and declarations) inside a task body may refer to entities declared outside it, for example other declarations in the parent unit. Thus one task may refer to entities declared in the specification of a sibling task, as well as other declarations of its parent.

Any task specification may declare entries, which provide services for use elsewhere in the parent unit (normally in its sibling tasks).

```
task ONE_MINUTE is
  entry GO;
  entry CHECK;
end ONE_MINUTE;

task body ONE_MINUTE is
begin
  loop
    accept GO;
    delay 60.0;
    accept CHECK;
  end loop;
end ONE_MINUTE;
```

Another task may call these entries:

```
ONE_MINUTE.GO;  -- starts the delay
-- other statements taking less than one minute
ONE_MINUTE.CHECK;
```

The CHECK entry waits until one minute after the GO entry. (This is an artificial example which is used only to introduce the interaction. A serious timer would have more facilities and checks built in.)

An entry may have parameters, for communicating data values between tasks. Here is a (passive) task to act as a simple communication channel, into which characters may be written and read by different tasks. The two services, WRITE and READ, must be used alternately. (It buffers one character at a time. A more complicated example which buffers several characters is given later.)

```
task SIMPLE_BUFFER is
  entry WRITE (CH : in CHARACTER);
```

```
      entry READ  (CH : out CHARACTER);
  end SIMPLE_BUFFER;

  task body SIMPLE_BUFFER is
    CHAR : CHARACTER;
  begin
    loop
      accept WRITE (CH : in CHARACTER) do
        CHAR := CH;
      end WRITE;
      accept READ (CH : out CHARACTER) do
        CH := CHAR;
      end READ;
      exit when CHAR = ASCII.EOT;
    end loop;
  end SIMPLE_BUFFER;
```

We might have two active tasks PRODUCER and CONSUMER, where the first produces characters to be dealt with in the second; we want to link them by the simple buffer.

```
  task PRODUCER;
  task body PRODUCER is
    C1: CHARACTER;
  begin
    -- loop
    -- produce C1
    SIMPLE_BUFFER.WRITE (C1);
    -- end loop
  end PRODUCER;

  task CONSUMER;
  task body CONSUMER is
    C2: CHARACTER
  begin
    -- loop
    SIMPLE_BUFFER.READ (C2);
    -- use C2
    -- end loop
  end CONSUMER;
```

We discuss the properties of entries and accept statements in section 8.2.

8.1.3   Controlling a task

There may be faults during the execution of a task (as in any other part
of a program), and the mechanism of exception handling allows
appropriate actions to be taken after detected errors. Additional modes
of control are possible, however, by one task influencing another:
typically a parent controlling its children.

Every task automatically has a special exception that may be raised
by another (controlling) task.   This may, for example, be used to
extract the task from an infinite loop.   The handler for this exception
should release any shared resources acquired by the task, make a report
if necessary, and safely close down any equipment associated with the
task.   The special exception takes the task name with the attribute
FAILURE. In the case of SIMPLE_BUFFER, if the writing task did not send
an EOT the reading task would wait indefinitely; if the parent task
decided to presume that the buffer task was faulty it could

```
raise SIMPLE_BUFFER´FAILURE;
```

to close down the buffer task.   This would cause SIMPLE_BUFFER to
execute its exception handler, known in this case as its "last wishes",
before finishing.   (If no last wishes are given, then the task
terminates when it receives the FAILURE exception.)

```
task body SIMPLE_BUFFER is
  CHAR : CHARACTER;
begin
  loop
    accept WRITE (CH : in CHARACTER) do
      CHAR := CH;
    end WRITE;
    accept READ (CH : out CHARACTER) do
      CH := CHAR;
    end READ;
    exit when CHAR = ASCII.EOT;
  end loop;
exception
  when SIMPLE_BUFFER´FAILURE =>
    NEW_LINE;
    PUT ("Buffering fault.");
end SIMPLE_BUFFER;
```

In contrast, CONTROL_LIFT must take steps to ensure safety in the case
of failure, or indeed of any other exception not handled internally:

```
task body CONTROL_LIFT is
begin
  --  normal execution
exception
  when CONTROL_LIFT'FAILURE =>  -- or when others
    EMERGENCY STOP;
    DISPLAY ("OUT OF ORDER");
end CONTROL_LIFT;
```

8.2   Communication between tasks

The normal method of communication between tasks in Ada is called a
rendezvous.   This means that two tasks coincide for a period of time,
after which they resume their parallel execution.   A rendezvous joins
together a task calling for a service and the task providing that
service; the caller is normally an active task and the provider a
passive task.

The task calling for the service does so by executing an entry call
statement (which is written like a procedure call statement, but with
the entry name instead of a procedure name); this says it wishes to
have the rendezvous.   The task providing the service expresses its
readiness to carry out the service by reaching an accept statement; this
says it is ready for the rendezvous.

Whichever of the tasks is first at the rendezvous, it waits for the
other to arrive.

When both calling and accepting tasks have arrived, the rendezvous
action takes place (as specified in the accept statement).   At the end
of the rendezvous, the calling task continues after the entry call
statement and in parallel the accepting task continues execution after
the accept statement.

If several tasks call the same entry, the accepting task carries out
the rendezvous with the first to arrive.   The accepting task usually
contains a loop so that the accept statement is repeated. This has the
effect of dealing with the entry calls one at a time, in their order of
arrival.

The action to be taken at the rendezvous is specified in an accept
statement (in the accepting task), and the specification for that task
makes the rendezvous visible by declaring it as an entry.   Every entry
in the specification must have a corresponding accept statement (perhaps

more than one) in the body:

```
    entry WRITE (CH : in CHARACTER);   -- in specification
    ---
    accept WRITE (CH : in CHARACTER) do   -- in body
      CHAR := CH;
    end WRITE;
```

The rendezvous action for WRITE is to copy the value of the parameter
given at the entry call into the local variable CHAR. Note that the
calling task cannot be doing anything else during the rendezvous, so any
actions involving variables of the calling task (through parameters) are
properly synchronised.

```
    entry GO;   -- in specification
    accept GO;   -- in body
```

Here the rendezvous action is null: as soon as both tasks have reached
the rendezvous (in either order), both may continue. This is purely a
synchronising device.

The parameters of the accept statement allow data values to be
communicated between two tasks, in both directions: in, (default) at the
beginning of the rendezvous, and out at its end (possibly both).

As well as the rendezvous method, tasks may communicate by sharing
variables. By virtue of the visibility rules, an object declared in the
parent task may be used in the children, and this can lead to trouble.
Distinct sibling tasks may refer to the same variable while they are
executing in parallel, so that one task may be accessing it while
another is changing it.

In order to ensure that a shared variable is updated with its proper
value in one task, so that another may use it, the generic procedure
SHARED_VARIABLE_UPDATE (see appendix A) may be used:

```
    S : ITS_TYPE;   -- to be shared
    procedure ENSURE is new
        SHARED_VARIABLE_UPDATE (SHARED => ITS_TYPE);
    --
    -- in task after changing S
    ENSURE (S);
```

(The declaration of ENSURE is an instantiation of the generic procedure
for the particular type of the shared variable: see chapter 10.)

8.3   Asymmetry of rendezvous

The junction of a calling task and an accepting task to form a
rendezvous is not symmetrical, and it is useful to appreciate the
implications of the difference.

   a. The calling task must know the name of the accepting task (and its
       entry point), but not vice versa.   Thus a task with entries offers
       a service to other tasks, limited only by the visibility rules.
   b. An accepting task may wait for the first of several entries to be
       called, whereas a calling task must state one specific entry it
       wishes to call. Thus there is greater non-determinism in the
       accepting task.
   c. Failure of a task in rendezvous is not passed from the calling to
       the accepting task, but is passed from the accepting to the calling
       task:

   The naming difference is perhaps the most fundamental.   To
understand it better, consider the alternatives: either the two
communicating tasks could each name the other, or they could both name
some common entity through which they communicate.

   If communicating tasks were required to name each other, the
redundancy would introduce further opportunities for checking, but it
would be impossible to write a general-purpose task that could be used
with arbitrary other tasks at run-time.

   If communicating tasks were required to name a common medium of
communication (such as a pipe or file), the kinds of communication which
could be expressed would be inherently bound to the facilities offered
by that medium;   and there would still be the asymmetry between each
task concerned and the common medium.

   Ada is designed with the latter scheme in mind, but the means of
communication are not built into the language - they are indeed
programmed. Although the language does not insist on a distinction being
made between different kinds of task, which we call passive tasks and
active tasks, it is probably helpful to design multi-task communication
on this basis. The passive tasks should be written to provide desired
means of communication, and the active tasks can then communicate
through them.

8.4   Active tasks

The normal pattern for Ada tasks then is for the declarative part of
some program unit (the parent) to contain passive and active tasks, with
the body of the parent controlling them. The passive tasks provide the
facilities needed for communication between the active tasks.

It can be expected that a few kinds of communication will be commonly
used (e.g. bounded buffers), and appropriate library units will be
written to provide them. The programmer using tasks will mainly write
active tasks, taking advantage of previously written passive tasks. We
defer to Chapter 13 the further discussion of passive taks, and
concentrate here on writing active tasks.

Writing an active task is almost indistinguishable from writing an
ordinary sequential program. As well as the sequential features, it
may call entries in its passive siblings, but these are very similar to
procedure calls.

The name is an entry call consists of the task name with its entry
name; there is no way of automatically eliding the task name as there is
for package names after a **use** clause. However, any individual entry may
be renamed as a procedure, for example in an active task

```
    procedure BUFFERED_WRITE (C : CHARACTER := ASCII.EOT)
       renames SIMPLE_BUFFER.WRITE;
    procedure BUFFERED_READ (C : out CHARACTER)
       renames SIMPLE_BUFFER.READ;
```

Note that the renaming can change the parameter names and defaults. We
have here given a default to BUFFERED_WRITE so that when called with no
parameter it marks the end of the sequence of characters.

From the point of view of the active task, an entry call is just like
a procedure call apart from timing: a procedure is started immediately
but an entry may have to wait for the passive task to be prepared to
accept it.   There are two programming features that may be used to deal
with this, both varieties of **select** statement (covered further in
chapter 13).

8.4.1   Entry time-out

If a task makes an entry call as an ordinary statement, it waits
(perhaps indefinitely) until the called task is prepared to accept that

entry. We can use a select statement to limit the period of time it is
prepared to wait.

```
select
  VALVE_STABLE;
  OK := TRUE;
or
  delay 0.5;
  OK := FALSE;
end select;
```

The call of VALVE_STABLE (which must be an entry) will be taken if the
called task accepts it within 0.5 seconds, otherwise the other arm will
be executed.

Notice that it is the start of execution of the entry which is
checked, not its finish. The time-out is cancelled as soon as the entry
is accepted.

8.4.2   Conditional entry call

Conditionally calling a rendezvous allows a task that calls an entry to
have an alternative action if the called task is not prepared to accept
the call immediately.

```
select
  GET_CHANNEL;  -- entry call
  -- statements using channel
else
  -- GET_CHANNEL is not immediately acceptable.
  -- alternative actions
end select;
```

Note that in both these forms of select statement there are only two
arms: the arm trying to call the entry, and the alternative.

8.5   Input/Output tasks

It is a common feature of embedded computer systems that they include
application specific input/output devices that must be programmed as
part of the project. We can do this in Ada using tasks to carry out the
input/output operations, including device handlers and interrupt

handlers.

8.5.1   Interrupt handling

An interrupt is considered in Ada to be a hardware-generated entry call. The programmer writes the necessary interrupt handler as an accept statement in a handling task. The Ada entry is linked with the appropriate interrupt entry address by giving its representation specification (see chapter 11).

In the PDP-11, character input from a keyboard generates an interrupt at location 8#100# (say), with the relevant character in the data buffer register. We write the handler for this, copying the character read into a local variable, from which another task can take it:

```
    task KB_HANDLER is
      entry TAKE (CH : out CHARACTER);
      entry KB_DONE;
      for KB_DONE use 8#100#;
    end KB_HANDLER;

    task body KB_HANDLER is
      CHAR : CHARACTER;   -- local variable
      DBR : CHARACTER;   -- hardware register
      for DBR  use 8#177462#;
    begin
      loop
        accept KB_DONE do
          CHAR := DBR;
        end KB_DONE;
        accept TAKE (CH : out CHARACTER) do
          CH := CHAR;
        end TAKE;
      end loop;
    end KB_HANDLER;
```

On reaching accept KB_DONE, the task enables the corresponding interrupt (indicating its readiness for the rendezvous); it sets the interrupt vector address to refer to the body of the accept statement. The interrupt is disabled for the rest of the task. Note that this task never ends.

The priority of a task may be given by a pragma; the possible values for priorities depend on the target computer used.

8.5.2   Input/Output Control

Between the interrupt handlers and the higher levels of a program, it is often useful to have distinct tasks to deal with particular aspects of the low-level device control. For example, the valves in the filtration unit are opened and closed in some particular way which is of no concern to the rest of the program.

```
task VALVE_ACTION is
  entry MOVE_VALVE (V : VALVE);
  entry VALVE_DONE;
end VALVE_ACTION;

task body VALVE_ACTION is
  C : NATURAL;
  S : VALVE_STATUS;
begin
  loop
    accept MOVE_VALVE (V : VALVE) do
      C := CONTROL_VALVE (V).CHANNEL;
      S := CONTROL_VALVE (V).CONDITION;
    end MOVE_VALVE;
    --  statements to establish status S on channel C
    accept VALVE_DONE;
  end loop;
end VALVE_ACTION;
```

Sibling tasks may call

```
VALVE_ACTION.MOVE_VALVE (AIR_VENT);
```

to get the valve into the position previously assigned to the appropriate valve parameter.

The entry VALVE_DONE must be called (for example by an interrupt) before another attempt to move a valve will be accepted.

The following program is for a small PDP-11, to make it ring a bell every second. The output is done by a simple task which puts a character in the printer buffer then waits for the ´i/o done´ interrupt. The delay is designed to use the line clock (which interrupts 50 times a second).

```
procedure BLEEP is
```

```
task XMIT is
  entry PUT(C:CHARACTER);
  entry DOIO;
  for DOIO use at 8#64#;
end XMIT;

task body XMIT is
  package PDP_11 is
    type BIT is (OFF,ON);
    type BITS is array (0..15) of BIT;

    for BIT use (OFF=>0, ON=>1);
    pragma PACK(BITS);

    procedure ENABLE(CSR:BITS) is
    pragma INLINE;
    begin
      CSR(6):=ON;
    end ENABLE;

    procedure DISABLE(CSR:BITS) is
    pragma INLINE;
    begin
      CSR(6):=OFF;
    end DISABLE;
  end PDP_11;

  use PDP_11;
  XBR:CHARACTER;
  XSR:BITS;
  for XBR use at 8#177566#;
  for XSR use at 8#177564#;
begin
  loop
    accept PUT(C:CHARACTER) is
      XBR := C;
    end PUT;
    ENABLE(XSR);
    accept DOIO;
    DISABLE(XSR);
  end loop;
end XMIT;


package TIMING is
  procedure DELAY_TICKS(N:NATURAL);
end TIMING;
```

```
        package body TIMING is
          TICK:constant DURATION:=0.02;
          procedure DELAY_TICKS(N:NATURAL) is
          begin
             delay N*TICK;
          end DELAY_TICKS;
        end TIMING;

        use TIMING;
     begin
        loop
          DELAY_TICKS(50);
          XMIT.PUT(ASCII.BEL);
        end loop;

     end BLEEP;
```

This program is written with nested units. The inner modules XMIT and TIMING deal with application-specific input/output.

Exercises

1. Write a piece of program to discover whether a pool of values contains an item with a particular key, giving the value if it is present. The items in the pool are being inserted, changed, and deleted by several concurrent tasks at a lower hardware priority.

2. Write an interrupt handler for a character printer. The character to be printed must be put in a hardware register; the interrupt indicates that it has been accepted.

CHAPTER 9

Program Structure

The principles of structured programming and the concept of abstract data types (in which details of the implementation are hidden), are essential for the reliable construction of large programs by many programmers. In this chapter we turn to the program text itself and the manner of its development and modification.

We deal with the general relationships among the entities in a program - particularly the identifiers and meanings they have in the program. We discuss the rules for visibility of declarations, which lead us to describe the structure of a program in terms of blocks and modules.

There can be many identifiers in an Ada program, denoting variables, constants, types, procedures, exceptions, tasks, etc., and each applies throughout a particular part of the program. This is true both for the predefined identifiers such as INTEGER and CONSTRAINT_ERROR as well as for identifiers defined by the programmer such as X, I, OBJECT, ASSOCIATED_TRACK. The meaning of an identifier is determined by the way it is introduced - usually in a declaration at the head of a block or module. The positions in the program where it may be used depend on the position of the declaration. The same applies also to the operator symbols such as + * (which may be overloaded by the programmer), and to enumeration literals (which may be characters). In this chapter we explain the structure of an Ada program, and consequently where in a program any particular declaration is "visible", so that the identifier it declares can be used.

A program in Ada has a logical and a physical structure. These are closely related but not identical. The logical structure consists of "program units", which may be nested inside one another. The physical structure consists of "compilation units" which are always separate from

101

one another.

A program unit can be a subprogram, package or task. For each kind of program unit there may be a specification and a body. Any kind of program unit may contain units of the same or different kinds inside it. Each compilation unit is a distinct program unit, with an appropriate context specification at its head.

The program as a whole consists of a collection of compilation units, all separate, and each compilation unit consists of a program unit that may contain other program units inside it, nested to any depth. It is possible for the text inside one compilation unit to refer to other compilation units, provided that the other compilation units are mentioned in the introductory context specification.

In this chapter we concentrate on the logical structure: program units; compilation units are explained in chapter 10.

9.1   Visibility of Declarations

Because it may happen that the same identifier is used for different purposes in different parts of the program (for example when different people are writing separate parts and decide independently to choose a particular name), we need to be able to associate any identifier used in the program with the proper meaning. We say that a declaration is "visible" in those parts of the program where its identifier can be used. The visibility rules ensure that there is no confusion: each use of the identifier has the meaning given by the corresponding declaration.

Each identifier (other than a statement label, block or loop identifier, or a loop parameter) which is used in a program must be declared somewhere in the program, or in the library packages it uses or the standard environment. The statement labels, block and loop identifiers and loop parameters are implicitly declared by their occurrence, as explained below.

9.1.1   Statement labels

A statement may be labelled, so that it may be referred to in a goto statement. The labelled statement is of course one of a sequence of statements, which may be part of a compound statement, and may contain other compound statements.

The first occurence of the label identifier in the program may be at the head of the labelled statement (for a backward - directed **goto** statement) or in a **goto** statement (for a forward jump). This first occurence acts as a declaration for the identifier as a label, and applies from that point until the end of the innermost enclosing program unit. This may be a subprogram body or a package body or a task body, whichever is the smallest.

A **goto** statement can specify the label of any statement which is in the same sequence of statements, or in an enclosing sequence of statements (if the **goto** statement is in a compound statement), subject to the rules given in section 4.7.4.

9.1.2   Block and loop identifiers

A block (declare statement) may be named, with a block identifier at the beginning and end of the block. Entities declared inside the block may be distinguished using this name. Similarly, a loop may be named, giving the loop identifier at the beginning and end of the loop. A loop identifier may be used in an exit statement.

```
OUTER: declare
  I,J : INTEGER;   -- these are OUTER.I, OUTER.J
begin
  -- see also section 9.3.1
end OUTER;

L1: loop
  -- any inner loop may contain
    exit L1 when REQUIRED;
  -- rest of loop(s)
end loop L1;
```

The occurrence of the identifier naming the block or loop acts as a declaration.

9.1.3   Loop parameters

A loop introduced by a **for** clause, such as

```
for I in 1 .. 200 loop
  VECTOR(I) := 0.0;
end loop;
```

establishes a new scope consisting of the sequence of statements which form the body of the loop. In the loop body, the loop parameter (I in this case) is available as though it had been declared as a **constant** of the type defined by the range part of the **for** clause, thus:

    I : **constant** INTEGER **range** 1 .. 200;

(The range in a **for** clause need not be of integers: it may be any discrete type, such as an enumeration type).

The fact that the loop parameter is effectively declared as a **constant** means that it is illegal to make any assignment to it inside the body, or to use it as an **out** or **in out** parameter of a procedure.

The fact that the loop parameter has a scope extending over the statements forming the body of the loop means that it has no significance in statements outside the loop, so there is no way by which statements outside the loop can refer to the loop parameter (for example, after an **exit** statement).

    for I **in** 0 .. 100 **loop**
       -- manipulate members of array A while positive
       exit when A(I) < 0.0;
    end loop;   -- value of I is now inaccessible

If there had been another declaration of the same identifier I in the program unit containing this loop, the outer declaration would be hidden. If it is necessary to know the value of the loop parameter outside, then its value must be assigned to another variable before leaving the loop.

9.2   Declared identifiers

For each declaration, there is a defined region of the program over which the declared identifier has the meaning given in the declaration; this is called the scope of the declaration. Within this scope, there is a particular region where the identifier may be immediately used, without any additional information. In this region, the declaration is said to be "directly visible".

Within the scope but not in the region of direct visibility, the declaration is said to be hidden; it is possible by appropriate additional information (of various kinds) to arrange for one or more hidden declarations to be made visible. The identifiers they declare can then be used with the declared meanings.

The regions of the program over which a declaration is relevant, both for scope and for direct visibility, are related to the program structure. We first explain the structures relevant to certain kinds of entities in the program, then proceed to the general position on scopes in an Ada program.

Scopes are mainly determined by the block and module structure of a program.   The block structure relates to subprogram bodies and declare statements; module structure relates to packages and tasks. Within the major units determined by the program structure, certain constructs introduce special regions relevant to enumeration types, records and procedure parameters.

9.3   Block Structure

The classical form of block structure, which is available in Ada, provides for declarations to be valid within the part of the program immediately following them.   We have declare statements, which are blocks in the executable part of the program, and subprograms, which are blocks in the declarative part of a program.

9.3.1   Block structure with declare statements

The declare statement is the simplest form of block structure in Ada. The word **declare** introduces one or more declarations, which are followed by **begin** then a sequence of statements, possibly with some exception handlers, and finally the word **end**. Each of the declared identifiers may be used in any subsequent declaration in the block, and throughout the sequence of statements and exception handlers. Thus any identifier introduced in the declarative part of the block has that meaning for all the executable part of the block. Its scope is all the block after the declaration.

There is no theoretical limit to the size of the block or the size of the declarations or statements inside it, but for practical purposes it is wise to keep declare blocks smaller than one page of text: for anything larger a module structure will be easier to handle, particularly for program maintenance.

The identifiers that are introduced in the declarative part of any block must all be distinct (with the exception of overloaded enumeration literals and procedures: see section 9.7). However, since the declare statement occurs in a position where many identifiers may already be visible, there is the possibility that an identifier declared inside the block is the same as an identifier visible in the context of the declare statement. In this case, the declaration at the head of the block takes precedence for the statements in the block, hiding the outer declarations for the same identifier. So in general, if the program has a nested block structure with declare statements in the executable part of larger declare statements, an identifier used in the program is interpreted according to the smallest enclosing block in which it is declared. (It is possible to have a block without any declarations, in which the statement starts with the word **begin** rather than **declare**; such a construct allows a particular set of statements to be guarded by specific exception handlers.)

An outer declaration that is hidden by a declaration for the same identifier in an inner block is still in scope, but its full name must be used to identify it. In the following block,

```
OUTER: declare
   I, J : INTEGER;   -- outer declarations
begin
   -- statements may use outer declarations
   INNER: declare
      J, K : INTEGER;   -- inner declarations
   begin
      -- J, K mean INNER.J, INNER.K
      -- I means OUTER.I
      -- OUTER.J needs full name
   end INNER;
   -- I, J mean OUTER.I, OUTER.J
end OUTER;
```

the identifier J is declared as a variable in the outer declarations and again in the inner declarations. Within the statements of the inner block, the inner declaration for J hides the outer declaration for J, so the simple name J in the inner block relates to the inner declaration rather than the outer one.

Although we illustrate this rule using identifiers for variables, the same principles apply to all declarations: types, procedures, packages etc. Furthermore, the kind of entity which an identifier denotes in an outer block need have no relationship at all with a declaration in an inner block.

There is a complicating possibility that an identifier declared in an outer block may be used (as opposed to declared) in the declarative part of an inner block – perhaps as an initialisation value for a variable, or as a type name. In this case it is dangerous to try to redeclare that identifier in the same inner block. So in the following block, the declarative part of the inner block should not redeclare the identifiers ITEM or P.

```
declare
  type ITEM is new INTEGER;
  P, Q : ITEM;
begin
  -- statements may use P and Q
  declare
    R : ITEM;
      -- subsequent declarations must not redeclare ITEM
    S : ITEM := P;
      -- subsequent declarations must not redeclare P
  begin
    -- statements may use P, Q, R, and S.
  end;
end;
```

9.3.2   Block structure with subprograms

A procedure or a function declaration is another form of block structure, which is basically similar to a declare statement but has the added feature of formal parameters.

The formal parameters of the procedure or function are introduced in the subprogram heading, and have the same effect on the subprogram body as declarations which may occur between the heading and the word **begin** at the start of the executable part of the subprogram. Thus the identifiers introduced as formal parameters may be used in any subsequent declaration and throughout the sequence of statements forming the executable part. The formal parameters are allowed only to be data objects, that is constants or variables. (They may not be types or other program objects such as procedures, exceptions, packages or tasks). The identifiers which are introduced as the formal parameters must be all distinct, from one another and from any local declarations. All these identifiers are visible in the subprogram body.

```
function PEX (I : NATURAL) return SHORT is
  S : SHORT := I;
begin
  return 6 - S;
```

```
   exception
     when CONSTRAINT_ERROR =>
       raise BAD_PARAMETER;
   end PEX;
```

Within this subprogram, we have the formal parameter I and the local variable S. The body also refers to two types (NATURAL and SHORT) and two exception (CONSTRAINT_ERROR and BAD_PARAMETER) which must have been declared outside the subprogram.

The subprogram declaration is itself in some context where many identifiers are visible, and the same rules apply as for a declare statement. Thus any identifier visible at the position of the subprogram declaration is also visible from inside the subprogram declaration unless that identifier is hidden by giving it a local meaning for the subprogram, either as a formal parameter or by a local declaration.

9.4   Module structure

Whereas blocks in a program serve the primary purpose of limiting the visibility of identifiers declared in them, modules (whether packages or tasks) serve the complementary purpose of expanding the visibility of identifiers declared in them. Certain of the declarations in a module have a scope which is greater than the module containing them. Identifiers which may have such an expanded visibility must be declared in the public part of the module - the specification part. We call these the public declarations. All other identifiers declared in the module, namely those declared in the implementation part or the private part of the specification, can never be visible outside the module, and are treated in the same way as identifiers in a block structure. (Note however that there may be separately compiled subunits of the module body, which although physically separate are logically inside the module.)

A package or a task (module) specification introduces the identifier for that module; as with other declarations, this identifier is directly visible in the context of the module declaration.

Throughout the scope of the package declaration, its public declarations are also in scope but they are hidden. They may be made visible throughout any specified program unit (provided that there is no ambiguity) by a use clause. Making the public identifiers visible throughout a unit is called exposing them. Because the current unit may happen to contain a declaration for the same identifier as is made public by the package, or several packages which are exposed in the same unit may happen to contain public declarations for the same identifier, the exposure of public identifiers applies only to those for which there is no such possible ambiguity.

Whether or not there is a use clause, any public identifier in scope may be accessed throughout the scope of the module by component selection, since there is then no possible ambiguity. In a context where the module name is visible, a component selection (consisting of the module name, a period, then the public identifier) constitutes the name of the entity which was declared in the visible part of the module. Thus with the module specified

```
package GINO_F is
   procedure DRAW2(X,Y : FLOAT);
   procedure MOVTO2(X,Y : FLOAT);
end GINO_F;
```

in a context where GINO_F is visible, the procedures can be called by statements such as

```
GINO_F.MOVTO2(X1, Y1);
GINO_F.DRAW2(X1 + 1.0E0, Y1);
```

The name so formed has all the properties of the declared entity: for example, if it is a record, its components may be selected, and if it is an inner module then the public identifiers of that may be accessed by further component selection. Using this technique, each time the public identifier is to be refered to, its full name must be given, starting with the visible module name.

Exposure is an alternative technique, by which all the public identifiers of a module or set of modules are made visible together, apart from potential ambiguities. A use clause may be written as though it were a declaration; it gives one or more module names, and exposes their public identifiers for the current block or module. So where GINO_F is visible, the following construction allows the unambiguous public identifiers of that package to be used without needing their full names:

```
declare
   use GINO_F;
   procedure DRAW2 (LENGTH, BREADTH : FLOAT) is
   begin
   -- local declaration
```

```
      end DRAW2;
   begin
      MOVTO2(X1, Y1); -- from GINO_F because no ambiguity
      GINO_F.DRAW2(X1+1.0, Y1); --explicitly from GINO_F
      DRAW2(3.0, 4.0);  -- implies local declaration
   end;
```

If the exposure of a particular identifier is inhibited by a local declaration, or by duplication of public identifiers in different modules exposed together, then any desired public declaration may be accessed by using the full name of the declared entity.

9.5   Uniqueness of identifiers

In all the various places where identifiers may be introduced, there are rules to ensure that the identifiers are distinguishable from one another. For most declared entities (including variables, constants, types, exceptions, modules) where the identifier stands alone, this requires that distinct identifiers must be used for the different entities declared together. This rule is relaxed for the values of an enumeration type: each individual enumeration type must have a distinct set of values, but the identifiers introduced as the values of one type do not have to be distinct from the identifiers introduced as the values of another type; such identifiers are said to be overloaded. The rule is also partially relaxed for subprograms, which can have parameters (and each subprogram has a specific number of parameters, which may be zero). Since their identifiers are always used with a list of parameters of specified types, it is possible for several subprograms to have the same identifier, provided that their parameters are sufficiently different. This is called overloading the subprogram, and is explained fully in section 9.7.

In each of the following, where several identifiers are introduced together, they must all be different:

a. Values of an enumeration type.
b. Components of a record type.
c. Entities introduced in a block or module (taking both specification and body together), apart from overloaded subprograms. These entities include formal parameters, local declarations, block and loop identifiers and statement labels.

Between any one set of declarations and another, an identifier may be repeated, and the rules of visibility determine which meaning is implied

by any use of the identifier. It is illegal to use an identifier where
no declaration for it is visible - it then has no meaning.

9.6   Local contexts

In some special constructions, identifiers from another part of the
program may be used, even though they are not normally visible. This
might arise because of potential ambiguity or to establish associations.
These special cases concern overloaded enumeration values, record
components, and name associations for aggregates or subprogram
parameters.

9.6.1   Values of Enumeration types

Each enumeration type declaration gives the set of identifiers (or
characters) that are the possible values in the enumeration type. These
identifiers or characters are known as enumeration literals; any such
identifier is normally available for use in expressions of the
appropriate enumeration type, provided that no other declaration is
given for it. For any individual enumeration type, the possible values
must of course all be distinct, but different enumeration types need not
have disjoint possible values. Thus:

```
type NUM_BASE is
   (BIN, OCT, DEC, HEX);
type MON_NAME is
   (JAN, FEB, MAR, APR,
    MAY, JUN, JUL, AUG,
    SEP, OCT, NOV, DEC);
```

can exist in the same context even though they both have possible values
OCT and DEC.

An identifier which is a possible enumeration value for more than one
enumeration type in the same context is said to be overloaded. In this
case, the identifier is not immediately available for use in an
expression : it is excluded from the context in which it is overloaded.
However, the enumeration type name (which can not be overloaded) is
available for use, to introduce a qualified expression.

Within this qualified expression the enumeration value may be given,
as any possible ambiguity has been eliminated. Thus the qualified
expression constitutes a local context, in which the identifier gives

the value in the specified enumeration type.

   In the context of MON_NAME and NUM_BASE, the identifiers BIN and JAN
may be used directly, but for the overloaded enumeration values one must
write NUM_BASE´(OCT) or MON_NAME´(DEC) if the context does not resolve
the ambiguity.

   An array which is indexed by an enumeration type implies
qualification for its index values. Consequently, an element of such an
array may be specified by using the enumeration value as the index
without needing explicit qualification. For example, with

   DAYS_IN_MONTH : **array** (MON_NAME) **of** NATURAL
      := (31, 29, 31, 30, 31, 30,
          31, 31, 30, 31, 30, 31);
          -- value for a leap year

any use of

   DAYS_IN_MONTH(OCT)

implies

   DAYS_IN_MONTH(MON_NAME´(OCT))

so automatically resolves the potential ambiguity.

9.6.2   <u>Record component identifiers</u>

The identifiers of record components are not necessarily visible in the
context of the declaration of either the record type or any of the
record objects; however, they become visible in the local contexts of
component selections and record aggregates. The type of the record must
be visible for any possibility of access to components of an object of
that type.

   type DATE **is**
     record
       YEAR : INTEGER **range** 1901 .. 2099;
       MONTH : MON_NAME;
       DAY : INTEGER **range** 1 .. 31;
     end record;

A record type declaration introduces the identifiers and types for its components. These identifiers (YEAR, MONTH, DAY in the above example) are <u>not</u> directly visible in the context of the type declaration. An object of that record type may be declared wherever the type declaration is visible, and in that context the type identifier may not be redeclared (as with ITEM in section 9.3.1). There may be an inner context in which the record type declaration is redeclared but the record object is still visible: in this context, all the constituents of the data object are hidden (as though it were of a private type: see section 7.4).

In a context where the type identifier is visible, a record aggregate may be specified, of the form shown in section 2.4.

```
(1900, JAN, 1)
(1999, NOV, 31)  -- legal but not sensible
(2000, FEB, 29)  -- component values given by position
(MONTH => FEB, DAY => 29, YEAR => 2000)
        -- components given by name
DATE´(1979, OCT, 13)  -- qualified expression
```

If there is no ambiguity over the aggregate, its type need not be stated explicitly. However, in general, the aggregate is given as a qualified expression, in which the record type is stated.

The association of a component with a value may be by position or by name, using the same notation as for subprogram parameters. This is a special context where the component identifiers are visible on the left hand sides of name-associated components, but not on right hand sides or in position-associated components, for which the outer context applies.

In a context where both the object identifier and the type identifier are visible, components of the record may be accessed by "component selection". The record object name followed by the component identifier constitutes the name of the component, and has all the properties of an object of the appropriate type - including the possibility of having components itself, if the component is a record within a record.

For example, in the context of the type declarations of POSITION and DISTANCE, there may be data object declarations

```
P, Q: POSITION;      -- data object declaration
SCAN : DISTANCE;
```

with components such as

```
P.EAST
```

Q.HEADING

Thus we might have

```
Q := POSITION´(
    EAST    => P.EAST + SCAN,
    NORTH   => P.NORTH - SCAN,
    HEADING => P.HEADING);
```

The identifiers EAST, NORTH and HEADING (the component identifier in type POSITION) are not directly visible here, and other declarations for these identifiers would be possible without confusion.

9.6.3   Formal parameters of subprograms

Within any context where a subprogram name is visible, the identifiers for the formal parameters of the subprogram are not directly visible, but may become visible in the local context of a subprogram call, for association by name with actual parameters.

A subprogram call consists of the procedure or function name followed by the list of parameter associations. This list constitutes a special context, in which the identifiers for the formal parameter of the subprogram are visible on the left hand sides of name-association parameters. They are not visible on right hand sides of name-associations or in positional parameters.

For example, with the declaration

procedure INSERT (IT: **in** ITEM; LIST: **in out** ITEM_PTR);

the identifiers ITEM and ITEM_PTR must be already visible at the points of declaration and use; the declaration introduces the identifier INSERT. The identifiers IT and LIST are not visible in that context, and if there happen to be declarations elsewhere in the block for these identifiers there is no confusion.

On a call of this procedure, the parameter list may contain the identifiers IT and LIST as parameter names.

```
declare
    A, B : ITEM;  -- inner declarations
    L : ITEM_PTR;
    IT:  INTEGER;  -- no confusion
begin
```

```
    INSERT(IT => A, LIST => L);
  end;
```

Both these parameter associations are by name; the first specifies that formal parameter IT is to be given the value A. Similarly the second parameter association specifies that the formal parameter LIST is to be taken as the object L. Note the inner declaration of IT. This is visible in parameter association by position and on the right of parameter associations by name: it could be used in an expression of the appropriate type.

9.7   Signature of subprograms

A subprogram (procedure or function) is distinguished by the combination of its declared identifier and the properties of its parameters. The relevant parameter properties are their formal identifiers, modes (**in**, **out** or **in out**), and types, with the type of the result, if any. This combination is called its signature. As a consequence of the parameter properties being involved in the signature, it is possible for a single subprogram identifier to be "overloaded", so that it can be declared with different bodies for different formal parameters. This is particularly important for the input/output procedures, where PUT and GET are defined for the various predefined data types.

The signature of the subprogram is used (at compile-time) to find which is the appropriate subprogram declaration for each subprogram call, and is composed of the information which must be specified in the call. The resolution of subprogram overloading is done at compile time, so there is no run-time overhead.

In order to give this information unambiguously, each subprogram parameter must have its type determinable (implying the need for a qualified expression if overloaded literals are used, such as numerical constants with user-defined types). For example, if a special output procedure were needed for data of type WEIGHT, it could be declared

```
  procedure PUT (X:WEIGHT) is
       -- appropriate body
  end PUT;
```

This could be used with variables of type WEIGHT

```
  W : WEIGHT;
  PUT(W);
```

but to apply this special procedure to a constant, say 0.0E0, the type qualifier must be used

    PUT(WEIGHT´(0.0E0));

to determine the right signature.

Exercises

1. Given

        A : **array** (0 .. 100) **of** FLOAT;

    write statements to find the negative element with smallest index value, and set

        I : INTEGER;

    to that index value. What happens if no element is negative?

2. Given character sets (which are in effect enumeration types) ASCII and EBCDIC, and a conversion array

        A_TO_E : **array** (ASCII) **of** EBCDIC;

    with variables

        C : ASCII;
        D : EBCDIC;

    write statements to assign to D the character corresponding to the current value of C unless it is a dollar sign, in which case assign a space. Remember that in this context, unqualified character strings would be ambiguous in type, different from both ASCII and EBCDIC.

3. In the sequence of statements following the declarations of section 9.6.2, including

        P,Q : POSITION;

    we have

        declare
          EAST : FLOAT;
          -- other declarations

```
begin
  -- statements
  PUT ( P.EAST );
end;
```

Does the above declaration of EAST affect the meaning of P.EAST ?
(No.)
Would any declaration there affect the meaning of P.EAST.?   (Yes:
redeclaration of P or POSITION)

CHAPTER 10

Separate Compilation and Generics

This chapter is concerned with compilation aspects of an Ada program: the physical structure of the program text, and the compile-time processing. The physically separate program units are called compilation units. Ada includes facilities for compile-time parametrization: as well as conventional run-time parameters for subprograms, both subprograms and packages may be written with compile-time parameters; they are then called generic program units.

In order that several programmers may be able to work concurrently on a project, each must be developing a distinct and clearly defined part of the eventual large program. Each must be able to handle and test his part without unnecessary dependence on other programmers, and without making other programmers unnecessarily dependent on him.

In general, each programmer is implementing certain facilities on the assumption that certain other facilities are available. The information which he needs to know is therefore the specification of these facilities, independent of the way they are implemented.

The textual structure of the part of a program developed by an individual programmer must be such as to contain and distinguish

    a. Specification of facilities provided;

    b. Implementation details of facilities provided;

    c. Specification of facilities assumed.

A rudimentary or dummy form of this textual structure could have the implementation details missing, and this might be the starting point for the programmer's task. It is clear from this that the style of project management has a strong relationship with the textual program structure. Depending on the working environment, it may be necessary to repeat in full the specifications of facilities assumed; alternatively it may be sufficient to name them and have the full specifications implied. A third possibility is to keep the full specifications centrally and have programmers name them when providing implementation details.

An Ada program is written as a collection of separately compiled program units, with compile-time type-checking across boundaries. Each unit may provide a set of facilities, and may use the facilities of other units. This kind of program structure determines the order in which units must be compiled: definition before usage. The context in which a unit is to be used must clearly be specified first if the unit is sensitive to that context. Library units are context insensitive so can be compiled before any unit which uses them. Ada separates the implementation part of a module from its specification part, so the specification parts can be compiled in the required order but the implementation parts subsequently in whatever order is convenient (provided that they conform to the previously compiled specification).

Here we consider how to design and construct an Ada program from a number of compilation units - how to express the relationship between them, and what the consequences of these relationships are in terms of the order in which compilation units are handled.

10.1   Compilation Units

A program in Ada is formed from a number of separate compilation units, which are translated individually and then linked together to form the target program load. If any changes have to be made to the program after the initial translation, it is only necessary to recompile the affected compilation units (and any others which depend on them) then relink them with the unaffected compilation units.

Although compilation units are translated separately, consistency checks are applied to ensure that their interfaces are compatible. This means that communication between separate compilation units is as well-checked as that between parts of a single compilation unit. In order to achieve this degree of security at compilation time, the translation of a compilation unit is not done in isolation but is associated by the compiler with information from other compilation units which are relevant. Similarly, after a compilation unit has been compiled, information is maintained for subsequent use in the translation of other compilation units which may depend on it. All this information for inter-compilation unit checking is maintained by the Ada translation system, forming a data base for each set of compilation units which comprise a complete program.

The fundamental idea in Ada is that each compilation unit, although compiled individually, is considered to be defined in some context which determines the visibility of declarations between one compilation unit and another. A compilation unit may use identifiers declared in that context (perhaps in other compilation units), but of course need not do so.

A basic distinction is drawn between compilation units that are effectively at the outermost level of declarations in a program, and those which are not. The former are called library units, the latter sub-units. A sub-unit must state which already existing unit effectively contains it; this is called its parent unit. A library unit makes no assumptions about declarations in the context of its definition; it could then be taken into other contexts as required. Tasks may only be sub-units; subprograms and packages may be library units or sub-units. A library unit may be a declaration or a corresponding body. All subunits of the same parent must have distinct names. All library units must have distinct names.

Once a library unit has been compiled, the facilities that it provides (by its public declarations) may be used in other compilation units by giving a suitable context specification.

We discuss how to specify the context of effective definition of a compilation unit; how to specify which other contexts it may refer to; and how these relationships affect the order in which the compilation units of a program must be compiled or recompiled after some change.

10.2   Effective context of a compilation unit

The rules of visibility of declarations apply between compilation units in the same way as they do between program units within the same compilation unit. Thus the identifiers declared in a separately compiled unit are visible in the context of the declaration and any context in which they are exposed, but nowhere else. It is of course possible to make the context of the declaration be the main level of the program and thereby get the identifiers visible throughout the program (apart from redeclarations), but this is by no means necessary.

A library unit has an effective context which is the whole program, i.e. all other library units. A subunit has a context which is which is explicitly specified as its parent unit: another unit (either a library unit or a subunit). Thus a program as a whole consists of a number of compilation units, of which some are library units and the rest are subunits. Every subunit has another unit as its parent unit.

A library unit may be the declaration or body of a subprogram or a package (not a task); a subunit may be the body of a subprogram, package or task. Library units are effectively global for the whole program, but subunits belong to particular contexts.

The context in which a particular subunit is to be effectively defined is somewhere in the outermost declarative level of its parent unit, as given by a body stub such as

```
package body FLUSHING is separate;
procedure PRINT_HELP_FILE is separate;
```

The parent unit must always contain the complete specification of the subunit, whether it is a package, task or subprogram. In the case of a subprogram, the specification gives the formal parameters and result, if any.

```
procedure DRAW2 (X, Y: FLOAT) is separate;
function ASK (QUESTION: STRING)
   return BOOLEAN is separate;
function MAT_MUL (X : MATRIX;
              (Y : COL_VEC)
   return COL_VEC is separate;
```

If the subunit is a module, the parent unit must contain the specification explicitly.

Suppose CLEAN_FILTER needs a package FLUSHING, which is written separately, then CLEAN_FILTER must contain the specification of FLUSHING among its local declarations:

```
-- in the declarative part of CLEAN_FILTER
package FLUSHING is     -- specification here
  procedure WATER_FLUSH ( N : NATURAL range 1 .. 2);
  procedure AIR_FLUSH;
end FLUSHING;
```

The corresponding package body must be indicated later in the same declarative part; it may be given either immediately here, or substituted by a "stub" here and compiled separately as a subunit.   The body is given immediately thus:

```
   -- later in declarative part of CLEAN_FILTER
   package body FLUSHING is
     -- local declarations
     -- bodies of WATER_FLUSH and AIR_FLUSH
     -- initialisation
   end FLUSHING;
```

or by substituting a stub:

```
   -- later in declarative part of CLEAN_FILTER
   package body FLUSHING is separate;    -- stub
```

with the separately compiled subunit:

```
   separate (CLEAN_FILTER)        -- stating parent
   package body FLUSHING is
     -- local declarations
     -- bodies of WATER_FLUSH and AIR_FLUSH
     -- initialisation
   end FLUSHING;
```

10.3   Contexts accessible to a compilation unit

The default context for a compilation unit is the package STANDARD
(given in Appendix A), allowing the unit to access the predefined
declarations for INTEGER, NATURAL, BOOLEAN, FLOAT etc.

A compilation unit may access the declarations of other compilation
units if they are explicitly stated in the context specification at its
head, in with clauses.

The package STORE specified in section 7.1 may be compiled separately
to form a library unit (since it needs no context beyond STANDARD).
Suppose we have another unit, GEOGRAPHY which needs to use the variables
in STORE, then GEOGRAPHY may be written

```
   with STORE;
   package GEOGRAPHY is
     -- may use STORE.ALAT etc
   end GEOGRAPHY;
```

The shorthand notation for entities specified in STORE may be used if we
write

use STORE;

either immediately after the with clause at the head (to expose the public declarations of STORE over all of GEOGRAPHY) or in the declarative part of any program units nested within GEOGRAPHY (to limit the exposure).

Any number of library units may be specified in the context specification. All the public declarations of these units are brought into scope for the unit being compiled.

10.4   Separate subunits

Consider two program units OUTER and INNER, related such that if they were written in a single compilation unit, then OUTER would contain INNER. The relationship has aspects pertaining to both units, which must be distinguished if the units are compiled separately. Each unit must indicate the relationship for itself: with separate compilation for the fact that OUTER contains INNER must be given in the OUTER unit, but also must be given (if relevant) in the INNER unit.

As a declaration in OUTER, the body stub

package body INNER **is separate;**

expresses the fact that OUTER contains INNER, and allows any subsequent declarations or statements in OUTER to use INNER as though the full text of the package body were there. This also expresses the fact that INNER is a subunit, and OUTER is its parent unit.

The heading for INNER

separate (OUTER)
package body INNER **is** --

connects this compilation unit to the specification for INNER given in OUTER; it expresses the fact that INNER may use the entities declared in OUTER, and allows any subsequent declarations or statements in INNER to refer to any of the other declarations of OUTER visible at the position of the body stub.

10.5   Order of compilation

The separate compilation units which form an Ada program may be
submitted for translation in any logical order. We here explain how the
ideas of context of effective definition and accessible contexts
influence the order of program construction whether by top-down or
bottom-up methods.

    The underlying principle is that if one compilation unit requires
information from another compilation unit, then the unit providing the
information must be translated before that requiring the information.

    The with clause is the main influence on order of compilation. For
each compilation unit governed by such a clause, the listed units'
specifications must have already been compiled before the unit naming
them in a with clause, so that their declarations may be accessible.
Thus if we have

    with TIME_SCALES, CHANNEL_VALUES;
    package body FILTER_OPERATIONS is
      -- text
    end FILTER_OPERATIONS;

then FILTER_OPERATIONS can not be compiled until after the
specifications of TIME_SCALES and CHANNEL_VALUES have been compiled. A
subunit must always be compiled after the specificaton of its parent:
the unit CLEAN_FILTER that contains

    package body FLUSHING is separate;

must be compiled before that which begins

    separate (CLEAN_FILTER)
    package body FLUSHING is

in order that the specification and body of FLUSHING are properly
associated.

    If a compilation unit does not have a context specification, then
there is no constraint on its order of compilation. This allows library
modules to be compiled in advance of programs which use them,

    The parent unit of a subunit contains the specification of the
subunit, so may use all its facilities. The other declarations in the
outermost level of the parent unit may also be used in the body of the
subunit, just as though it were textually present in the parent.

In bottom-up program construction, we build the program progressively from subprograms into larger units, generally completing the body of a unit before working in detail on the unit that calls it. This allows each unit to be easily tested as all its subsidiary units have been completed by the time work on it begins. In this method, compilation units would generally be library units, which might refer to previously written library units. Perhaps a project-specific package would be written first to contain basic declarations for the project, and all subsequent units would be compiled with that package as their context.

In top-down program construction, we build the program by refinement, with increasing amount of implementation detail, generally completing the specification of entities and the body of the unit using those entities, before working in detail on the implementation of the specified entities. This allows each unit to be easily verified, as all the units are specified in advance of implementation and the implementation of each unit can be validated on its own. In this method, compilation units might well be subunits, sensitive to the context in which the unit is effectively declared.

In practice, of course, programs are constructed using both bottom-up and top-down methods, and Ada allows both to be accommodated.

10.6   Order of recompilation

If there is a change to the program, either because an error has been corrected, or some change to the specification has been taken into account, or a different programming technique is adopted, or for any other reason, one or more compilation units are immediately affected and the new versions of them must be recompiled.

There are circumstances in which other compilation units not immediately concerned are nethertheless possibly affected; these must also be recompiled, to make sure that all the consistency checks for an Ada program still hold.

The guiding principle is to maintain software interfaces as far as possible, and explicitly check changes. If a change does not affect an interface, then parts of the program beyond the interface need no attention. But if a change does affect an interface, then all other units which can access that interface are potentially affected.

If a separate subprogram is changed so that its body is different but its specification (formal parameters and result) remains the same, then recompilation of the subprogram has no effect on the other compilation units of the program.

However if a subprogram is changed and given a different
specification in any respect (e.g. changing the number of parameters, or
even the name of a formal parameter) then all other compilation units
which refer to this subprogram are invalidated, and must be recompiled
before the program load can be linked together again.

Similarly, if a module body is changed (but its specification remains
the same), there are no consequential effects, but if a module
specification is changed in a recompilation, then the corresponding
module body (whether included explicitly or written as a separate
subunit) must also be recompiled.

Any compilation unit carrying a **with** clause is also invalidated by
recompilation of any of the units mentioned in this context
specification. A subunit is invalidated by recompilation of the unit
containing its stub.

To summarise, after a change to a compilation unit, THIS_UNIT, the
recompilation of THIS_UNIT invalidates (and consequently requires
recompilation of) all units with any of the following properties:

   a. If THIS_UNIT is a parent unit, then all its subunits, which
       must begin

          separate (THIS_UNIT)

   b. If THIS_UNIT is a library unit, then every unit with a
       context specification containing THIS_UNIT, i.e. every unit
       including

          with THIS_UNIT;

       in its heading.

   c. If THIS_UNIT is a specification, then the corresponding
       body, if any.

After recompilation of each of these, further compilation units may be
invalidated by the same rules.

Note that no consequential recompilations are necessary as a result
of recompiling a module body or a subprogram declaration whose
specification is not changed, provided that it has no subunits and the
name is not in any unit's context specification.

10.7   Generic Program Units

A universally valuable technique in programming is to write once a piece
of code which will be used many times. This underlies the ideas of
loops, procedures and libraries in Ada as in other programming
languages; generic program units are another case of the idea in Ada. A
generic program unit is a compile-time parametric subprogram or package,
that can be written once (usually as a library unit) and then used as
many times as needed, as the program is being compiled. The generic
program unit forms a model or pattern that may involve compile-time
parameters.

A generic unit is not itself directly executable, but instances of
the model (formed at compile-time) have the properties of the
appropriate program unit. Only subprograms and packages may be made
generic.

Generic program units are pieces of program which define patterns for
subprograms or packages, such that the patterns can be filled out to
form proper subprograms or packages by the program translator. The act
of making a particular instance of the unit given generically is called
instantiation.

Note that all the processing to do with generic program units takes
place at translation-time. After a unit has been compiled, there is no
difference in meaning between one which was written individually and one
which was an instance of a generic unit.

Just as subprograms may have parameters, so may generic program
units, allowing the different instances of the pattern to have
individual features. Generic parameters offer a wider range of
possibilities than subprogram parameters, because they are handled at
translation time rather than execution time. Generic parameters may be
data values or data objects (like subprogram parameters, but excluding
out mode), or types or subprograms.

Whenever an instance of a generic unit is required in a program,
actual entities must be specified for the generic parameters. This
corresponds to giving actual subprogram parameters in a subprogram call,
but takes place at compile time rather than run-time.

10.7.1   Comparison of direct, separate and generic styles

We can compare three ways of writing a program unit: directly, separately, or generically. Suppose in a certain context R we need to declare a procedure P. One way is to write

```
procedure P is    -- direct style
begin
    -- statements to be executed for P
end P;
```

In this style, the statement to be executed for P are entirely specific to the context.

Another way is to write (in the declarative part of R) a body stub

```
procedure P is separate;      -- separate style
```

with the required body given as

```
separate (R)
procedure P is  -- separate style
begin
  -- statements to be executed for P
end P;
```

In this style, the separate procedure body is again specific to its context of use, even though it is written separately from it. However, different versions of the body could produced by file editing (independent of Ada).

The third way is to write (in the declarative part of R) a generic instantiation

```
procedure P is new P_PATTERN;   -- generic style
```

with the required pattern given as

```
generic
procedure P_PATTERN is  -- generic style
begin
  -- statements to be executed for P_PATTERN
end P_PATTERN;
```

In this, the generic style, the body may be given in terms of parameters whose actual meanings are specified on instantiation, and the program can have any number of declarations containing

   new P_PATTERN;

with the same or different actual parameters.

10.8   Generic Parameters

The parameters of a generic program unit are given in much the same way
as those of a procedure - as identifiers in the declaration of the
generic program unit, and may then be used inside the body which
follows.   When the generic program unit is instantiated, actual
parameters are given which replace the generic parameters in the body.
There are two major differences from the formal parameters of a
procedure:

    a.   The substitution is at compile-time (so that generics are in
        this repect more like macros than procedures); consequently

    b.   The kinds of entity which can be parametrized generically
        are more varied than those for procedures.

The parameters of a subprogram carry values of data objects at run-time;
those of a generic program unit may similarly carry data values at
compile_time, but in addition they can be used to give types or
subprograms.

   If a generic parameter is given as a data item, it may be of mode **in**
(the default), meaning a constant determined at compile-time, or of mode
in out, meaning an object whose identity is determined at compile-time.

   If a generic parameter is given as a type, then the generic formal
parameter must indicate what kind of type it is, to permit strict
checking. The kinds of type recognised are indicated in the heading of
the generic unit when introducing the identifier:

    (<>)   -- discrete (enumeration or integer)
    range <>   -- integer
    delta <>   -- fixed point,
    digits <>   -- floating point,

for scalar types, or the actual definition of an array type, access
type, or private type.   The notation for the formal parameter shows
which of these is intended, and allows the consistency of the contents
of the generic unit to be checked (e.g. a discrete type used as an index

for an array type).

If a generic parameter is given as a subprogram, the full specification of the subprogram must be stated (introduced by the word **with**). The parameter may be provided with a default, in which case the corresponding parameter may be omitted when the program unit is instantiated. The default is shown by writing **is** after the subprogram specification. Two forms of default are allowed: either the name of a subprogram visible at the position where the generic program unit is declared, or the subprogram with the same name as the formal parameter, visible at the position where the generic program unit is instantiated. For the first default write the required name after **is**, for the second write **is** <>.

10.9   How to use generics

A principal use for generic program units is to specify the pattern of a package for dealing with entities of different types, where similar but not necessarily identical actions are needed.

Thus we may, for example, have a generic package for stack manipulation. It is necessary in a stack for all items to be basically the same type (refinements allow a variety of types to be represented in terms of the basic type), but different stacks may have different base types. For each stack, operators are needed to push new items on and pop existing items off, which will depend in detail on the base type of the stack items, although their general pattern is the same.

Similarly we may have a generic package for manipulating lists of elements. Since a list is to be such that in principle any item could be used in place of any other, all the items on the list must be basically of the same type. (Elaborations are possible to allow a variety of types to be represented in terms of the base type). In general we will want to be able to deal with a number of lists all containing elements of the same type, with procedures to search, append and remove items, or move items for one list to another. These will follow a general pattern which does not depend on the base type, although there will be particular places where the item type is relevant.

A generic program unit is written by prefixing a generic part to a subprogram specification or package specification. The generic part gives the generic parameters, which may then be used within the specification and corresponding body. The generic program unit would usually be a library unit, in which case the corresponding body would be

written as another library unit. However, it may be written wherever a
declaration is allowed, in accordance with the ordinary Ada rules about
specification and body.

10.9.1   Queue Handling

The following generic package deals with a doubly-linked list of
objects, where the type of the objects is left parametric. No
operations on the objects are carried out in the generic package, so
they can be considered to be of a private type.

```
generic
   type OBJECT is private;      -- generic parameter
package QUEUE_HANDLING is

   type ITEM;      -- incomplete, needed for access
   type POINTER is
     access ITEM;

   type ITEM is
     record
       CONTENTS : OBJECT;
       NEXT     : POINTER; -- null for last item in queue
       PREVIOUS : POINTER; -- null for last item in queue
     end record;
   -- invariant :
     -- ANY_POINTER.NEXT = null or else
     -- ANY_POINTER.NEXT.PREVIOUS = ANY_POINTER;
   -- invariant :
     -- ANY_POINTER.PREVIOUS = null or else
     -- ANY_POINTER.PREVIOUS.NEXT = ANY_POINTER;

   type QUEUE is
     record
       FIRST : POINTER;  -- null if queue is empty
       LAST  : POINTER;  -- null if queue is empty
     end record;
   -- invariant:
     -- ANY_QUEUE.FIRST = null or else
     -- ANY_QUEUE.FIRST.PREVIOUS = null;
   -- invariant:
     -- ANY_QUEUE.LAST = null or else
     -- ANY_QUEUE.LAST.NEXT = null;

   procedure STRIP (ONE, ANOTHER : QUEUE);
```

```
                     -- move ONE.FIRST to become ANOTHER.LAST

      end QUEUE_HANDLING;
```

The list structure uses **access** types (see section 12.5). The body of
the package shows how the queues are manipulated (see figure 10a).

```
      package body QUEUE_HANDLING is

         procedure STRIP (ONE, ANOTHER : QUEUE) is
         -- move ONE.FIRST to become ANOTHER.LAST
           -- assert ( ONE /= null );   -- something to move
           THIS : POINTER := ONE.FIRST;   -- item to be moved
         begin
           ONE.FIRST := THIS.NEXT;
             -- a: new first item (may be null)
           if ONE.FIRST /= null then
             ONE.FIRST.PREVIOUS := null;
             -- b: mark it as first item in queue
           end if;

           -- Join old ANOTHER to THIS :
           -- assert ( THIS.PREVIOUS = null );
             -- since it was the first item
           THIS.PREVIOUS := ANOTHER.LAST;
             -- c: attach it to other queue (may be null)
           if THIS.PREVIOUS /= null then
             THIS.PREVIOUS.NEXT := THIS;
             -- d: adjust previous last item
           end if;

           -- Make new ANOTHER :
           THIS.NEXT := null;
             -- e: mark it as last item in queue
           ANOTHER.LAST := THIS;
             -- f: new last item
         end STRIP;

      end QUEUE_HANDLING;
```

To get a version (instance) of this package called FQH suitable for use
with lists of objects of type FLOAT, we would write

```
      package FQH is new QUEUE_HANDLING (FLOAT);
```

This counts as a declaration of the package (both specification and
body), so can be followed by declarations of objects of type

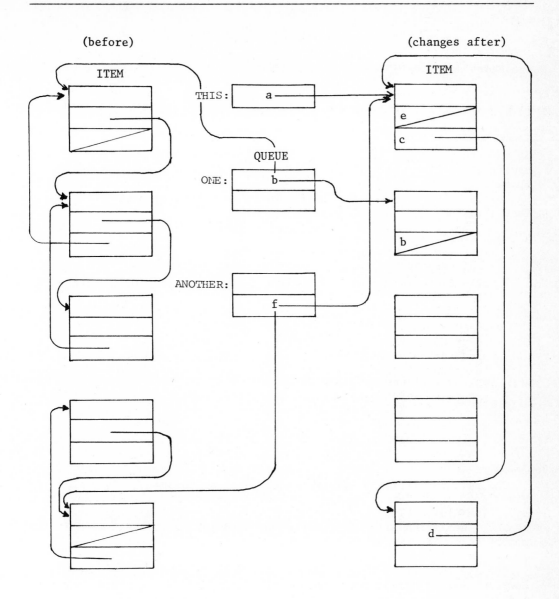

Figure 10a: Strip item from one queue to another

FQH.POINTER, FQH.QUEUE and calls of the procedure FQH.STRIP, or after use FQH;

the short names POINTER, QUEUE and STRIP.

10.9.2   Table with keys

As a further example of a generic program unit, we give this package for
handling an indexed data set, where the key values are presumed to be
sparse. (A simpler version, assuming compact keys, is given in
MASCOT_POOL in chapter 13.) This version presumes that each
instantiation will be used in only one task.

```
generic
  type KEY is private;
  type ITEM is private;
  with function HASH(K:KEY) return INTEGER range 0..INTEGER'LAST;
  SIZE : NATURAL;

package ASSOCIATIVE_MEMORY is
  procedure ENTER(K:KEY;X:ITEM);
  procedure REMOVE(K:KEY);
  function VALUE(K:KEY) return ITEM;
  function CURRENT_KEY return KEY;
  function ADVANCE_KEY return KEY;

  NONEXISTENT, MEMORY_FULL : exception;
end ASSOCIATIVE_MEMORY;
```

The main facilities provided are to enter or remove an item with a
given key, or to determine the value of a current item. These may raise
exceptions in certain cases. Also, in order to be able to scan the
memory, facilities allow the current key and key of the next item in the
memory to be discovered.

The implementation uses a number of working variables, set by a
common search procedure. These are used in the relevant procedure
bodies to detect errors, and refer to relevant positions in the memory.

```
package body ASSOCIATIVE_MEMORY is
  type STATUS is (VALID,DELETED,EMPTY);
  type INDEX is 0..SIZE-1;
  type ASSOCIATION is
    record
      LOCATOR : KEY;
```

```
           CONTENTS : ITEM;
           CHECK : STATUS :=EMPTY;
        end record;
MEMORY : array (INDEX) of ASSOCIATION;
START, CURRENT, POSSIBLE : INDEX;
THIS_KEY : KEY;
GAP,FULL : BOOLEAN;

procedure SEARCH(K:KEY) is
   -- on exit:
   -- THIS_KEY = K;
   --CURRENT,POSSIBLE are such that
   --(MEMORY(CURRENT).CHECK = VALID and
   -- MEMORY(CURRENT).LOCATOR = K) or else
   --(MEMORY(POSSIBLE).CHECK/= VALID and
   -- this is a suitable place to locate K);
   -- FULL indicates whether all memory has been examined;
   -- GAP indicates whether there is space for insertion;
begin
   FULL:=FALSE;
   GAP :=FALSE;
   START:=HASH(K) rem SIZE;
   CURRENT:=START;
   THIS_KEY:=K;
   while MEMORY(CURRENT).CHECK /= EMPTY loop
     if MEMORY(CURRENT).CHECK = DELETED then
        if not GAP then
           POSSIBLE := CURRENT;
           GAP := TRUE;
        end if;
     if MEMORY(CURRENT).LOCATOR /= K then
        CURRENT:=(CURRENT+1) mod SIZE;
     else -- found
        if not GAP then
           POSSIBLE:=CURRENT;
        end if;
        return;
     end if;
     if CURRENT = START then
        FULL := TRUE;
        exit; -- searched all memory
     end if;
   end loop;
   -- not found
   if not GAP then
     POSSIBLE := CURRENT;
   else
```

```
      CURRENT  := POSSIBLE;
    end if;
    return;
end SEARCH;

procedure ENTER ( K:KEY ; X:ITEM ) is
begin
    SEARCH(K);
    if FULL and not GAP then
      raise MEMORY_FULL;
    end if;
    MEMORY(CURRENT).CHECK := DELETED;
    MEMORY(POSSIBLE) := (K,X,VALID);
end ENTER;

procedure REMOVE (K:KEY) is
begin
    SEARCH (K);
    if MEMORY(CURRENT).CHECK /= VALID then
      raise NONEXISTENT;
    end if;
    MEMORY(CURRENT).CHECK := DELETED;
end REMOVE;

function VALUE (K:KEY) return ITEM is
begin
    SEARCH (K);
    if MEMORY(CURRENT).CHECK = VALID then
      return MEMORY(CURRENT).CONTENTS;
    else
      raise NON_EXISTENT;
    end if;
end VALUE;

function CURRENT_KEY return KEY is
begin
    return THIS_KEY; -- may not have an entry
end CURRENT_KEY;

function ADVANCE_KEY return KEY is
begin
    START := CURRENT;
    CURRENT := (CURRENT+1) mod SIZE;
    while MEMORY(CURRENT).CHECK /= VALID loop
      if CURRENT = START then -- no other entries
        return THIS_KEY;
      end if;
```

```
        CURRENT := (CURRENT+1) mod SIZE;
      end loop;
      THIS_KEY := MEMORY(CURRENT).LOCATOR;
      return THIS_KEY;
    end ADVANCE_KEY;

  end ASSOCIATIVE_MEMORY;
```

Exercises

1. Write a library unit to define the type for control and status registers in a PDP-11, with procedures to enable and disable interrupts by adjusting bit 6 in a control and status register.

2. Package MAJOR_PHASES is a library unit. Write the heading of a separately compiled procedure that uses the facilities provided by this package.

3. Package INPUT_OUTPUT is generic with respect to the ELEMENT_TYPE. Write a declaration for an instance of this package to handle card images, and declare a read-only files of card images called CR.

4. Function UNCHECKED_CONVERSION is generic with respect to two types, SOURCE and TARGET. Declare a function to do unchecked conversion from type FP_REP to type FLOAT.

CHAPTER 11

Input/Output and representations

Ada allows the programmer to deal with input/output on any peripherals which may be connected to a computer – not only conventional peripherals, such as card readers, line printers and backing store devices, but also those which are important for embedded computer systems such as communication data-links and on-line instrumentation for real-time monitoring and control.

Input/output is concerned with communication between internal and external processes, using shared variables such as data buffer registers and intercommunication stimuli which are recieved by the computer as interrupts. No special features or additional program structures are needed to deal with these in Ada, but the programmer needs the ability to specify data structures and their representations.

The facilities required for input/output are achieved by making extensive use of the module (package and task) features, rather than by having many special features in the language. We can define the input/output operations in Ada, and put them in a library for other programmers to use.

Input/output is necessarily machine dependent, and the aim of this style of programming in Ada is to keep the machine dependency in as limited a context as possible. Where equivalent operations exist in different computers, then a package specification gives the common interface to the operations, and different computers would have different package bodies to implement these operations in the appropriate ways.

Each input/output operation consists of a type conversion between an internal value and a value at the shared interface between the computer and the peripheral. The program has to treat concrete representations, and relate the desired internal types to the hardware-determined types of the physical devices.

The Ada Language Reference Manual defines such common Input/Output facilities in two packages : INPUT_OUTPUT (a generic package) for general handling of files, and TEXT_IO (a package which contains inner generic packages) for handling streams of characters intended for communicating with people.

In order to handle the details of input/output transfers, or to program application specific devices, it is necessary for the Ada program to specify particular representations of data objects and particular addresses in the computer where data objects are located. These are done by representation specifications.

The physical configuration of peripherals is specified by values in a data structure determined by the computer architecture (e.g. channel number, subchannel number, device address; or unibus address of principal control and status word). The hardware/software interface is specified by another data structure determined by the device controller (e.g. structure of control registers, layout of buffer registers).

11.1   Files

Ada treats input/output as the transfer of sequences of data values between the program and some external sources or destinations. There can be a number of logically independent sequences being operated on concurrently. They are called files, and are distinguished as values in special types which are defined in the package INPUT_OUTPUT (see Appendix A).

Ada requires the programmer to state two fundamental facts about each input/output activity, which of their nature seem to imply a restriction on the kinds of input/output that can be carried out. Each input/output sequence (file) has a particular direction and a particular element - type.

The direction indicates the permissible transfer operations: either reading data values into the program from the external source, or writing data values from the program to the external destination, or both reading and writing data values between the program and the external file. We refer to the external source or destination as the partner for the input/output operation.

A file available for read-only access (such as from a card reader) must be given as an IN_FILE; a file available for write-only access (such as to a line printer) must be given as on OUT_FILE; a file available for both reading and writing (such as with an interactive terminal) must be given as a INOUT_FILE. The purpose of this distinction is to allow checks at compile time that reading or writing are intended.

The sequence of operations applied to a file always determines the particular data values used – thus a sequence of write operations will send to the destination the given data values in the given order.

This rule appears trivial in the case of an IN_FILE or an OUT_FILE, but it is particularly important for an INOUT_FILE. It means that a write operation (giving a prompt to the user) followed by a read operation (getting the reply he gives) will be carried out in the order stated in the program, in other words ensuring that the write operation has been completed before the read operation is started.

Specifying the element-type for a file is the way of stating the type of the data values which will be transferred. Note that this has to be fixed in the program and cannot change during execution. This rule is a consequence of the "strong typing" style of programming in Ada. Since each data object has to have a particular type known at compile-time, any data object whose value is obtained by input (or which gives its value for output) must have a particular type, and consequently all the data values in the sequence which might be transfered to it during input/output must be of the same type. The rule makes logical sense when considered as a means of converting the values from their external form into a suitable internal form for use in the program. What is actually input (or output) is a bit-pattern, and the input/output procedures in the program must convert this to or from the appropriate internal values. To make this conversion, the procedures must know the type of the internal values.

Although the element-type for a file must be fixed, there is no restriction on using the file to hold values of different types, provided that they can all be represented as sequences of elements of the common element-type. It is then a matter of programming appropriate conversion procedures to be used in association with the actual data transfer operations.

Ada does not specify which particular external source or destination is to be used for each file: the way of identifying the external partners and their connection is so machine-dependent that it has to be programmed explicitly.

Thus the presumption is that for any input/output package, there would be a procedure to establish the association between a file and a partner, using whatever scheme is appropriate for the machine to identify the partner.

The package INPUT_OUTPUT in Ada presumes a system in which files have permanent names, used to identify them when several programs may access the same file. The package is generic, with the type of the elements in the file as the parameter. For any particular element-type, such as WORD, the package must be instantiated, by a declaration such as

package WORD_IO is new INPUT_OUTPUT(WORD);

This establishes all the file-types and file-operations:

    WORD_IO.IN_FILE   -- for read-only files of words
    WORD_IO.OUT_FILE   -- for write-only files
    WORD_IO.INOUT_FILE -- for read-write files

and the appropriate operations. A different instantiation would be needed for files of card images where

    type CARD_IMAGE is array(1..80) of CHARACTER;
    package CARD_HANDLING is new INPUT_OUTPUT(CARD_IMAGE);

Thus for a card reader we would use a read-only file, and for a card punch a write-only file:

    CR : CARD_HANDLING.IN_FILE;
    CP : CARD_HANDLING.OUT_FILE;

Operations on these are written

            CARD_HANDLING.READ (FILE => CR,
                                ITEM => IMAGE);

The input/output procedures and functions can be called using their full names, or, if CARD_HANDLING is the only instantiation of INPUT_OUTPUT, by

    use CARD_HANDLING;

and the local names of the package.

11.2   Preparing to use a file

To create a new file to recieve output, the program must declare a
variable of the appropriate type (OUT_FILE or INOUT_FILE), say

   use WORD_IO;
   DAC : OUT_FILE;

and call the procedure CREATE to set up the control block for that file,
with a permanent name:

   CREATE (DAC, "MAGNET WAVE_FORM");

This would be done only once in the life of a file. If it is impossible
or illegal to create a file with the name given, an exception is raised.
STATUS_ERROR means that the file variable (DAC in this example) is
already in use, so is not available for a new file; NAME_ERROR means
that the permanent name specified is already in use or is not allowed
for some reason.

   For a program to use a file which already exists, a variable must be
declared of the appropriate file type, say

   ADC : IN_FILE;

and the procedure OPEN must be called to set up the control block for
the file and on the basis of the file's permanent name, to make the
connection between the external partner and the current program.

   OPEN (ADC, "VOLTAGE SENSOR");

   If the OPEN operation cannot be carried out, an exception is raised.
These are the same exceptions as can be raised by CREATE, with slightly
different conditions applying. STATUS_ERROR again means that the file
variable (ADC here) is already in use. This exception would be raised if
by mistake the OPEN procedure was called twice in succession with
identical arguments: the second call would detect this error, even
though the file name happened to be the same. NAME_ERROR means either
that there is no file in existence with the specified name, or that it
exists but access to it is prohibited.

   Every file used in a program must have a variable of the proper
file-type which is initialised by calling one of the procedures CREATE
or OPEN. No other operations may be carried out on the file until it has
been opened (creation implies opening) - if any is attempted, the

exception STATUS_ERROR is raised.

Other exceptions may be raised during the course of input/output operations once a file has been opened: DEVICE_ERROR means that there are difficulties in the underlying system (software or hardware - not distinguished), which prevent the operation being completed; USE_ERROR means that the specified operation is physically impossible or prohibited. In other words, DEVICE_ERROR is something which might arise when the user program is itself correct and sensible, but USE_ERROR indicates a fault in the logic of the user program.

After use of a file by a program, some post-processing may be necessary before the connection is actually severed. Corresponding to CREATE and OPEN, there are two procedures which reverse their effects.

```
CLOSE(ADC);
```

causes the file ADC to be closed but to remain in existence with its permanent name for future use.

```
DELETE(DAC);
```

causes the file DAC to be closed and all information about it deleted, including its permanent name.

The permanent name of a file may be discovered using the function NAME:

```
S : constant STRING := NAME(ADC);
```

and the current state (open or closed) may be tested using the function IS_OPEN. thus

```
if IS_OPEN(ADC) then
   -- file ADC is open
else
   -- file ADC is closed
end if;
```

11.3   Data Transfers

The primary operations of transfering data to or from a file are done by the procedures READ and WRITE. Each transfers a single element of the appropriate type. Thus with

---

```
W1 : WORD;
```

we can have

```
WORD_IO.READ(ADC, W1);
WORD_IO.WRITE(DAC, W1);
```

to read the next value from the file controlled by ADC into the local variable W1, then to write that value to the file controlled by DAC.

Note that the use of READ and WRITE is checked at compile time for compatibility of the direction of transfer: READ may be used only with an IN_FILE or INOUT_FILE; WRITE may be used only with an OUT_FILE or an INOUT_FILE.

Each READ or WRITE operation carried out refers to the next element in sequence in the file, unless there is a reposition operation (see section 11.4 below). In the simplest case, each WRITE adds one new element to the file, until an eventual CLOSE marks the end of the file. If a READ operation is executed when there are no more elements in the file, the exception END_ERROR is raised.

With an INOUT_FILE, the READ and WRITE operations refer to consecutive elements in sequence: WRITE adds a new element to the file and a subsequent READ takes the next element after that. (This means that if there is any buffering of elements, any READ must flush out the buffer of elements waiting to be written, and ensure that all the previous WRITEs have been completed before the READ is allowed to procede.)

The READ operation implies checking that the next element in the file is a proper value of the declared element-type for the file. If the element is not of the proper type then the exception DATA_ERROR is raised.

In the presence of repositioning operations, each READ or WRITE applies to the current ´next´ position in the file for the appropriate direction of transfer. This means that elements may be skipped, reread, or overwritten, assuming that such operations are physically possible. If the position has been set to a value outside the range of existing positions for the file, a READ operation will raise the END_ERROR exception In similar circumstances a WRITE operation is carried out with automatic adjustment of the file size. Any intermediate positions have indeterminate values – a subsequent READ might give an arbitrary value or might raise DATA_ERROR.

11.4   File Positioning

As a file consists of a sequence of elements, the number of elements   in
it is in principle countable. At any stage during processing, there is a
current read position and a current write position, which establish   the
next element to be read or written. Unless specific instructions are
given, a series of read or write operations apply to consecutive
positions in the file.

   For some kinds of file there is no possibility of working other   than
sequentially. However, other kinds of file have possible control actions
to reposition them (such as backspacing a magnetic tape, or seeking a
track on a disk file). The package INPUT_OUTPUT provides procedures to
manipulate the position of a file, but recognises that particular
operations may be physically impossible. There is no systematic
distinction between files which can or cannot have particular operations
applied to them: there is no check at compile-time on the use of
positioning procedures, but if such a procedure is executed on a file
which cannot substain the operation, the exception USE_ERROR is raised.

   The positions in the file are counted from 1, with one position
occupied for each element of the file. Thus in the context of
CARD_HANDLING each card image occupies one position. The functions
NEXT_READ and NEXT_WRITE return values of type FILE_INDEX giving the
position of the next element available to be read or written:

   I1 := NEXT_READ(CR);   -- serial number of next card

and the function SIZE returns an integer value giving the   total   number
of elements currently in the file

   I2 := SIZE(CP);   -- number of cards punched

When a file has just been created, its size is 0 and its position is 1.
As each element is written to it, its size and position both increase by
one. When a file is closed, its current size may be recorded in a
directory (but this is not required by the package). When a file that
already exists is opened, its size is the same as when it was last
closed (but this information may not be available); the newly opened
file is set at position 1.

   The position of a file is changed by reading from it or writing to
it, or (if the external partner has the ability) by repositioning. The
procedures SET_READ and SET_WRITE change the position number, making the
element at the specified position be the next one available to be read
or written. Consequently

```
    SET_READ(FILE1, 1);
```

sets the file to position 1, in other words rewinds it;

```
    SET_READ(FILE1, NEXT_READ(FILE1) - 1);
```

sets it before the previous element, as a back-space operation;

```
    SET_READ(FILE1, SIZE(FILE1) + 1);
```

sets it to access the next element position after the last current
element, in other words spacing forwards to the end of the current file.
If the position given in SET_READ is outside the current range of
positions for the file, there is no immediate error, but if there is an
attempt to READ from such a position then the exception END_ERROR is
raised.

The procedures RESET_READ and RESET_WRITE set the current read and
write positions to 1, in other words rewind the files.

11.5   Text Input/Output

Ada includes a package providing facilities for input/output of strings
of characters, such as are needed for communication between a computer
and an operator or programmer. The principal use of this package would
be in conventional computer contexts, rather than embedded computer
systems, where each program runs under the control of an operating
system that handles its input/output as sequences of characters, which
we call streams.

The package presumes that a particular source and destination are by
convention used as standard input and standard output for each program.
The identification of these standard partners is not specified by Ada,
but is presumed to be arranged by the implementation, in other words by
the operating system. The package is called TEXT_IO, and uses the
facilities of the standard file package INPUT_OUTPUT, with the addition
of extra facilities to cover textual layout and input/output of values
in the various data types in Ada. Easy procedure calls are provided for
working with the standard input and output streams but other files (of
the right type) may be specified if required. The specification of
package TEXT_IO is given in Appendix A.

The standard input and output streams are automatically opened when
the progam begins execution. If any other files are to be used with
TEXT_IO, they must be opened or created using the facilities of

CHARACTER_IO, with IN_FILE and OUT_FILE.   Remember to put

   with TEXT_IO;

at the head of your program, and

   use TEXT_IO;

to make all the names directly visible.   The inner generic packages for
integer, floating point, fixed point and enumeration types must be
instantiated if they are needed:

   package CENT_IO **is new** INTEGER_IO (CENTS);
   package ANGLE_IO **is new** FLOAT_IO (ANGLE);

for those types declared in chapter 2.

11.5.1   Simple Text Output

All text output is done by the procedure PUT, which can take parameters
of different types for the values to be output, together with parameters
defining the layout. Presuming that we had declared

   LINE_NO, TOT_CHARS : NATURAL;
   package NAT_IO **is new** INTEGER_IO (NATURAL);
   package FLT_IO **is new** FLOAT_IO (FLOAT);

and had accumulated counts of lines and characters in them, the
statements

   NEW_LINE;
   PUT("Number of lines:");
   PUT(LINE_NO, 5);   -- NAT_IO.PUT
   PUT("; average length:");
   PUT(FLOAT(TOT_CHARS)/FLOAT(LINE_NO), 10, 4);   -- FLT_IO.PUT

would give on the standard output a new line containing something like

 Number of lines: 874; average length: 3.012E01

The string parameters are output unchanged, as many characters as given.
In the statement to output the value of LINE_NO, the second parameter
specifies the desired field-width, that is the minimum number of columns
to be used for this value.   No BASE parameter is specified, so by
default the value is output in base 10.   The declaration of LINE_NO

gives its subtype as NATURAL, which implies that its type is INTEGER.
The current value of LINE_NO is converted from internal INTEGER format
to a decimal integer in the desired field (or longer if necessary to
hold the value).

In the final statement, an expression is given whose value is to be
output. This value is of type FLOAT, so two extra parameters are used
to specify the layout. The second parameter specified the desired
field-width, and the third parameter specifies the number of digits to
be printed in the mantissa. No EXPONENT parameter is specified, so by
default two digits are used.

The procedure PUT can be used directly to output characters, strings,
or truth values (BOOLEAN). The appropriate inner package must be
instantiated before it can be used for integers, floating point, fixed
point or enumeration types: after

    package DAY_IO **is new** ENUMERATION_IO(DAY_NAME);

we may output values of type DAY_NAME by

    DAY_IO.PUT(TODAY);

or

    use DAY_IO;
    PUT(TODAY);

Each enumeration value is output as an identifier in upper case
(unless explicitly requested to be in lower case) or as a character
literal, padded out on the right with spaces if a field-width parameter
is given.

11.5.2   Simple Text Input

All text input is done by the procedure GET, which has an **out** parameter
(i.e. a variable) to receive the value input. The type of the parameter
determines what kind of conversion (if any) is done as the value is
taken in. GET takes the characters from the input stream to make a
value of the required type, automatically going over line boundaries as
necessary.

Thus if we have

```
I : INTEGER;
X : FLOAT;
J : NATURAL;
```

then after instantiating the package as described above, the statements

```
SKIP_LINE;
GET(I);
GET(X);
GET(J);
```

will start on the next line of the input file, first read the characters to form an integer (terminated by a space or end of line), then a floating point number, and then another integer, whose range will be checked. This is free-format input, and the values are not dependent on the number of spaces or lines between them.

The following procedure has the same effect as the default form of SKIP_LINE to force input from a new line: it reads any remaining characters on the current line, so that a subsequent GET starts on a new line.

```
procedure READLN is
  CH : CHARACTER;
begin
  loop
    GET(CH);
    exit when END_OF_LINE();
  end loop;
end READLN;
```

If an error or inconsistency is detected during input, an exception is raised. If the characters read are not consistent with the type of the parameter given (for example a letter is detected instead of an integer) then DATA_ERROR is raised. If the value of an integer or approximate number read is outside the range implemented, then NUMERIC_ERROR is raised. If the value is outside the range constraint of a subtype, then CONSTRAINT_ERROR is raised.

Similar facilities are available for Boolean input, and for programmer-defined fixed point or enumeration types.

For boolean and enumeration values, the characters may be in upper case or lower case without distinction. If the characters read form an identifier which is not one of the values in the expected type, then the exception DATA_ERROR is raised.

11.5.3   Fixed format input

This package provides facilities for fixed format input, but only of character strings. Thus:

```
S : STRING(1 .. 5);
GET(S);
```

takes the next 5 characters (whether printable or control characters) and assigns them to S for further inspection. There are no automatic facilities for discovering what type this string might refer to (and because of overloading, the value may not be unique); but when the program has decided what type is required - say INTEGER - the appropriate value in that type can be obtained by using the attribute VALUE in a conversion function:

```
I := INTEGER´VALUE(S);
```

11.5.4   Layout control

The characters in a text file consist of printable characters and control characters. The printable characters are considered to be arranged as a series of lines of text, each line consisting of a number of columns. Line lengths may be fixed or may be indicated by the control characters.

The line length in a file is set by calling the procedure

```
SET_LINE_LENGTH(FILE => F1, N => 80);
```

or

```
SET_LINE_LENGTH(F1, 80);
```

to set the length for file F1 to be 80.

A series of printable characters occupy consecutive columns in the same line; control characters affect the line or column numbers. Line numbers and column numbers are both counted from 1. The effect of the package is defined only for the printable characters: Ada does not specify what happens with control characters.

At any stage during processing with a text file, there is a current line and a current column, which establish the next character to be taken or provided. With GET and PUT operations, sequences of characters occupy consecutive columns in one line, then the next line and so on. In some circumstances it is possible to specify the line length (for fixed sized lines) or the next column to be used. TEXT_IO includes procedures and associated functions for doing this, but that does not guarantee that they can always be used - if an attempted action is not possible, the exception USE_ERROR is raised. If the column number gets beyond the line length, LAYOUT_ERROR is raised.

The current line number is set (say to 25) by

    SET_LINE(F1, 25);

Similarly the column number may be set (say to 72) by

    SET_COL(F1, 72);

and the current line and column numbers may be discovered by using functions LINE and COL respectively. In all of these the file must be stated explicitly, and may be either an IN_FILE or an OUT_FILE.

11.5.5   Implied Streams

The procedures PUT and GET can work with either an implied file or an explicitly specified file. If the file is specified, it must have been declared as an IN_FILE for GET, and an OUT_FILE for PUT. (Note that there are no INOUT_FILES with TEXT_IO). If the file is not specified, an implied input or output stream is used.

The implied streams are initially set to the standard input and output streams, but subsequently may be set by procedures

    SET_INPUT(NEW_SOURCE);
    SET_OUTPUT(NEW_DESTINATION);

their current values may be discovered at any stage by using statements as follows:

    SRCE := CURRENT_INPUT();
    DSTN := CURRENT_OUTPUT();

(where SRCE is a variable of type IN_FILE and DSTN is a variable of type OUT_FILE). The right hand sides of these assignments are actually calls of functions with no parameters. The functions STANDARD_INPUT and STANDARD_OUTPUT deliver the default initial values of these files.

11.6   Representation Specifications

The input/output of a real embedded computer sustem will have to specify not only sequences of operation but detail to the level of particular bit-patterns and particular hardware addresses which have to be used. Ada provides facilities for doing this as representation specifications.

   The normal declarations in Ada are sufficient to define the logical properties of the entities involved, but do not give all the physical details. For normal purposes it is appropriate that the compiler should make choices for these, and apply them consistently. When input/output is concerned, the program has to relate to other parts of the system about which independent decisions have been taken, and the compiler is not free to choose physical representations unilaterally.

   Guidance for input/output is therefore:

   a. Identify as a data type the structure of device addresses
       determined by the computer architecture, and define the
       various peripherals by the values of this type.

   b. For each kind of peripheral, identify (as a data type) the
       structures of the registers which constitute the
       hardware/software interface for communication with it, both
       for device control, status monitoring and data transfer.

   c. Regard each peripheral as a task which cannot be
       reprogrammed; design a corresponding device driver as a task
       which communicates with it using variables of the defined
       types for device addressing, device control and data
       transfer, and synchronised to it by the device interrupt.
       The driver task can only transfer data of a predetermined
       type. For other more abstract types, higher level procedures
       must include any conversions necessary to use that type as a
       concrete representation.

   This approach leads to a program in which there can be representation dependencies in certain parts, to specify hardware addresses and bit positions for interface registers.

Various kinds of representation specifications may be included in a program, giving implementation details for different entities involved in the program. The most important of these are for the layout of a record type and the location of a data object (variable); in addition we can state the representation for values of an enumeration type and various details about storage allocation. All representation specifications use the keywords **for** and **use**, with various other words to denote particular details. Representation specifications must be given after all the declarations in a program unit, before any inner unit bodies or the executable part.

11.6.1   Record layout

The layout of a record type is specified by giving the positions of its components, stating for each component which location it is in (relative to the start of the record) and which range of bit positions it occupies. Ada presumes that there are addressable storage units which are used consecutively, and bit numbers which identify the bits within a storage unit (or extending to adjacent storage units).

The type declaration

```
type OUTPUT_DEVICE is
  record
    PSR : CSR_WORD;
    PBF : CHARACTER;
  end record;
```

would be used in connection with a PDP-11 where CSR_WORD is a previously defined type consisting of bits for special purposes.

The components in this record always occupy consecutive words starting on a multiple of 4 bytes. This is indicated by the representation specification

```
for OUTPUT_DEVICE use
  record at mod 4;
    PSR at 0 * WORD range 0 .. 15;
    PBF at 1 * WORD range 0 .. 7;
  end record;
```

where WORD has the value 2 in a PDP-11 (each word consists of two bytes, and the byte is the addressing unit : hardware addresses are given in bytes). The range specifies the bit numbers used in the stated location for the given component.

Similarly, we could give the representation for floating point values by writing

```
type FP_REP is
  record
    SIGN    : BOOLEAN;
    EXPONENT: INTEGER range -128 .. 127;
    MANTISSA: delta 16.0 ** -14
              range 0.0 .. 1.0 - 16.0 ** -14;
  end record;
```

with representation specification

```
for FP_REP use
  record
    SIGN     at 0 range 0 .. 0;
    EXPONENT at 0 range 1 .. 7;
    MANTISSA at 1 range 0 .. 55;
  end record;
```

Bit numbering extends over consecutive storage units as far as necessary. There is no check that the specified fields are distinct.

11.6.2   Address Specification

In the PDP-11, all devices connected to the computer communicate with it and are controlled through registers at particular Unibus addresses; in general each device is identified by the Unibus address of its principal control and status register. (The situation is more complicated for multiplexed devices, but the same principles apply.) In other computers, devices are connected to particular ports or channels, which are similarly represented.

A PDP-11 output device (e.g. LA36 printer) would be declared thus

```
LA36 : OUPUT_DEVICE;
```

and the actual location to be used for its contol and status register could be specified by stating

```
for LA36 use at 8#177564#;
```

(Note the use of the based integer to give the location in octal.)

The representation specifications thus allow devices to be referred
to explicitly through ordinary Ada names, and for example a character C
can be sent to the printer by the assignment

    LA36.PBF := C;

Checks on the status word can similarly be programmed. This is of course
for direct output to the device with no hidden buffering. Any buffering
needed can be programmed explicitly.

11.6.3   Enumeration representations

The idea of an enumeration type is that identifiers, rather than
internal codes, are used as the values of the type. This makesit very
much easier to understand and maintain the program. However, when an
enumeration value is input or output directly (e.g. in a message format)
a code value is required rather than an identifier. For example,
messages may carry a precedence field which uses a particular code to
denote the several possibilities.

To deal with this, Ada allows the code for an enumeration type to be
specified. The identifiers would still be used in the program, but their
internal representations would be as specified. The code values are
stated as integers, and the correspondence between the symbolic values
of the enumeration type and the integers are given as an aggregate,
thus:

```
    type PRECEDENCE is
      (ROUTINE, PRIORITY, FLASH);

    type SECURITY_CLASSIFICATION is
        (UNCLASSIFIED, RESTRICTED, CONFIDENTIAL,
         SECRET, TOP_SECRET) ;

    for PRECEDENCE use
      (ROUTINE  => 1,
       PRIORITY => 2,
       FLASH    => 4);

    for SECURITY_CLASSIFICATION use
      (UNCLASSIFIED => 0,
       RESTRICTED   => 1,
       CONFIDENTIAL => 2,
       SECRET       => 4,
       TOP_SECRET   => 8);
```

11.6.4   Representations affecting storage allocation

Without specifying in complete detail the layout of a record or array
type, it is possible to state that it is to be stored compactly
(possibly at the expense of access time) by the specification

    pragma PACK (CSR_WORD);

Giving slightly more detail about a type, we can specify the maximum
number of bits to be allocated for objects of the type

    for SMALL_INTEGER´SIZE **use** 10;

    We can also specify the number of storage units to be reserved for
the collection of objects in an access type by writing

    K : **constant** := 1024;
    for POINTER´STORAGE_SIZE **use** 2 * K;

    The same format is used to specify the amount of working storage to
be allocated for an activation of a task.

    In the case of a subprogram or module, the code may be provided from
outside the Ada program; the position at which it is loaded can be
specified in the Ada program by a representation specification.   Suppose
there is a kernel subroutine for resetting the system clock, whose entry
point is at 220 octal, we would specify the procedure thus:

    procedure RESET_CLOCK;
    for RESET_CLOCK **use at** 8#220#;

The program could then call RESET_CLOCK and thereby enter the kernel
subroutine.

11.6.5   Manipulating representations

As well as allowing the programmer to state the representation to be
used for objects of specified types, Ada provides an ´escape´ from the
strong typing rule, for use in special situations such as input/output.

    When a value has to be converted for input/output, the low-level
program may have to manipulate the bit-patterns which represent values.

In order to be able to do this, we must be able to treat representations of values of one type by the operations appropriate to another type. Clearly this is a very dangerous thing to do, as mistakes cannot be detected by the compiler. Manipulations like this should only be done within the body of a package whose body is carefully checked manually.

There is a predefined library unit called UNCHECKED_CONVERSION (see Appendix A), which is a generic function to return a value in one type which has the same representation as the value in another type. (It actually does nothing, but satisfies the type rules.)

Any program unit which needs to use this must be headed

   with UNCHECKED_CONVERSION;

to access the library unit; the context specification acts as a warning to the maintenance programmers that it may do strange things. Inside the unit, the generic function must be instantiated for the particular source and target types required:

```
function FLOAT_OF_REP ( R : FP_REP ) return FLOAT is
   new UNCHECKED_CONVERSION
      ( SOURCE => FP_REP,
        TARGET => FLOAT );
```

11.6.6   Packaged Input/Output

The input/output for special peripherals will usually be written individually for each particular system. However, it may be that classes of peripherals are sufficiently common to justify library packages being prepared. For example, CAMAC devices may be controlled using a package which implements the CAMAC operations:

```
package CAMAC_IML is

   type CRATE_NUMBER is range 0 .. 63;
   type STATION_NUMBER is range 0 .. 31;
   type SUB_ADDRESS is range 0 .. 15;

   type CAMAC_ADDRESS is record
      C : CRATE_NUMBER;
      N : STATION_NUMBER;
      A : SUB_ADDRESS;
   end record;
```

```
type F_CODE is range 0 .. 31;
type F_READ is new F_CODE range 0 .. 7;
type F_WRITE is new F_CODE range 16 .. 23;
type F_OP1 is new F_CODE range 8 .. 15;
type F_OP2 is new F_CODE range 24 .. 31;

procedure SA (CNA : CAMAC_ADDRESS; F : F_READ;
              DATA : out WORD);

procedure SA (CNA : CAMAC_ADDRESS; F : F_OP1);

procedure SA (CNA : CAMAC_ADDRESS; F : F_WRITE;
              DATA : in WORD);

procedure SA (CNA : CAMAC_ADDRESS; F : F_OP2);

  end CAMAC_IML;
```

The procedures would be implemented differently on different systems; for example with a particular crate controller on a PDP_11 we have these declarations in the package body

```
type NAF is
  record
    N : STATION_NUMBER;
    A : SUB_ADDRESS;
    F : F_CODE;
  end record;

CAR : CRATE_NUMBER;
NAFR : NAF;
DBR : WORD;
```

with representation specifications giving their hardware addresses and layout. Each procedure body is declared like this:

```
procedure SA (CNA : CAMAC_ADDRESS; F : F_OP1) is
begin
  CAR := CNA.C;
  NAFR := NAF (CNA.N, CNA.A, F_CODE´(F) );
end SA;
```

This selects the required crate then applies the F code for the operation to the specified station and subaddress.

11.6.7   Code Statement - executable machine code

On any particular target computer, there may be useful machine
instructions which are not normally generated by the Ada translator.
You can program then explicitly in Ada by giving the values for fields
of the machine instruction as a qualified expression, thus:

    VAX_11.OPCODE´(BPT);

where VAX_11 is the name of a package that includes

    type OPCODE **is** (HALT, NOP, REI, BPT, RET,
      RSB, MTPR, MFPR);

    for OPCODE **use**
      (HALT => 0, NOP => 1, REI => 2,
        BPT => 3, RET => 4, RSB => 5,
        MTPR => 16 # DA #, MFPR => 16 # DB #);

If the instruction needs operands, the type must express what they can
be, and the code statement must include suitable values given as an
aggregate value, thus

    VAX_11.OP2´(MFPR, SID, W´ADDRESS);

using another type from package VAX_11 that defines the operations
taking two operands, and

    type VAX_REGISTER **is**
      (KSP, ESP, SSP, USP, ISP, SID); -- and others

    for VAX_REGISTER **use**
      (KSP => 0,
        ESP => 1,
        SSP => 2,
        USP => 3,
        ISP => 4,
        SID => 62);

11.6.8   Low-level input/output

For computers that require special instructions to initiate input/output
actions, the normal technique is to make suitable procedures with code
bodies. Two procedures are predefined for sending control information
to a physical device, and requesting status information back from it.

```
package LOW_LEVEL_IO is    -- see Appendix A
  -- type declarations for devices
  -- type declarations for control and status
  procedure SEND_CONTROL (DEVICE : {device_type};
                DATA : in out {control_and_status});
  procedure RECEIVE_CONTROL (DEVICE : {device_type};
                DATA : in out {control_and_status});
end LOW_LEVEL_IO;
```

There may be several such procedures, overloaded for different device
types.

11.7   Interrupts

For programmer-defined input/output, the program sets an operation going
then either has to test status repeatedly or wait for an interrupt
before carrying out the next operation on the same device. The
facilities for having tasks in Ada mean that the driver for the device
can be written as one task, containing an **accept** statement to wait for a
call of the corresponding entry, which can be set as the representation
specification for a hardware interrupt.

To illustrate this technique, we show a simple timer using the PDP-11
line clock. The hardware clock causes an interrupt at regular intervals
(1/50 or 1/60 second) and the program increments a counter by 1 on each
occasion.

```
package SIMPLE_TIMER is
  TICK_COUNT : INTEGER := 0;
end SIMPLE_TIMER;

package body SIMPLE_TIMER is
  task TIMER_CONTROL is
    entry DOIO;
    for DOIO use at 8#100#;
    pragma PRIORITY (5);
  end TIMER_CONTROL;
```

```
      task body TIMER_CONTROL is
      begin
        loop
          accept DOIO;
          TICK_COUNT := TICK_COUNT + 1;
        end loop;
      end TIMER_CONTROL;
    end SIMPLE_TIMER;
```

(Note that this program uses a priority mechanism to ensure that TICK_COUNT cannot be accessed while it is being incremented.)

The representation specification for DOIO gives the address of the hardware interrupt to which the entry is linked. Whenever the interrupt occurs, there is an entry call to DOIO. The task is initiated by the enclosing program unit which enables the line-clock interrupt.

For a slightly more complicated case, consider output of a series of characters to the LA36 printer. Assigning a character to the register PBF starts the print operation; when the printing is completed there is an interrupt through location 64 octal. The important thing is to prevent a new character being assigned to PBF before the previous one has been printed. We do this as follows:

```
    task SIMPLE_PRINT is
      entry PRINT (C : CHARACTER);
      entry DOIO;
      for DOIO use at 8#64#;
      pragma PRIORITY (4);
    end SIMPLE_PRINT;

    task body SIMPLE_PRINT is
      LA36 : OUTPUT_DEVICE;
      for LA36 use at 8#177564#;
    begin
      loop
        accept PRINT (C : CHARACTER) do
          LA36.PBF := C;
        end PRINT;
        accept DOIO;
      end loop;
    end SIMPLE_PRINT;
```

This task would similarly be initiated after enabling the LA36 interrupt in another part of the program.

Exercises

1. Write statements to input two unsigned decimal integers and print out their sum (up to three digits).

2. Write a function to ask the user a question, and return a Boolean result, depending on whether the reply is yes or no.

3. Using the GINO-F procedure DRAW2, draw a horizontal line of length one unit.

4. Write an interrupt handler for input from a keyboard, where each key depression causes an interrupt with the character code in a hardware register.

5. Reserve 200 blocks of storage, each sufficient to hold a track image, for allocation with track pointers.

CHAPTER 12

More on types

The description of types and values in chapter 2 deliberately left out a number of finer points in order to concentrate on the basic ideas. In this chapter we complete the exposition of types in Ada. There are a number of separate issues to be covered, which all combine to give a very powerful and flexible scheme.

The type specifies more than the range of possible values - it also determines the way the data values are represented, and which operators are valid for a data item. Ada has a fixed set of operator symbols; their meanings with certain elementary types are predefined, but the program may give additional meanings for an operator symbol by defining it with other types. Thus the operator + is defined for addition of integers and real values, as used in

```
3 + 2        -- 5
4.1 + 3.3    -- 7.4 (approximately)
```

or other expressions involving similar values, but not immediately for values of other types, such as in ´A´ + ´x´ (i.e. unless the programmer has taken steps to define + applied to characters).

Every type has a representation (such as a series of distinct bit patterns for an enumeration type). Different types sometimes have the same representation, but are nevertheless kept distinct by the translator. The representation is usually chosen by the translator, but in some circumstances (particularly in connection with input/output) it may be necessary to specify explicit details. Section 11.6 explains this.

The fundamental "strong typing" idea means that programs should contain distinct types for all the different kinds of data item with which they deal. Ada allows new types to be introduced easily. Derived types (section 12.1) take their properties from already existing types, so that there are similar values in the new type, and the operations applicable to them are the same. Abstract data types (section 12.2) are more general, in that the new type has an explicitly specified set of properties - the programmer gives the complete set of operations applicable to values of the new type. Variant records (section 12.3) are more flexible, in that different values of the type may have different components.

Further sections in this chapter deal comprehensively with the idea of constraints on types (section 12.4), and dynamic objects which are the values of access types (section 12.5). Finally, we discuss how types may be used to clarify ideas during the design stage of a program (section 12.6).

12.1   Derived Types

There may be occasions when we wish to use the typing rules of Ada to maintain a distinction between similar values - such as between lengths, weights and speeds. We want to be able to add lengths together, but not to add a length to a weight. The way of doing this in Ada is to use derived types.

```
type LENGTH is new FLOAT;
type WEIGHT is new FLOAT;
type SPEED  is new FLOAT;
```

The fact that the types are distinct means that even though they are all handled as floating point quantities, they are logically different. Although we can add together floating point values, we can not add a length to a weight, or a weight to a speed.

We can construct a new type as a derivative of another, so that the new type "inherits" all properties of the original one (in particular its literals and the operators which may be applied to it) yet nevertheless the values in the new type are treated as distinct, and assignments between different types are prevented.

So with

```
L1, L2 : LENGTH;
W1, W2 : WEIGHT;
```

we can have

```
L1 := 5.0;          -- literal of type LENGTH
L2 := L1 + 1.0;     -- addition of type LENGTH
W1 := 2.2;          -- literal of type WEIGHT
W2 := 0.5 * W1;     -- multiplication of type WEIGHT
```

but not for example L1 + W1 or W1 := L2 or a comparison W2 < L1 -- all of which are clearly nonsense and in Ada are detected at compile-time.

(Note that the checking which Ada provides is not a full dimensional analysis: there would be no challenge to the physically meaningless statement

```
W1 := W1 * W2;
```

since there is no infringement of the type matching rules).

A derived type is introduced by writing the word **new** before the original type name, and then possibly putting a constraint. The derived type is given a name by introducing it in a type declaration

type NEW_TYPE **is new** OLD_TYPE;

to allow objects and parameters to be introduced for this type.

Any type (predefined or user-defined) may be used as the basis for derived types, including arrays and records. However, the most useful cases are likely to be derivatives of the predefined scalar types FLOAT and INTEGER. These are explained below, in the secion on Constraints and Derived Types.

12.2   Abstract data types

For some purposes it is necessary to control access to the values in a type, to provide security between one part of a program and another. For example, a system may have several input/output channels with a package to handle the physical input/output using a control block for each channel. It is important that the rest of the program should not interfere with the control blocks, or even with the control block for the channel which it might be using. It might even be important to prevent unauthorised copying of control blocks. We deal with this situation in Ada using an abstract data type, in which the type is given a name and operations on objects of the type are defined, but nothing is shown about the implementation details for the type.

An abstract data type in Ada is said to be private, and is declared
thus:

type CHANNEL **is private**;

The private type must always be introduced in the visible part of a
package module, and the same visible part must contain the declarations
for all the other information related to that type – any constant values
of the type that may be used, and the subprograms that can manipulate
objects of that type. Several abstract data types may be introduced in
the same module if required, by approprite private type declarations.
The rest of the program (wherever the package is visible) can use the
private type – declaring objects of that type, and using them as
parameters to the given subprograms. But the rest of the program cannot
directly investigate or interfere with the values of any object of the
private type, or even determine what its structure is (i.e. whether a
scalar, a record or an array).

So if the package consists of

package IO_HANDLING **is**
   type CHANNEL **is private**;
   INACTIVE : **constant** CHANNEL:
   procedure CONNECT (C : **out** CHANNEL);
   procedure DISCONNECT (C : CHANNEL);
      -- further declarations, including private part
   end IO_HANDLING;

then the program elsewhere can contain

   use IO_HANDLING;
   C1, C2 : CHANNEL;

   C1 := INACTIVE;
   CONNECT (C2);
   CONNECT (C1);

If the private type is introduced as shown above, then it is
permitted for objects of that type to be copied using assignment
statments, and compared for equality. However, the assignment and
equality operations can be eliminated by declaring

   type SPECIAL_CHANNEL **is limited private**;

where the word **limited** indicates that only the operations defined by the
subprograms in the visible part of the package are available for objects

of the private type. Objects of a limited private type may not be assigned (copied) using assignment statements, nor may they be compared with one another, unless suitable relational operators are given in the same visible part as the type definition.

A common use for limited private type would be when the values are records containing linkages to other records, and cross references have to be maintained, so copying by assignment would bypasss the maintenance of the cross references.

12.3   Records with variants

A record may have variants in which certain components are only present in particular circumstances. For example, in a message switching system, we might have a directory which will give the disposition of messages according to their destination address - some local (for immediate delivery), and some remote (for passing to a neighbouring node). The record for each destination address must contain information for either local or remote destinations, together with some common information. The whole directory would be an array of such records, indexed by the telephone number of the relevant entry. Each entry in the directory would have components as shown, according to whether it was local or remote.

```
type TRUNK is range 1 .. 9;
type LINE is range 1 .. 99;
type WHERE is (LOCAL, REMOTE);
type DIRECTORY_ENTRY (PROXIMITY: WHERE) is
  record
       ANSWER_BACK : STRING(1..5);
       case PROXIMITY is
         when LOCAL =>
             LINE_NUMBER : LINE;
         when REMOTE =>
             TRUNK_NUMBER : TRUNK;
  end record;
```

Similarly, in an air traffic control system there will be observed tracks, flight plans, and advance warning of tracks from adjacent geographical areas; each track will require a record with some common information plus some further specialised information depending on which kind of track it is. Variants allow the value of the record to take account of the possibility that certain components may sometimes be "not applicable" or "not relevant".

In general, a record consists of a fixed part (containing one or more components) and possibly a number of variant parts, which are mutually exclusive. Each variant part contains any number of components (which may themselves be records with variants). The several variants are distinguished by the value of a special component called the discriminant: PROXIMITY in the above example. The discriminant is introduced as a special component in the heading of the type declaration; all the variants are collected together in a **case** clause which uses values of the discriminant to select each particular variant.

As usual with a **case** clause, the values given for the discriminant to select the different variant parts must be all different. Any number of components may be introduced for each variant; if it happens that a particular variant has no components, then **null** must be written to indicate this explicitly. Usually the discriminant is an enumeration type, and the selections in the case clause correspond to the values of that enumeration type, as with LOCAL and REMOTE in the above example. A number of special forms are possible for the cases where several values for the discriminant all determine the same variant, as in a **case** statement (section 4.3.2): the list of values or a range denotation for a compact set of values may be given as the selection.

In any value of type DIRECTORY_ENTRY, there is the PROXIMITY component (the discriminant), which specifies whether the particular value is LOCAL or REMOTE, and always a component called ANSWER_BACK which is a string of five characters; if PROXIMITY is LOCAL then there is a further component called LINE_NUMBER, whose value is an integer in the range 1 to 99; but if the PROXIMITY is REMOTE the DIRECTORY_ENTRY contains a component called TRUNK_NUMBER, whose value is an integer in the range 1 to 9. The notation of the variant record ensures that a line-number exists for a local directry-entry and a trunk number only exists for a remote directory-entry. (In practice, the implementation may use the same storage location for these components, but they are logically distinct).

Thus with

        D1, D2: DIRECTORY_ENTRY;

we could have assignments to the complete record:

```
D1 := (LOCAL, "CMDHQ", 1);
      -- by position

D2 := (ANSWER_BACK => "DIVN5";
       PROXIMITY => REMOTE;
       TRUNK_NUMBER => 5);
```

```
                -- by name
```

and to individual components:

```
    D1.LINE_NUMBER := 91;
    D2.TRUNK_NUMBER := 6;
```

(with appropriate range checks on the integer values given).

A similar notation is used to denote a record containing an array of
variable length; the length is the discriminant. Each value of the
record must have a particular length, but different records may have
different lengths. This is illustrated by the component SRC in
WAIT_CONTROL_BLOCK, whose length is given by S_COUNT.

```
    PROC_MAX : constant INTEGER := 5;
            -- maximum number of processes

  type PROC_NO is range 1 .. PROC_MAX;

  type SOURCE is
    record
      HOST : BYTE;
      NAME : BYTE;
    end record;

  type WAIT_CONTROL_BLOCK (S_COUNT : range 0 .. PROC_MAX) is
    record
      W_TYPE : W_CODE;
      SRC : array (PROC_NO range 1 .. S_COUNT) of SOURCE;
    end record;
```

A record may contain several variable-length arrays, but the bounds on
their indices must be simple (not expressions), and all variable bounds
must be written in the heading as discriminants. This is to ensure that
each object of the record type is allocated the right amount of space
when it is declared.

The variants of a record always come after the non-variant component.
However, any component (including variants) may be of any type, so may
itself be a record containing variants. Thus a nested variant structure
is possible. This is illustrated in type MESSAGE below.

```
    K : constant INTEGER := 1024;

  type TIMER_IDENTIFIER is range 0 .. 255;
```

```
type TIMER_TIME is range 0 .. 64 * K - 1;
       -- counts seconds

type NET_B_PTR is range 0 .. NET_BUF_MAX;

type OP_CODE is (MODIFY, OPEN, CLOSE,
                  RESET_LINK,
                  RESET_VC,
                  RESTART);

type DETAILS (OP_CMD : OP_CODE) is
  record
    case OP_CMD is
      when MODIFY  =>
        MODIF : ADDRESS;
      when OPEN .. RESET_LINK  =>
        LINK : LINK_NO;
      when RESET_VC  =>
        L_C : L_CHANNEL_NO;
      when RESTART =>
        SUBSCRIBER : SUBSCR_NO;
    end case;
  end record;

type M_CODE is (OPERATOR, IN_DONE, OUT_DONE,
            DO_OUTPUT, TIMER, LOCAL, NET_IO,
            BUFF_MAN);

type MESSAGE (M_TYPE : M_CODE) is
  record            -- use array (1 .. 4) of BYTE
    case M_TYPE is
      when OPERATOR  =>
        CMD : OP_CODE;
        OP  : DETAILS(CMD);
      when IN_DONE .. DO_OUTPUT  =>
        STATUS : S_CODE;
        BUFF : NET_B_PTR;
      when TIMER  =>
        ID : TIMER_IDENTIFIER;
        T : TIMER_TIME;
     .when others  =>
        null; -- to be defined
    end case;
  end record;
```

12.4   Constraints and subtypes

Within the set of values comprising a type, there may be useful subsets, which we may want to use in the program. This can be used to give names to a particular range of values relevant to the problem, e.g. for different parts of a week:

>   **subtype** WEEKDAY **is** DAY_NAME **range** MONDAY .. FRIDAY;
>   **subtype** WEEKEND **is** DAY_NAME **range** SATURDAY .. SUNDAY;

so that a variable could be declared to hold values in a weekend

>   SS : WEEKEND;

and this would be always in the specified range.

We often require particular ranges of integers. The type INTEGER includes all whole-number values from an extreme negative value to a large positive value; but a useful subset is the set of non-negative numbers starting at zero and going up to the same large positive value. We can write

>   **subtype** NON_NEGATIVE **is** INTEGER **range** 0..INTEGER´LAST;

and then declare objects such as

>   TRACK_COUNT : NON_NEGATIVE;

This means that TRACK_COUNT is a variable whose values will be of type INTEGER but always constrained to the range 0 up to the largest integer value. Since its type is INTEGER, all the usual integer operations can be used with it, but whenever there is an assignment of a new value to TRACK_COUNT, an implicit check is made that the value is in the proper range. If this check fails, the exception CONSTRAINT_ERROR is raised.

The object declaration could have been written equally well

>   TRACK_COUNT : INTEGER **range** 0 .. INTEGER´LAST;

with the type given explicitly, and the constraint to be applied for this object. The subtype declaration is simply a shorthand notation, giving a simple name for the type and constraint.

The values in a range constraint need not be constants or even static expressions: the values will be calculated if necessary when the declaration is met in the course of executing the program. So we might have a subprogram with a formal parameter MAX and a local declaration

    subtype INDEX **is** INTEGER **range** 1 .. MAX;

12.4.1   Range constraints

There are various kinds of constraint which are used with different
types. We have already met a range constraint used with type INTEGER;
it can equally apply to other scalar types. Thus we can have subtype
declarations:

    subtype UC_LETTER **is** CHARACTER
                          range ´A´ .. ´Z´;
    subtype LC_LETTER **is** CHARACTER
                          range ´a´ .. ´z´;
    subtype HIGH_GRADE **is** SECURITY_CLASSIFICATION
                          range CONFIDENTIAL..TOP_SECRET;

and object declarations

    START_DAYLIGHT : MONTH **range** FEB..MAY;
    END_DAYLIGHT   : MONTH **range** AUG..NOV;

A range constraint may be used by itself to form an implied derived
type, for numerical values (integer or floating-point). The bounds of
the range must be of the same type, and the range implies a derivative
of that type. Thus

    range 1 .. 10;

as a type definition implicitly means

    new SHORT_INTEGER **range** 1 .. 10;

(on a computer with SHORT_INTEGER covering this range).

A range constraint may be given for a floating point type and <u>must</u> be
given for a fixed point type. It is needed to determine the
representation for values of the type. The actual range implemented will
cover the specified range, but need not exactly match it. A value
outside the specified range will raise CONSTRAINT_ERROR. A value
outside the implemented range will raise NUMERIC_ERROR.

12.4.2   Accuracy constraints

For a real type (i.e. fixed or floating point), we use accuracy constraints. The sets of abstract values concerned are approximations to mathematical real numbers (for example, measurements of continuous physical quantities such as length, voltage, temperature or weight). A fundamental distinction is made in Ada between approximations which are relative and those which are absolute. This is shown by the accuracy constraint given in the declaration. You either specify the number of decimal digits of precision needed (indicating that the approximation is relative) or the magnitude of the acceptable error bound for the approximation (indicating that the approximation is absolute).

a. Relative precision: Floating point.

The type declaration

    type SPEED **is digits** 5;

says that the possible values for SPEED are approximations to real numbers, with a relative accuracy of at least five decimal digits. (It is left to the compiler to decide for each computer whether this needs single precision or double precision floating point.)

We could the use this type to declare objects

    AIR_SPEED : SPEED;
    GROUND_SPEED, WIND_SPEED : SPEED;

or components of records:

    record
      MAGNITUDE : SPEED;
      ORIENTATION : ANGLE;
    end record;

The predefined environment of Ada includes the built-in floating-point types SHORT_FLOAT, FLOAT and LONG_FLOAT; the particular number of digits of precision in each depends on the computer concerned. Any floating-point type is effectively derived from one of these, appropriate for the constraint:

    type SPEED **is new** FLOAT **digits** 5;

(on a computer with at least five decimal digits of precision in FLOAT).

b. Absolute precision: Fixed point.

The type declaration

type COMPASS **is delta** 0.1 **range** 0.0 .. 360.0;

says that the possible values for COMPASS are approximations to real numbers, with an absolute precision of 0.1 (and the range specified). In other words, the possible values of COMPASS will cover the range and will allow discrimination between real values at least 0.1 apart. (It is left to the compiler to decide for each computer whether to use more finely spaced approximations: usually it will choose a suitable power of 2 to achieve an efficient representation.)

Every object declared with absolute precision must have its range specified. This might be done in the type declaration itself as above, or in two stages:

type POTENTIOMETER **is delta** 0.0001;

followed by

X, Y : POTENTIOMETER **range** 0.0 .. 1.0;

or by using an intermediate subtype:

subtype LOW_POT **is** POTENTIOMETER **range** 0.0 .. 0.1;
Q : LOW_POT;

There are no predefined fixed point types in Ada: any absolute precision quantities needed must have an explicit type definition.

12.4.3   Discriminant constraints

A type defined as a record may have discriminant constraints. For example, the type DIRECTORY_ENTRY implies that we can have local or remote values with appropriate line numbers or trunk numbers. There will be an occasion when we wish to deal only with values of that type which are local; to specify this we can declare

```
    subtype LOCAL_ENTRY is DIRECTORY_ENTRY
                            (PROXIMITY => LOCAL);
```

and declare objects such as

```
    L1 : LOCAL_ENTRY;
```

or combine the declarations together as in

```
    R1 : DIRECTORY_ENTRY (PROXIMITY => REMOTE);
```


The objects so declared have all the components of the stated variant of the base type (including of course the components which are in the fixed part of the record). These components may be accessed in just the same way as those of an object of the base type, but any assignment of a new value to L1 is checked to ensure that the component PROXIMITY has the value LOCAL. If this check fails, the exception CONSTRAINT_ERROR is raised.

The discriminant constraint is written after the name of the type (or subtype) to which it applies, and consists of an aggregate specifying the required value of the discriminant. In general, a record with variants is written

```
    type RECORD_WITH_VARIANTS (DISCRIMINANT : SOME_DISCRETE_TYPE) is
      record
        case DISCRIMINANT is
          when SOME_DISCRETE_VALUE =>
            VARIANT_COMPONENT : SOME_TYPE;
            -- etc
        end case;
      end record;
```

where SOME_DISCRETE_VALUE is in SOME_DISCRETE_TYPE; a discriminant constraint which selects this particular variant would be

```
    (DISCRIMINANT => SOME_DISCRETE_VALUE);
```


A discriminant constraint may also be applied to an access type, where the base type is a record with variants. (In this case the constraint refers to the objects in the collection denoted by the values in the access type.)

12.4.4   Index constraints

A type defined as an array may have index constraints. These give the lower and upper bounds (and hence the type) of each index of the array. Index constraints are particularly important with array parameters for subprograms, and for arrays whose sizes are not fixed in the type definition.

For example, the predefined declaration

    type STRING **is array** (NATURAL **range** <>) **of** CHARACTER;

defines STRING as a one-dimensional array but does not give the bounds for the index. Any object declaration for a string must specify the bounds to be used, either by attaching an index constraint or by giving an initial value:

    CARD_IMAGE : STRING (1 .. 80);
    PROMPT : **constant** STRING := "TYPE NEXT VALUE";

Since array indexes may be of any discrete type (not just integers), an index constraint must be of the same type as is given in the array definition. For example, with

    type RATE **is array** (DAY_NAME, 0 .. 23)
                of FLOAT;

we could have constrained arrays defined as

    DAY_RATE : RATE (DAY_NAME **range** MONDAY .. FRIDAY, 9..18);
    WEEKEND_RATE : RATE
            (DAY_NAME **range** SATURDAY .. SUNDAY, 0..24);

An index constraint is written after the name of the type (or subtype) to which it applies, and consists of one or more discrete ranges that specify the bounds for the array indices. For each index position, the discrete range is written either

        LOWER .. UPPER

where the expressions for LOWER and UPPER are of the proper type (and there is no ambiguity, which is usually the case with indices of type INTEGER), or

        INDEX_TYPE **range** LOWER .. UPPER

giving the index type explicitly.

If a parameter of a subprogram is specified as an array, the formal parameter may leave the bounds unspecified so that the subprogram body can be applied to any array of the appropriate dimensionality and element type. (The types of the indices must also be fixed, in order that statements in the subprogram body can manipulate them.) So we can have

        type VECTOR **is array** (NATURAL **range** <>) **of** FLOAT;
        procedure SCALAR_PRODUCT(X, Y : VECTOR) **return** FLOAT;

where the procedure can be applied to any two vectors. On each occasion the procedure is called, there is an implied index constraint applied to the parameters, taking the bounds of the actual parameters.

12.4.5   Constraints and Derived Types

A type may be defined by a constraint clause (or combination of constraint clauses) on its own. This is implicitly taken to be derived from an appropriate built-in type, chosen by the implementation to satisfy the constraint. Depending on the constraints given, this could be an integer, a floating-point type or a fixed-point type.

A **range** constraint with integer values for its range bounds, say

        range 0 .. 5280;

has the effect of

        new INTEGER **range** 0 .. 5280;

or perhaps SHORT_INTEGER or LONG_INTEGER, to cover the stated range.

A **digits** constraint, say

        digits 5;

is taken as a type definition for a floating point type

        new FLOAT **digits** 5;

or perhaps SHORT_FLOAT or LONG_FLOAT, to provide at least the stated number of digits of precision.

A digits constraint may be followed by a range constraint with real bounds, such as

    digits 5 range −1.0 .. 1.0;

this is taken as

    new FLOAT digits 5 range −1.0 .. 1.0;

A **delta** constraint may not be given by itself, but both a **delta** and a **range** may be given together to define a new fixed-point type: for example

    delta 0.125 range 0.0 .. 255.0;

There are no built-in fixed-point types, and this is the complete definition of such a type.

Types which are derived from these numeric types may have further constraints applied, provided that the additional constraint does not try to extend the set of possible values in the type.

Thus if an additional range constraint is given for an existing scalar type S_TYPE, the new bounds must be contained in

    S_TYPE´FIRST .. S_TYPE´LAST

If an additional **digits** constraint is given for an existing floating-point type, the new precision must have no more digits than the existing type. If an additional delta constraint is given for an existing fixed part type, the new delta must be no finer than that of the existing type.

The values in accuracy constraints may be given by expressions, but they must be static, that is independent of any dynamically computed value, so that they are determinable when the program is translated.

In general, if a derived type definition is given with constraints, the effect is as though a new type had been set up by definition, then the constraints applied to that. Thus the type definition

    new W_VALVE range WATER_INLET .. FLUSH_WATER;

makes a distinct type with the same operators and literals as for W_VALVE, but only the given range of values in it.

We may use these ideas to show constraints on values returned by functions, such as

```
subtype POSITIVE_FLOAT is FLOAT
        range FLOAT'SMALL .. FLOAT'LARGE;

subtype UP_TO_ONE is FLOAT range -1.0 .. 1.0;

function SIN(X:FLOAT) return UP_TO_ONE;

function SQRT(X:POSITIVE_FLOAT) return POSITIVE_FLOAT;
```

Another use for constraints and derived types is to deal with posible index values in an array containing cross references:

```
MAX_SIZE : constant := 200;

type POSSIBLE is range 0 .. MAX_SIZE;

subtype DEFINITE is POSSIBLE range 1 .. POSSIBLE'LAST;

type LIST_ITEM is
  record
    PREV, NEXT : POSSIBLE;     -- value 0 means none
    VALUE : FLOAT;
  end record;

A : array ( DEFINITE ) of LIST_ITEM;
```

12.5   Access Types

An access type is used for a collection of objects, all of the same type (usually a record) where the number of objects currently relevant can change during the execution of the program, and it is necessary to note relationships between one object in the collection and another. For example, in an air defense system, there will be a collection of tracks (changing as aircraft pass through the region under surveillance) and relationships between them, such as between targets and interceptors. The type of the individual objects in the collection is called the base type.

The access type both establishes the collection, and introduces the possibility of values denoting particular members of the collection. Each access type establishes a collection of a particular base type; any value of that access type can denote one of the objects currently in that collection, or be **null** denoting no object at all.

Quantities of an access type have values which are closely related to values of the corresponding base type. All the objects in the collection must have values of the base type, and a value of the access type may denote any one of them. (Note that there may be other objects having values of the base type, which are <u>not</u> in the collection; these can not be denoted by values of the access type.)

For example, with

```
type TRACK_IMAGE is
  record                    -- basic components
      TRACK_NAME : STRING(1 .. 5);
      X_COORD : DISTANCE;
      Y_COORD : DISTANCE;
      HEIGHT  : KFEET;
  end record;
```

The corresponding access type is

```
type TRACK_POINTER is
   access TRACK_IMAGE;
```

This establishes a collection of objects of type TRACK_IMAGE. The type TRACK_POINTER may then be used to access objects in that collection. We can show this by drawing the access-value as an arrow, pointing at the appropriate object of the base-type (or a diagonal line for **null**). We might have values of these types as shown in figure 12a.

The key point in understanding access types is to appreciate that the access type definition itself implies the collection of base-objects, and that the set of possible values in that access type consists of **null** and the collection of base-objects so implied. (In other words, the access type definition causes space for the collection to be allocated, with its own local storage manager called for each **new** object in the collection.)

Thus with

```
type POINTER is access BASE_TYPE;
```

the declaration itself implies a collection of objects of type BASE_TYPE, which can be referred to only by objects of type POINTER. Access objects may be isolated, such as

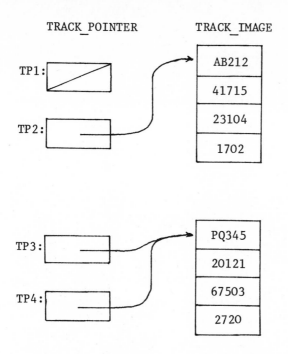

TRACK_POINTER   TRACK_IMAGE

Figure 12a: Track pointers and track images

    P1, P2 : POINTER;

or be components of a record (including the BASE_TYPE to which they refer).

The rules of type-matching apply as usual, so if we have several access type definitions, they are distinct types, having different collections of base-objects, even though the base-types may be the same.

Any number of access-type objects (including components in records) may denote the same base object. This means that if any of them is a variable which makes a change to the object it denotes, then all other variables necessarily denote the changed object. This is an important difference from the normal behaviour of variables, and is a possible source of errors in programs. For variables not of an access type, and not shared between different tasks, the value of the variable is that which was most recently assigned to it. In the case of access types, it is true that the object denoted by the variable is the same as that which was most recently assigned to it, but the properties of that object are not necessarily the same. Since when dealing with access types we normally think directly of the properties of the object denoted, this can be confusing.

12.5.1   Access objects

We can introduce access objects to denote possible objects of the base type by an ordinary object declaration, specifying the required access type:

    TP1, TP2 : TRACK_POINTER;

The variables TP1 and TP2 will have values which in general may denote objects in the collection, not necessarily different objects, and perhaps denoting no objects at all. The top pointer in figure 12a might have been the result of

    TP1 := null;

whereas the bottom pointer could have been made to point to the same object as the third by

    TP4 := TP3;

    The notation for a component of a record can also be used for the component of an object denoted by an access value: thus

    TP1.TRACK_NAME

means the value of the TRACK_NAME component in the object currently denoted by TP1, in this case "AB212". The special notation

    TP1.all

means all components of the base object currently denoted by TP1.

    There is a crucial difference between values of a base type and values of a corresponding access type. Consider:

    T1, T2 : TRACK_IMAGE;

then

    T1 := T2;

asigns all the current value of T2 to T1, making two identical copies of that value. Any subsequent change to T2 or any of its components such as T2.X_COORD has no effect on T1.

In contrast, the assignment

    TP1 := TP2;

sets TP1 to denote the same object as is denoted by TP2: two identical references to the same object. Any subsequent change to a component of that object such as TP2.X_COORD necessarily implies the same change to TP1.X_COORD. However, if TP2 is changed so that it denotes a different object than there is no effect on TP1.

If we want to copy the value of an object denoted by an access value, we must write

    TP1.all := TP2.all;

this sets all the components of the object denoted by TP1 to have the same values as the components of the object denoted by TP2, making the objects equal but not necessarily identical (see figure 12b).

12.5.2   Constructing new objects

A new object in the collection is formed by allocation in an expression (see section 3.5d). An allocator consists of the word new followed by an appropriate typed expression to give the value of the allocated object. Each new object is different from all previously allocated objects in the collection, even though the value of the object may be the same as that of another object. The allocator both creates the new object, and gives an access value denoting that object as its result. Thus

    TP1 := new TRACK_IMAGE (T1);
    TP2 := new TRACK_IMAGE ("AB212", X, Y, H);

generates two new objects in the TRACK_POINTER collection (since that is the type of TP1 and TP2), and assigns values denoting them to TP1 and TP2.

Notice the significance of each new allocating a distinct object: the two statements

    TP1 := new TRACK_IMAGE (T1);
    TP2 := new TRACK_IMAGE (T1);

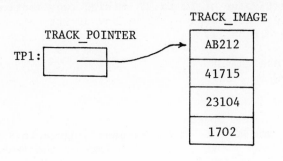

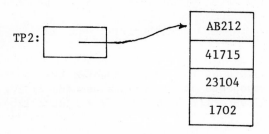

Figure 12b: Pointers to equal objects

allocate two objects with the same values (figure 12b), whereas

```
    TP1 := new TRACK_IMAGE (T1);
    TP2 := TP1;
```

allocates one object with two access values denoting it.

12.5.3   Access values as record components

The principal use of access types is for working with inter-
relationships between the objects in the collection. For each such
relationship an object might have, its record has a component of the
appropriate access type, denoting the object (if any) with which it has
the relationship. Thus a track may be that of an interceptor, which may
be associated with a target.

We can link any track with another if we include a component for the link in the type for TRACK_IMAGE:

```
record
   -- basic components plus
   ASSOCIATED_TRACK: TRACK_POINTER;
end record;
```

We make the link by assigning the required track pointer to the ASSOCIATED_TRACK component. The link may be changed during the course of execution, or broken by

```
TP1.ASSOCIATED_TRACK := null;
```

There is a notational problem that follows from the rule that every identifier in Ada must be declared before it may be used. Since the declaration of an access type must specify the type of the objects in the collection, and the type of the objects is usually a record containing components whose type is the access type, each declaration depends on the other, and therefore (according to the rules of scope for declarations), must be written after it. The way to write the declarations in the right order is to give the base type a name, but not to specify its details until after the access type has been declared, thus:

```
type TRACK_IMAGE_LINKED;        -- with no details yet
type TRACK_POINTER_LINKED is
  access TRACK_IMAGE_LINKED;
type TRACK_IMAGE_LINKED is      -- now with details
  record
     TRACK_NAME : STRING (1..5);
     ASSOCIATED_TRACK : TRACK_POINTER_LINKED;
  end record;
```

Notice that there are two declarations for TRACK_IMAGE_LINKED; the first is incomplete: it simply says that this identifier refers to a type, without giving the type definition; the second gives the necessary type definition. A similar technique of splitting name and details is used for private types (see section 7.4).

12.5.4   Relations between access objects

Components which are themselves access values are the crucial ones for dealing with the inter-relationships.

        TP1.ASSOCIATED_TRACK

denotes the track (if any) associated with TP1.

   Suppose TP1 denotes the linked track image with name PQ345, and that TP2 denotes track XY678, neither having an associated track. We can establish the association between these two tracks (see figure 12c) as follows:

```
   TP1.ASSOCIATED_TRACK := TP2;   -- make link a
   TP2.ASSOCIATED_TRACK := TP1;   -- make link b
```

The two tracks now stand associated in both directions, and the variables TP1 and TP2 could be used for other purposes without affecting these track images.

   Similar techniques are used to express inter-relationships between objects of different types, for example tracks of interceptors and their controllers. Now we need an access type for each distinct collection of objects, and the record for any of the objects may include components of an access type corresponding to the kind of related object.

   Thus we may also have

```
   type CONTROLLER;

   type CONTROLLER_POINTER is
     access CONTROLLER;

   type TRACK_IMAGE_CONTROLLED is
     record
       -- basic components plus
       TRACK_CONTROLLER : CONTROLLER_POINTER;
     end record;

   type CONTROLLER is
     record
       INTERCEPTOR : TRACK_IMAGE_CONTROLLED;
       TARGET : TRACK_IMAGE_CONTROLLED;
     end record;
```

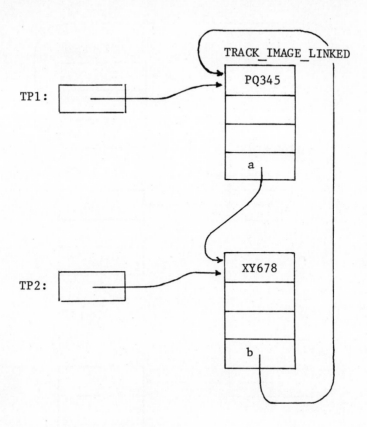

Figure 12c: Links between tracks

This allows each controller to be able to refer to two distinct tracks,
an interceptor and a target, while each track can denote the controller
responsible for it (in either capacity). A typical situation is shown in
figure 12d.   In the second case a target is linked to a controller but
an interceptor has not yet been set up.

Another arrangement might be

```
type POSSIBLE_TRACKS is (NORMAL, TARGET, INTERCEPTOR);

type TRACK_IMAGE_SPLIT (TRACK_TYPE : POSSIBLE_TRACKS ) is
  record
      -- basic components
      case TRACK_TYPE is
        when NORMAL =>
```

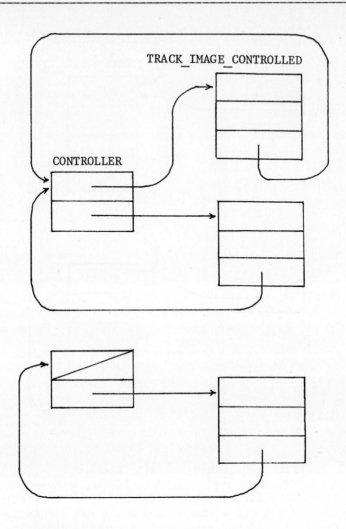

Figure 12d: Track controller links

```
         null;
      when TARGET =>
         ASSOCIATED_TRACK : TRACK_POINTER;
      when INTERCEPTOR =>
         TRACK_CONTROLLER : CONTROLLER_POINTER;
      end case;
   end record;
```

or the pointers could be kept distinct by

```
type NORMAL_TRACK is
  record
      -- basic components
  end record;

type TARGET_TRACK;

type INTERCEPTOR_TRACK;

type NORMAL_POINTER is
  access NORMAL_TRACK;

type INTERCEPTOR_POINTER is
  access INTERCEPTOR_TRACK;

type TARGET_POINTER is
  access TARGET_TRACK;

type TARGET_TRACK is
  record
      -- basic components plus
      ASSOCIATED_TRACK : INTERCEPTOR_POINTER;
  end record;

type INTERCEPTOR_TRACK is
  record
      -- basic components plus
      TRACK_CONTROLLER : CONTROLLER_POINTER;
  end record;
```

12.5.5   List processing

The same linking technique is used for maintaining a list (of varying
length) of items for processing. The relationship in this case is the
ordering of the list: each item (except the last) has a successor.
Suppose we have queues of messages awaiting transmission along several
trunks, we would make a collection of message items as follows (see
figures 12e and 12f):

```
type MESSAGE_ITEM;      -- without details
type MESSAGE_PTR is
  access MESSAGE_ITEM;
type MESSAGE_ITEM is       -- details now
  record
```

```
      DESTINATION : PORT;
      CONTENTS : STRING (1..80);
      SEQUEL : MESSAGE_PTR := null;      -- default for last item
   end record;

   DIRECTORY   : array (PORT) of TRUNK;
   PENDING : array (TRUNK) of MESSAGE_PTR;
      -- first element in queue
   NEW_MESSAGE : MESSAGE_PTR;      -- with SEQUEL = null
```

PENDING points to the first message (if any) for each trunk, and we wish to attach a new message to the pending queue for its destination.

The SEQUEL component in MESSAGE_ITEM allows a chain of these items to be formed, each containing a pointer to the next (and the last in the chain containing null), as shown in figure 12e.

Note that since an access-object may have the value null there might be no object component denoted by a name such as TP1.TRACK_NAME or M.SEQUEL. This possibility cannot be detected at compile time, and if it occurs during execution then the exception ACCESS_ERROR is raised. Any use of an access value with a component selector implies the possibility of ACCESS_ERROR, and the programmer should specify the action to be taken in the case of this error by writing an appropriate exception handler.

The possibility can be avoided by explicit programming, thus (see figure 12f):

```
   -- attach NEW_MESSAGE to appropriate queue
   M : MESSAGE_PTR;
   T : TRUNK;
begin
   T := DIRECTORY (NEW_MESSAGE.DESTINATION);
         -- find trunk to use.
   M := PENDING (T);
         -- start of queue pending transmission on
         -- this trunk.

   if M = null then
         -- a: no messages pending
      PENDING (T) := NEW_MESSAGE;
   else
         -- b: attach message
      while M.SEQUEL /= null loop
         -- assume that few repetitions are needed
        M := M.SEQUEL;
```

MESSAGE ITEM

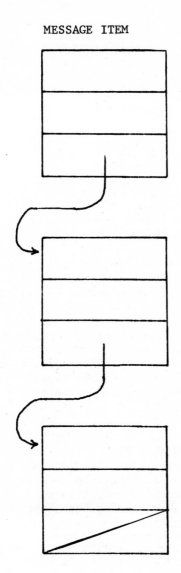

Figure 12e: Sequence of messages

```
end loop;
    -- advance to the last current message
-- assert ( M.SEQUEL = null );
M.SEQUEL := NEW_MESSAGE;
    -- c: attach message
```

```
      end if;
   NEW_MESSAGE.SEQUEL := null;
            -- d: mark end
   end;
```

Notice that M.SEQUEL always occurs in positions where M is not **null**, thus avoiding the possibility of ACCESS_ERROR.

12.5.6   Limited number of objects

In principle, the number of objects in a collection for an access type may change during execution without limit. In practice, because a finite amount of storage must be reserved for the collection, there is a limit to the number of new objects which may be allocated in each collection.

If the program tries to allocate an object when there is no space available for it in the collection, then the exception STORAGE_ERROR is raised. Any use of an allocator (with **new** in an expression) implies the possibility of a STORAGE_ERROR, and the programmer should specify the action to be taken in case of this error by writing an appropriate exception handler.

The representation for an access type should include a length specification, which gives the amount of storage space to be reserved for all objects of that access type. For example

```
   for TRACK_POINTER´STORAGE_SIZE use 200 * TRACK_IMAGE´SIZE;
```

provides space for nearly 200 new track images. (The space reserved may have to contain special variables for the allocator, so the maxium number of possible objects is not precisely determined). The number of objects which can be allocated in the collection is independent of how many variables are declared for the access type, and also of the possibility that any object of the access type may cease to be relevant. When any variable or record component of the access type is given a new value by an assignment, the old value is lost, but the object denoted by that value continues to exist.

If as a result of such an assignment there is no access value at all denoting some particular object, then there is no way of ever subsequently referring to that object: it has in effect ceased to exist. The storage space is still occupied by the object, however, and there is not necessarily any automatic recovery of the inaccessible space (i.e. no garbage collection). Once a new object has been allocated, it continues to occupy space until the whole collection is lost when the

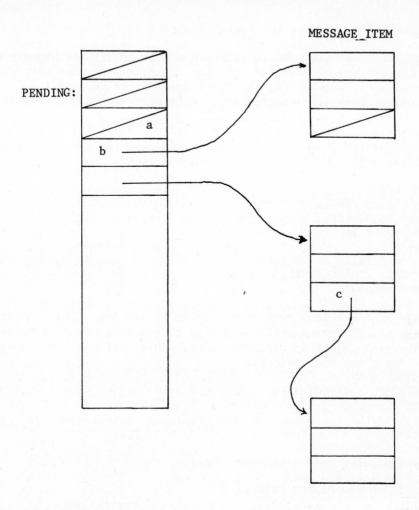

Figure 12f: Attach message to queue

program reaches the end of the block in which the access type is declared.

12.5.7   Storage control with access types

When objects are entering and leaving the collection dynamically, some improvement is needed on the primitive technique by which storage is allocated for a new object but never recovered. The program must itself control the use of storage for these objects.

The simplest technique is to maintain a list of all the objects which are currently unused, called a free list, and arrange that when an object enters the collection, the first free object is used for it, and when an object leaves the collection, it is attached to the free list.

To maintain a list of objects, the usual method is for each record to contain a component which is an access value denoting the next object in the list (or **null** for the last object in the list).

```
type OBJECT;
type OBJECT_REF is
   access OBJECT;
type OBJECT is
   record
      -- details of object
      NEXT : OBJECT_REF;
   end record;
```

A variable of the access type is needed to denote the first object in the free list. (A second variable of the access type may also be used to denote the last object in the free list. This spreads the usage of objects throughout the collection).

```
FIRST,THIS : OBJECT_REF;
```

To initialise the list, new objects must be constructed and linked together:

```
FIRST := null;   -- marks end of list
for I in 1 .. 200 loop
   FIRST := new OBJECT (FIRST);
            -- sets object with link to previous one
end loop;
```

The loop is executed once for each object to be put on the free list, each time using the previous value of FIRST as its NEXT component, and setting FIRST to point to the newly created object. Initialising FIRST to **null** causes the list to be properly terminated. (It is constructed from the end, so that the last one actually allocated will be denoted by FIRST.)

When an object is needed for use, the first one from the free list is unlinked and denoted by THIS:

```
THIS := FIRST;        -- get object
```

```
      FIRST := THIS.NEXT;   -- adjust free list start
      THIS.NEXT := null;
```

Similarly when an object is no longer needed, it is put on the free list (before the variable denoting it is changed). Suppose THIS denotes the object to be freed:

```
      THIS.NEXT := FIRST;   -- attach free list to it
      FIRST := THIS;        -- adjust free list start
```

Now THIS can be changed without damaging the list.

The following sequence of statements manipulate a list, exchanging the head items of lists A and B (see figure 12g).

```
      THIS := A.NEXT;       -- save rest of A list (object Q)
      A.NEXT := B.NEXT;     -- a. attach rest of B list to A
      B.NEXT := THIS;       -- b. attach rest of A list to B
      THIS := A;
      A := B;               -- c.
      B := THIS;            -- d.
```

(Notice the structure: the first three statements exchange A.NEXT and B.NEXT; the second three statements exchange A and B.)

The set of procedures for obtaining and freeing objects can conveniently be formed into a package, so that all changes to the membership of the collection would be carried out properly.

12.6   Use of types in program design

The notation of a type definition gives valuable assistance in program design, by allowing the programmer to show the contents of tables and control blocks (as records) and the possible values for coded fields (as enumeration types). While the program is partially designed, it is likely that many types will be declared using type names which are introduced but not yet declared. The following example illustrates this, in which some types (such as AB_CODE) are given in full, but others use type names which have not yet been declared (such as L_S_CODE in LINK_STATUS)

```
      type AB_CODE is (      -- CCITT X25 sections
         TIMER_RECOVERY,     -- 3.7.10
         DTE_BUSY,           -- 3.7.8
```

(before)

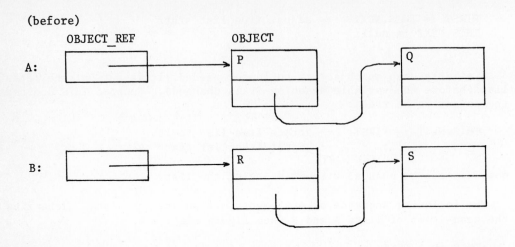

(after)

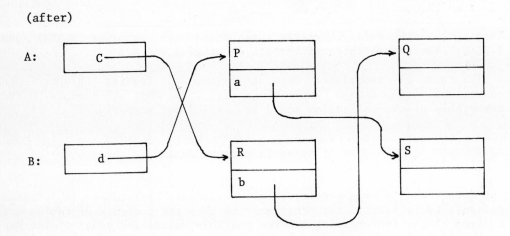

Figure 12g: Exchange list head items

```
DCE_BUSY,           -- 3.7.9
FC_REJECT,          -- 2.3.20,  3.10,  table 2.7
RETRANSMISSION      -- 2.4.3,  3.7.5  (ii),  3.7.7
RESET);
```

```
type LINK_STATUS is
  record          -- ref CCITT definition of X 25 sections
    STATE    : L_S_CODE;  -- 1.7 to 1.9
    AB_COND  : AB_CODE;
    MODE_B   : B_CODE;
    V_S, V_R : SR_STATE;    -- 2.2.2, 2.2.4
    TRIES    : SHORT_INTEGER range 0 .. MAX_TRIES;    -- II-40
    UNACK_I  : SHORT_INTEGER range 0 .. MAX_UNACK_I;  -- II-40
    U_I_Q    : QUEUE;       -- of unacknowledged I frames
    T_I_Q    : QUEUE;       -- of I for transmission
    GOING    : NET_B_PTR;  -- frame being output
    NEXT_F   : SHORT_NETWORK_BUFFER;
                -- piggyback for next frame

  end record;

type MESSAGE_CONTROL_BLOCK is
  record
    PRIORITY  : PRI_CODE;
    BUFFERING : BUF_CODE;
    SENDER    : PROC_NO;
    TARGET    : PROC_NO;
    USER_DATA : MESSAGE;
  end record;

type NETWORK_BUFFER_HEADER is
  record
    NEXT   : NET_B_PTR;
    VCN    : VIRTUAL_CCT_NO;
    IN_USE : BOOLEAN;
    LINK   : LINK_NO;
    FRAME_LENGTH : SHORT_INTEGER range 0 ..  MAX_FRAME_LENGTH;
  end record;

type NETWORK_BUFFER_FRAME is
  record
    ADR_FIELD : BYTE;
    CTR_FIELD : BYTE;
    PKT       : PACKET;
  end record;

type BUFFER is
  record
    HDR : NETWORK_BUFFER_HEADER;
    FRAME : NETWORK_BUFFER_FRAME;
  end record;
```

```
POOL : array (NET_B_PTR range 1 .. NET_BUF_MAX)
         of BUFFER;

procedure SEND_MSG(M : MESSAGE_CONTROL_BLOCK)
   return STATUS range SUCCESS .. NO_IPM_BUFF;

procedure WAIT_MSG(W : WAIT_CONTROL_BLOCK;
                   B : NET_B_PTR)
   return STATUS range SUCCESS .. NO_MESSAGE;

procedure GET_BUFF(B : NET_B_PTR) return STATUS;

procedure RELEASE_BUFF(B : NET_B_PTR) return STATUS;
```

Such text would of course give rise to diagnostic messages if submitted for compilation before all the types had been completely defined – but there messages could be a useful aid for the program designer.

Exercises

1. Write the type declarations for a track image which may be normal, a target or an interceptor; if it is a target it must be able to be associated with another track (its interceptor), and if it is an interceptor, it must be able to denote a controller. A normal track needs none of these.

2. Write three separate type declarations for normal tracks, targets and interceptors as in exercise 1, and declare separate access types for collections of each. What are the differences between the two techniques, regarding (a) storage for each track, (b) flexibility between the number of tracks of each type, (c) possibility of execution-time errors?

3. A message switching system handles messages of type

    ```
    type MESSAGE is
      record
        DESTINATION : PORT;
        CONTENTS : STRING (1..80);
      end record;
    ```

    At a node with no local lines, destinations are interpreted using

    ```
    DIRECTORY : array (PORT) of TRUNK;
    ```

to determine which trunk is to be used for forwarding. Messages arrive spontaneously; they have to be sorted according to their trunk number into queues pending onward transmission. Assume they are forwarded sufficiently quickly that queues are short. Write a suitable declaration for the collection of messages, capable of holding a list of messages for each trunk number, and appropriate variables to define the queue of messages for each trunk number. Write a sequence of statements to add a new message to the appropriate queue.

4. To maintain a list in order as a queue, with new items arriving at one end and items being taken off the other end for further processing, it is common to include with each item a pointer to the next item in the queue and also another pointer in the previous item in the queue. Define a type for the queued items (assuming that the information to be carried is of type OBJECT) and an access type for a collection of them. Define a queue control type to denote the first and last items in a queue (which may be empty). Write a sequence of statements to take the first item from one (non-empty) queue and put it as the last item in another queue.

CHAPTER 13

More on Tasking

In this chapter we deal with advanced tasking facilities, mainly concerned with writing the passive tasks used to provide communication media between sibling active tasks. We cover grouping techniques, non-determinism, and faults. The grouping techniques provide for handling similar tasks (section 13.1), or similar entries within a task (section 13.2). These are basically notational matters, that are not intrinsically novel. Non-determinism, on the other hand, introduces an entirely new principle into programming (section 13.3). Failures (section 13.4) are particularly tricky in multi-task systems, because of the dangers of a domino effect between tasks communicating with one another. We illustrate how to write tasks for two kinds of communication, including the use of a generic package, in section 13.5. Section 13.6 concludes the book.

13.1   Task types

When a number of tasks have similar properties (specifically the same body with corresponding entries), they may be written together as a task type. The notation here draws on the ideas of task declarations and object declarations: the task declaration is treated like a type rather than an object, and an object declaration must be given (with the task type as its type) for each particular task with the given properties. (Remember that there is no provision in Ada for generic tasks.)

The specification of a task type is written just as for an individual task, except for the introductory words:

```
task type SIMPLE_CHANNEL is
   entry GIVE (M : in MESSAGE);
```

200

```
      entry TAKE (M : out MESSAGE);
    end SIMPLE_CHANNEL;
```

The body is written exactly as for an individual task

```
    task body SIMPLE_CHANNEL is
      MESS : MESSAGE; -- local
    begin
      loop
        accept GIVE (M : MESSAGE) do
          MESS := M;  -- caller gives M to channel
        end GIVE;
        accept TAKE (M : out MESSAGE) do
          M := MESS; -- caller takes M from channel
        end TAKE;
      end loop;
    end SIMPLE_CHANNEL;
```

The idea is that the several instances of the task type may use reentrably the same code for the body (although this is not guaranteed by the language). The task body may be written separately as a subunit, with a stub in its place in the program unit containing the specification.

Having declared a task type, we can introduce task objects:

```
      C1, C2 : SIMPLE_CHANNEL;
```

and refer to their entries by the dot notation:

```
      C1.TAKE (M1);  -- take M1 from channel C1
      C2.GIVE (M1);  -- give M1 to channel C2
```

Task objects may also be declared as components of records or arrays.

13.2   Families of entries

When a number of entries to a task have similar properties (specifically, the same formal part), they can be written together as a family. In effect this is like an array of entries, although it is not officially called an array to avoid giving the impression that it has general array properties. A family of entries has a single dimension; the members of the family are distinguished by the index value.

The entry declaration for a family is written with the discrete range for the family index:

```
task TRUNK_MONITOR is
  entry CHECK_TRUNK (TRUNKS);
  ---
end TRUNK_MONITOR;
```

Any formal parameters are given in the usual way after the family index:

```
task SETTLE is
  entry VALVE_STABLE (VALVE)        -- name with index
    (STATE : out VALVE_STATUS);     -- parameters
  ---
end SETTLE;
```

The two parts in parentheses here are entirely different, giving the index and parameters respectively. The notation for entry calls and accepts are similar.

To call an entry in a family, we must give the particular index value and relevant parameters, this

```
TRUNK_MONITOR.CHECK_TRUNK (T1);    -- no parameters
SETTLE.VALVE_STABLE (CLEAN_WATER) (S); -- parameter S
```

There is no notational distinction between the parameters for an ordinary entry call and the index for a member of a family. When the family entry takes parameters, there are two adjacent parts in parentheses. The first is always evaluated to establish which member of the family is called; the second may be evaluated, according to the mode of the formal parameters.

Within the body of the task declaring the family of entries, accept statements specify the rendezvous actions for members of the family. The index may be a constant or a variable (of the right type), and its value determines which member of the family is accepted by that statement. Thus for a particular value E of type TRUNKS

```
accept CHECK_TRUNK (E);
```

will accept a call of CHECK_TRUNK for that index value, and no other. The value E could be given as a constant, but most commonly would be a loop index covering all the members of the family. This is explained in the section on conditional rendezvous (13.3.5).

13.3   Non-determinism

The facilities described previously are all deterministic: the actions
in the program are determined by the previous actions that have taken
place. We now turn to non-determinism programs, in which the actions in
one task depend not only on the previous actions in the task, and the
data communicated to it from other tasks, but on the relative timings of
actions taking place in other tasks.   In general non-deterministic
programs are not precisely repeatable, so are particularly difficult to
debug.   This is of course characteristic of real-time embedded computer
systems.

The most vivid form of non-determinism is the time-out.   A task
contains a series of actions to be carried out, but if a certain action
cannot be done by a given time,   then an alternative action may be
attempted.   We have met this in Chapter 8. Non-determinism also arises
with buffer handling: one task may be producing items for the buffer,
another task consuming items from the buffer, but the precise order of
producing and consuming may be arbitrary and unrepeatable.

The statement in Ada used to indicate non-determinism is **select**.   It
is used in a variety of forms, which we describe here. A select
statement is a compound statement, which contains several sequences of
statements, one of which is executed.

The principal form of select statement introduces a set of accept
statements, to achieve mutual exclusion between the execution of the
corresponding bodies. Other forms are used to achievee time-outs and
conditional rendezvous.

13.3.1   Selective rendezvous

A task may have several entries, and at a certain stage be prepared to
have a rendezvous with any of them, whichever might be called first.

```
loop
  select
    accept READ (X : out ITEM) do
        X := STORED;
    end READ;
  or
    accept WRITE (X : ITEM) do
        STORED := X;
    end WRITE;
```

```
   end select;
end loop;
```

This uses a local variable STORED, of type ITEM, presumed to be
initialised in some way, which can be read or written in any order,
either to READ the current value or to WRITE a new value.

A select statement frequently occurs in a loop, so that each READ
gives the value of the most recent WRITE.

Notice the important difference between this and a program with
procedures for READ and WRITE.   Because procedures are reentrable,
there is nothing to stop a task calling one procedure while the same or
an associated procedure is in the course of execution for another task.
The loop select construct gives disjoint execution of the several accept
statements.

If the relevant entries have been called before the select statement
is reached, one (only) of the accept statements is executed, chosen
arbitrarily.

Each arm of a select statement must begin with a special kind of
statement, so that the appropriate choice can be made.   As well as
accept (described above), the possibilities are an entry call, **delay**, or
terminate.   The delay is used to give a time-out on the accepting side
(similar to time-out on the calling side, see section 8.4); the
terminate is used to indicate that the task may be terminated at this
point.   A further form provides for alternative action if no task is
ready for a rendezvous when the select statement is executed.   We
explain these in detail below.

13.3.2   Watchdog timer

We can check that an entry is called within a prescribed time as
follows:

```
select
  accept OK;
or
  delay 3.0;
  PUT ("something wrong here");
end select;
```

This will expect the entry OK to be called within the next 3.0 seconds;
if this happens, the statement is executed and the delay is ignored.

But if the delay expires, the second arm of the statement is executed and the message is output: the entry OK is no longer acceptable.

There may be several delay arms, but only the one with the shortest duration can be effective. They can be used with any number of accept arms.

13.3.3   Conditional task termination

In the loop select construct, we have to be able to allow the task to be cleanly terminated in case the enclosing task needs to be terminated. (Remember the rule that when a task reaches its end, all its child tasks have to terminate before the parent task can finish.) Typically a child task may offer a number of entries by the loop select, and may properly terminate between executing any of the corresponding accept statements, but not within an accept statement. We express this by writing **terminate;** as another arm of the select statement, being an option that is chosen if another task is trying to terminate this one when the select statement is executed.

```
loop
  select
    accept READ (X : out ITEM) do
        X := STORED;
    end READ;
  or
    accept WRITE (X : ITEM) do
        STORED := X;
    end WRITE;
  or
    terminate;
  end select;
end loop;
```

There may not be more than one terminate arm, or a terminate arm with any delay arms in the same select statement.

13.3.4   Inhibition

The arms of a select statement may be preceded by clauses which inhibit the possibility of those arms being executed.

```
select
  when SET =>
    accept READ (X : out ITEM) do
       X := STORED;
    end READ;
or
  accept WRITE (X : ITEM) do
     STORED := X;
     SET := TRUE;
  end WRITE;
or
  terminate;
end select;
```

This uses a BOOLEAN variable SET, which is initially FALSE, to ensure
that READ will not be accepted until a WRITE has been given.

   The same technique is used when working with a buffer to ensure that
the producer cannot give more data when the buffer is full, nor the
consumer take more out when the buffer is empty:

```
loop
  select
    when COUNT < MAX =>
      accept GIVE (X: DATA) do
        --
      end GIVE;
  or
    when COUNT > 0 =>
       accept TAKE (X : out DATA) do
         --
       end TAKE;
  or
    terminate;
  end select;
end loop;
```

This assumes that the bodies of GIVE and TAKE make suitable adjustments
to COUNT.   The inhibition conditions are evaluated each time the select
statement is executed.   Any arms for which the condition is false are
not considered eligible for execution.

   If all of the arms of a select statement are inhibited, so that there
is no entry which it can ever accept, the exception SELECT_ERROR is
raised, unless there is an else part.

13.3.5   Conditional rendezvous

A further possibility in the select statement is to give an alternative
sequence of statements to be executed if, at the time the select
statement is met, no other task is ready to rendezvous with it.   This
is used to give a conditional rendezvous: performing the rendezvous if
another task is immediately ready, but taking other action if not.
There   are   two forms of this, depending on whether the condition is put
at the calling side or the accepting side of the rendezvous.   We have
already introduced (in Chapter 8) the selection in an active task
(calling on entry); here we describe selection in a passive task, where
an entry is accepted.

For conditional acceptance of a rendezvous, we write

```
    select
      accept SEIZE do
        --
      end SEIZE;
    else
      AVAILABLE := TRUE;
    end select;
```

Another task could have called SEIZE, but if none has, then AVAILABLE is
set TRUE.   (It is presumably set FALSE elsewhere.)

Logically, the else arm in a select statement is the same as

delay 0.0;

but the different notation is used to show a different intent.

A typical situation when this might be necessary would be to select
from entries in a family:

```
    for E in TRUNKS loop
      select
        accept CHECK_TRUNK (E) do
          --
        end CHECK_TRUNK (E);
      else
        null;
      end select;
    end loop;
```

Each time round the loop, any call alredy waiting for the corresponding
entry CHECK_TRUNK (E) will be accepted, but no further time is wasted if
it has not been called. The same technique is used to provide one of
several resources.

The accept arms may be preceded by inhibition clauses, in which case
the else arm is executed if none of the uninhibited entries is called.
This includes the case where all the arms are inhibited: if there is an
else part, it is executed rather than raising the exception.

In general, an else part, if used, must be the last arm of a select
statement.   There may be any number of other arms beginning with accept
statements, or a single arm beginning with an entrycall.   A selective
entry may not be optional or inhibited.   (An else arm may not be used
in a select statement with a terminate arm or any delay arms.)

13.4   Task and rendezvous failures

As any action might fail, it is possible that a task may fail
unexpectedly, even while it is in rendezvous with another task.   Here
we discuss what happens, arranged to minimise the spread of damage.   In
general, a failure in a task may be detected within the task (shown by
raising an exception) or by another task to which it is visible.

The normal rules of exception propogation and handling apply when a
failure is detected within a task, with special cases only when the
propagation passes out of an accept statement or when it reaches the
complete task body (when there is no handler at the outermost level for
the exception that has arisen).   These two cases are explained in the
following subsections.

If one task decides that another task has failed, then it has two
possible courses of action, of increasing severity.   It may raise the
special exception FAILURE in the faulty task (thus getting it out of a
possibly infinite loop).   This allows the faulty task to close down
gracefully, if a suitable exception handler is present.   If the faulty
task does not respond properly to this, the monitoring task may abort
it, causing it to be terminated abruptly with no chance of graceful
close-down.   If the fault is detected during a rendezvous, the task in
communication is prevented from adverse effects as far as possible.

It is of course possible that the suspected task was not really
faulty, but the mistake was in the task that tried to stop it.   This
kind of program error cannot be detected automatically.   Another
possibility is that two tasks watch one another, and both decide that

the other is faulty. On a single-processor machine, one task (non-deterministically) is likely to succeed in stopping the other before it could itself be stopped, so would survive. On a multi-processor machine, both attempts could be successful: no survival would be guaranteed.

Other error conditions arise if a task terminates when another task is trying to make a rendezvous with it.

13.4.1   Exception propagation out of an accept statement

An accept statement is executed when another task calls the entry: the rendezvous then takes place. If an exception is raised during the rendezvous, there might be a handler for it so that the rendezvous can take place normally. But if the exception propagates past the accept statement, the rendezvous has failed. In this case, the propagation spreads to both tasks involved in the rendezvous, from the accept statement in the accepting task, and from the entry call in the calling task.

13.4.2   Exceptions at the outermost level of a task

When an exception propagates to the outermost level of a task, and there is no handler there for it, the task is terminated with no further action - the exception is not propagated any further.

It may be thought that this is rather an unsatisfactory action: apparently ignoring the exception. The reason for it is that the action to be taken must depend on the application concerned, and should therefore be programmed in Ada. In other words, it is the programmer's responsibility to ensure that there is a handler at the outermost level of a task: every task body should contain

```
exception
   when others =>
      TERMINATION_ACTION;
```

The termination action may be to report the fault or to close down the part of the application system covered by this task. (The same argument applies to an exception reaching the outermost level of a program, as illustrated in the example in section 1.3). The termination action is known as the task's 'last wishes', to be carried out before it finishes.

13.4.3   Stopping a faulty task

One task may decide that another task is faulty, and try to stop it. The preferred way is to raise an exception, which allows the suspected task to close down properly. Every task T has an implied exception declaration

    T´FAILURE: **exception**;

and any task to which T is visible may

    raise T´FAILURE;

to stop normal execution of T.   If the task is currently engaged in a rendezvous, the rendezvous is handled as explained below. Otherwise whatever T is doing at this time (awaiting a rendezvous, delayed, temporarily suspended, or executing on another processor), it now reacts to the exception condition, and searches for the appropriate exception handler.   In any exception part, T may contain

    when T´FAILURE =>
       RECOVERY_ACTION;

and the normal rules of propagation apply.

This is the only exception that one task can raise in another task.

13.4.4   Abnormal termination of a faulty task

As a last resort, if a misbehaving task does not respond to the task failure exception, the task watching it may abort it:

    abort T;

Several tasks may be aborted together. If the task is currently engaged in a rendezvous, the rendezvous is handled as explained below. Otherwise it is stopped abruptly.

This is a drastic action, and prevents the task from carrying out any last wishes.   Before it is aborted, a task should be given a chance to carry out its last wishes by a previous

    raise T´FAILURE;

The abort statement is available in case this is ineffective.

Abnormal termination applies to all tasks dependent on T, including those dependent on subprograms and blocks currently being executed.

13.4.5   Faulty rendezvous

Faults may arise (or be detected) in either task involved in a rendezvous. In general a fault in the calling task has no effect on the accepting task; but a fault in the accepting task will always affect the calling task.

If the calling task is stopped before the rendezvous has started (i.e. before the entry call has been accepted), then the attempted rendezvous is simply ignored. If the calling task is actually in the rendezvous when the task is stopped (by a failure exception or abort), the rendezvous is allowed to complete normally, so that the accepting task can continue.

If the accepting task is stopped, then any other tasks awaiting or attempting to rendezvous with it are notified by

   raise TASKING_ERROR;

in each.

13.5   Inter-task communication in Mascot

Mascot is a technique for developing embedded computer systems, in which the several activities in a system are distinguished, with two prescribed kinds of communication between them: channels and pools.   A channel passes data in order from one activity to another; a pool allows data to be shared between several activities.

To write a program in Ada designed in this style, each Mascot activity corresponds to an active Ada task, and the channels and pools for inter-task communication are given as passive Ada tasks.   In the next two subsections we give the Ada programs for these.

13.5.1   Implementation of Mascot channels

A channel in Mascot is a means of sequential communication between two or more tasks. The type of data items communicated would be fixed for any particular channel, but any tasks could use it. There is an implication of a buffer within the channel, containing data items in the course of communication.

We write the channel as a task type, where the data item will be declared in the surrounding environment. This would probably be a generic package, with parameters ITEM and BUFFER_LENGTH.

```
task type MASCOT_CHANNEL IS
    entry GIVE (D : in ITEM);
    entry TAKE (D : out ITEM);
end MASCOT_CHANNEL;

task body MASCOT_CHANNEL is
    type BUFFER_POSSIBLE is new INTEGER range 0 .. BUFFER_LENGTH;
    subtype BUFFER_ACTUAL is BUFFER_POSSIBLE range 1 .. BUFFER_LENGTH;
    BUFFER : array (BUFFER_ACTUAL) of ITEM;
    INX,OUTX : BUFFER_ACTUAL := 1;
    CONTAINS : BUFFER_POSSIBLE := 0;
    -- invariant:
    -- (CONTAINS - INX + OUTX) mod BUFFER_LENGTH = 0;
begin
loop
    select
      when CONTAINS < BUFFER_LENGTH =>
        accept GIVE (D : in ITEM) do
            BUFFER (INX) := D;
          end GIVE;
        INX := INX mod BUFFER_LENGTH + 1;
        CONTAINS := CONTAINS + 1;
    or
      when CONTAINS > 0 =>
        accept TAKE (D : out ITEM) do
            D := BUFFER (OUTX);
          end TAKE;
        OUTX := OUTX mod BUFFER_LENGTH + 1;
        CONTAINS := CONTAINS - 1;
    or
        terminate;
      end select;
    end loop;
  end MASCOT_CHANNEL;
```

This structure is characteristic of a server task.   The   specification
provides   entries for communication between the user tasks.   The server
task body consists of a loop select that covers the several entry points
(and terminate).

13.5.2   Implementation of Mascot pools

A pool in Mascot is an indexed dataset,   accessible   by   several   tasks,
capable   of   random   access   with protection against interference during
each read or write.   The types of data items in the pool and the   keys
used   to   distinguish them would be fixed for any particular pool.   The
facilities imply memory within the pool,   containing   the   current   data
items,   with   markers distinguishing valid from invalid memory elements.
In this implementation, we assume   that   the   possible   key   values   are
compact,   so   that   an   array   is a suitable format for the memory.   An
alternative, where the key values are sparse, would follow the lines   of
the generic package ASSOCIATIVE_MEMORY given in chapter 10.

   We write the pool as a generic package, whose body uses a server task
to   ensure   mutual   exclusion   between access from different user tasks.
(Remember that procedures in Ada are reentrable.)

```
generic
   type KEY is (<>);
   type ITEM is private;
package MASCOT_POOL is
   procedure READ (K :KEY; D : out ITEM);
   procedure WRITE (K : KEY; D : in ITEM);
   procedure UPDATE (K : KEY;
       REVISED : in ITEM;
       PREVIOUS : out ITEM);
   procedure DELETE (K : KEY);
   function IS_THERE (K : KEY) return BOOLEAN;
   NONEXISTENT, OVERWRITTEN : exception;
end MASCOT_POOL;

package body MASCOT_POOL is

   task POOL_MANAGER is
      entry EXAMINE (K : KEY; D : out ITEM; PRESENT : out BOOLEAN);
      entry SET (K : KEY; D : in ITEM; PRESENT : out BOOLEAN);
      entry CHANGE (K : KEY; REVISED : in ITEM;
              PREVIOUS : out ITEM; PRESENT : out BOOLEAN);
      entry REMOVE (K : KEY; PRESENT : out BOOLEAN);
      entry X_IS_THERE (K : KEY; PRESENT : out BOOLEAN);
```

```
      end POOL_MANAGER;

      procedure READ (K : KEY ; D : out ITEM) is
         IS_THERE : BOOLEAN;
      begin
         POOL_MANAGER.EXAMINE (K, D, IS_THERE);
         if not IS_THERE then
           raise NONEXISTENT;
         end if;
      end READ;

      procedure WRITE (K : KEY; D ; in ITEM) is
         WAS_THERE : BOOLEAN;
      begin
         POOL_MANAGER.SET (K, D, WAS_THERE);
         if WAS_THERE then
           raise OVERWRITTEN;
         end if;
      end WRITE;

      procedure UPDATE (K :KEY; REVISED : in ITEM;
                    PREVIOUS : out ITEM) is
         WAS_THERE : BOOLEAN;
      begin
         POOL_MANAGER.CHANGE (K, REVISED, PREVIOUS, WAS_THERE);
         if not WAS_THERE then
           raise NONEXISTENT;
         end if;
      end UPDATE;

      procedure DELETE (K :KEY) is
         WAS_THERE : BOOLEAN;
      begin
         POOL_MANAGER.REMOVE (K, WAS_THERE);
         if not WAS_THERE then
           raise NONEXISTENT;
         end if;
      end DELETE;

      function IS_THERE (K :KEY) return BOOLEAN is
         WAS_THERE : BOOLEAN;
      begin
         POOL_MANAGER.X_IS_THERE (K, WAS_THERE);
         return WAS_THERE;
      end IS_THERE;

      task body POOL_MANAGER is
```

```
        POOL_VALUES : array (KEY) of ITEM;
        EXISTS      : array (KEY) of BOOLEAN;
                      := (others => FALSE);
      begin
        loop
          select
            accept EXAMINE (K : KEY ; D : out ITEM;
                          PRESENT : out BOOLEAN) do
              PRESENT := EXISTS (K);
              if PRESENT then
                  D := POOL_VALUES (K);
              end if;
            end EXAMINE;
          or
            accept SET (K : KEY; D : in ITEM;
                          PRESENT : out BOOLEAN) do
              PRESENT := EXISTS (K);
              POOL_VALUES (K) := D;
              EXISTS (K) := TRUE;
            end SET;
          or
            accept CHANGE (K : KEY; REVISED : in ITEM;
                        PREVIOUS : out ITEM; PRESENT : out BOOLEAN) do
              PRESENT := EXISTS (K);
              if PRESENT then
                      PREVIOUS := POOL_VALUES (K);
              end if;
              POOL_VALUES (K) := REVISED;
              EXISTS (K) := TRUE;
            end CHANGE;
          or
            accept REMOVE (K : KEY; PRESENT : out BOOLEAN) do
              PRESENT := EXISTS (K);
              EXISTS (K) := FALSE;
            end REMOVE;
          or
            accept X_IS_THERE (K : KEY; PRESENT : out BOOLEAN) do
              PRESENT := EXISTS (K);
            end X_IS_THERE;
          or
            terminate;
          end select;
        end loop;
      end POOL_MANAGER;

  end MASCOT_POOL;
```

Note the way the server task communicates with the procedures which
provide the externally visible facilities, in particular the exceptions.
The server gives a status flag to the calling procedure, which then
decides whether to raise the exception. Many tasks may have access to
the package, and provide their own handlers for the exceptions.

13.6   Conclusion

The rendezvous technique of Ada is one of the most novel features of the
language, and there is very little actual experience of using it.
Similar remarks also apply to the use of generics, exceptions, and (to a
lesser extent) private types. The examples given here have not been
tried out in practice, and are as tentative as any programs in Ada at
this early period of its life. If they are found useful as guides to
the development of real programs, the purpose of this book will have
been achieved.

APPENDIX A

Predefined specifications

Certain library units are predefined in Ada, so that any other unit may
be compiled in their context. The predefined units are specified here.
Package STANDARD is available to every compilation unit automatically,
and need not be mentioned in the context specification. If any of the
other units are needed, their names must be written in the context
specification of the unit being compiled.

package STANDARD **is**

    type BOOLEAN **is** (FALSE, TRUE);

    function "not" (X : BOOLEAN) **return** BOOLEAN;

    function "and" (X,Y : BOOLEAN) **return** BOOLEAN;
    function "or" (X,Y : BOOLEAN) **return** BOOLEAN;
    function "xor" (X,Y : BOOLEAN) **return** BOOLEAN;

    type SHORT_INTEGER **is range** {implementation defined};
    type INTEGER   **is range** {implementation defined};
    type LONG_INTEGER **is range** {implementation defined};

    function "+"   (X : INTEGER) **return** INTEGER;
    function "-"   (X : INTEGER) **return** INTEGER;
    function ABS   (X : INTEGER) **return** INTEGER;

    function "+"   (X,Y : INTEGER) **return** INTEGER;
    function "-"   (X,Y : INTEGER) **return** INTEGER;
    function "*"   (X,Y : INTEGER) **return** INTEGER;
    function "/"   (X,Y : INTEGER) **return** INTEGER;
    function "rem" (X,Y : INTEGER) **return** INTEGER;
    function "mod" (X,Y : INTEGER) **return** INTEGER;

```
    function "**"  (X : INTEGER; Y : INTEGER
                    range 0..INTEGER'LAST) return INTEGER;

-- similarly for SHORT_INTEGER and LONG_INTEGER

    type SHORT_FLOAT is digits {implementation defined}
                         range {implementation defined};
    type FLOAT       is digits {implementation defined}
                         range {implementation defined};
    type LONG_FLOAT  is digits {implementation defined}
                         range {implementation defined};

    function "+"   (X : FLOAT) return FLOAT;
    function "-"   (X : FLOAT) return FLOAT;
    function ABS   (X : FLOAT) return FLOAT;

    function "+"   (X,Y : FLOAT) return FLOAT;
    function "-"   (X,Y : FLOAT) return FLOAT;
    function "*"   (X,Y : FLOAT) return FLOAT;
    function "/"   (X,Y : FLOAT) return FLOAT;
    function "**"  (X : FLOAT; Y : INTEGER) return FLOAT;

-- similarly for SHORT_FLOAT and LONG_FLOAT

    -- The following characters comprise
    -- the standard ASCII character set.
    -- Character literals corresponding to control characters
    -- are not identifiers;
    -- They are indicated in lower case in this definition:

    type CHARACTER is

    (nul, soh, stx, etx, eot, enq, ack, bel,
     bs, ht, lf, vt, ff, cr, so, si,
     dle, dc1, dc2, dc3, dc4, nak, syn, etb,
     can, em, sub, esc, fs, gs, rs, us,

     ' ', '!', '"', '#', '$', '%', '&', ''',
     '(', ')', '*', '+', ',', '-', '.', '/',
     '0', '1', '2', '3', '4', '5', '6', '7',
     '8', '9', ':', ';', '<', '=', '>', '?',

     '@', 'A', 'B', 'C', 'D', 'E', 'F', 'G',
     'H', 'I', 'J', 'K', 'L', 'M', 'N', 'O',
     'P', 'Q', 'R', 'S', 'T', 'U', 'V', 'W',
     'X', 'Y', 'Z', '[', '\', ']', '^', '_',
```

```
      ´`´, ´a´, ´b´, ´c´, ´d´, ´e´, ´f´, ´g´,
      ´h´. ´i´, ´j´, ´k´, ´l´, ´m´, ´n´, ´o´,
      ´p´, ´q´, ´r´, ´s´, ´t´, ´u´, ´v´, ´w´,
      ´x´, ´y´, ´z´, ´{´, ´|´, ´}´, ´~´, del);

  package ASCII is
  -- Control characters:

     NUL : constant CHARACTER := nul;
     SOH : constant CHARACTER := soh;
     STX : constant CHARACTER := stx;
     ETX : constant CHARACTER := etx;
     EOT : constant CHARACTER := eot;
     ENQ : constant CHARACTER := enq;
     ACK : constant CHARACTER := ack;
     BEL : constant CHARACTER := bel;
     BS  : constant CHARACTER := bs;
     HT  : constant CHARACTER := ht;
     LF  : constant CHARACTER := lf;
     VT  : constant CHARACTER := vt;
     FF  : constant CHARACTER := ff;
     CR  : constant CHARACTER := cr;
     SO  : constant CHARACTER := so;
     SI  : constant CHARACTER := si;
     DLE : constant CHARACTER := dle;
     DC1 : constant CHARACTER := dc1;
     DC2 : constant CHARACTER := dc2;
     DC3 : constant CHARACTER := dc3;
     DC4 : constant CHARACTER := dc4;
     NAK : constant CHARACTER := nak;
     SYN : constant CHARACTER := syn;
     ETB : constant CHARACTER := etb;
     CAN : constant CHARACTER := can;
     EM  : constant CHARACTER := em;
     SUB : constant CHARACTER := sub;
     ESC : constant CHARACTER := esc;
     FS  : constant CHARACTER := fs;
     GS  : constant CHARACTER := gs;
     RS  : constant CHARACTER := rs;
     US  : constant CHARACTER := us;
     DEL : constant CHARACTER := del;

     -- Other characters

     EXCLAM     : constant CHARACTER := ´!´;
     SHARP      : constant CHARACTER := ´#´;
     DOLLAR     : constant CHARACTER := ´$´;
```

```
    QUERY        : constant CHARACTER := ´?´;
    AT_SIGN      : constant CHARACTER := ´@´;
    L_BRACKET    : constant CHARACTER := ´[´;
    BACK_SLASH   : constant CHARACTER := ´\´;
    R_BRACKET    : constant CHARACTER := ´]´;
    CIRCUMFLEX   : constant CHARACTER := ´^´;
    GRAVE        : constant CHARACTER := ´`´;
    L_BRACE      : constant CHARACTER := ´{´;
    BAR          : constant CHARACTER := ´|´;
    R_BRACE      : constant CHARACTER := ´}´;
    TILDE        : constant CHARACTER := ´~´;

    -- Lower case letters

    LC_A : constant CHARACTER := ´a´;
     ---
    LC_Z : constant CHARACTER := ´z´;

end ASCII;

-- Predefined types and subtypes

subtype NATURAL is INTEGER range 1 .. INTEGER´LAST;
subtype PRIORITY is INTEGER range {implementation_defined};

type STRING    is array (NATURAL range <>) of CHARACTER;

type DURATION  is delta {implementation_defined}
        range {implementation_defined};

-- The predefined exceptions

CONSTRAINT_ERROR : exception;
NUMERIC_ERROR    : exception;
SELECT_ERROR     : exception;
STORAGE_ERROR    : exception;
TASKING_ERROR    : exception;


package SYSTEM is    -- machine dependent
  type SYSTEM_NAME is {implementation_defined_enumeration_type};

  NAME: constant SYSTEM_NAME := {implementation_defined};
  STORAGE      : constant    := {implementation_defined};
  MEMORY-SIZE  : constant    := {implementation_defined};
  MIN_INT      : constant    := {implementation_defined};
  MAX-INT      : constant    := {implementation_defined};
```

```
       ---
   end SYSTEM;

private

   for CHARACTER use -- 128 ASCII character set without holes
   (0,1,2,3,4,5,6,7,8,9,10,11,12,13,14,15,
    16,17,18,19,20,21,22,23,24,25,26,27,28,29,30,31,
    32,33,34,35,36,37,38,39,40,41,42,43,44,45,46,47,
    49,49,50,51,52,53,54,55,56,57,58,59,60,61,62,63,
    64,65,66,67,68,69,70,71,72,73,74,75,76,77,78,79,
    80,81,82,83,84,85,86,87,88,89,90,91,92,93,94,95,
    96,97,98,99,100,101,102,103,104,105,106,107,108,109,110,111,
    112,113,114,115,116,117,118,119,120,121,122,123,124,125,126,127);

   pragma PACK(STRING);

end STANDARD;
```

```
generic
   type ELEMENT_TYPE is limited private;
package INPUT_OUTPUT is
   type IN_FILE    is limited private;
   type OUT_FILE   is limited private;
   type INOUT_FILE is limited private;

   type FILE_INDEX is range 0 .. {implementation_defined};

   -- general operations for file manipulation

   procedure CREATE (FILE : in out OUT_FILE;
                     NAME : in STRING);
   procedure CREATE (FILE : in out INOUT_FILE;
                     NAME : in STRING);

   procedure OPEN   (FILE : in out IN_FILE;
                     NAME : in STRING);
   procedure OPEN   (FILE : in out OUT_FILE;
                     NAME : in STRING);
   procedure OPEN   (FILE : in out INOUT_FILE;
                     NAME : in STRING);

   procedure CLOSE  (FILE : in out IN_FILE);
   procedure CLOSE  (FILE : in out OUT_FILE);
   procedure CLOSE  (FILE : in out INOUT_FILE);

   function   IS_OPEN (FILE : in IN_FILE)    return BOOLEAN;
   function   IS_OPEN (FILE : in OUT_FILE)   return BOOLEAN;
   function   IS_OPEN (FILE : in INOUT_FILE) return BOOLEAN;

   function   NAME    (FILE : in IN_FILE)    return STRING;
   function   NAME    (FILE : in OUT_FILE)   return STRING;
   function   NAME    (FILE : in INOUT_FILE) return STRING;

   procedure DELETE   (NAME : in STRING);

   function   SIZE    (FILE : in IN_FILE)    return FILE_INDEX;
   function   SIZE    (FILE : in OUT_FILE)   return FILE_INDEX;
   function   SIZE    (FILE : in INOUT_FILE) return FILE_INDEX;

   function   LAST    (FILE : in IN_FILE)    return FILE_INDEX;
   function   LAST    (FILE : in OUT_FILE)   return FILE_INDEX;
   function   LAST    (FILE : in INOUT_FILE) return FILE_INDEX;

   procedure TRUNCATE(FILE : in OUT_FILE;
                      TO :  in FILE_INDEX);
```

```
procedure TRUNCATE(FILE : in INOUT_FILE;
                   TO :  in FILE_INDEX);

procedure READ    (FILE : in IN_FILE;
                   ITEM : out ELEMENT_TYPE);
procedure READ    (FILE : in INOUT_FILE;
                   ITEM : out ELEMENT_TYPE);

function NEXT_READ (FILE : in IN_FILE)    return FILE_INDEX;
function NEXT_READ (FILE : in INOUT_FILE) return FILE_INDEX;

procedure SET_READ (FILE : in IN_FILE;    TO : in FILE_INDEX);
procedure SET_READ (FILE : in INOUT_FILE; TO : in FILE_INDEX);

procedure RESET_READ (FILE : in IN_FILE);
procedure RESET_READ (FILE : in INOUT_FILE);

procedure WRITE(FILE:in OUT_FILE;   ITEM:in ELEMENT_TYPE);
procedure WRITE(FILE:in INOUT_FILE; ITEM:in ELEMENT_TYPE);

function NEXT_WRITE (FILE : in OUT_FILE)   return FILE_INDEX;
function NEXT_WRITE (FILE : in INOUT_FILE) return FILE_INDEX;

procedure SET_WRITE (FILE : in OUT_FILE; TO : in FILE_INDEX);
procedure SET_WRITE (FILE : in INOUT_FILE; TO:in FILE_INDEX);

procedure RESET_WRITE(FILE : in OUT_FILE);
procedure RESET_WRITE(FILE : in INOUT_FILE);

function  END_OF_FILE(FILE : in IN_FILE)     return BOOLEAN;
function  END_OF_FILE(FILE : in INOUT_FILE)  return BOOLEAN;

-- exceptions that can be raised

NAME_ERROR    : exception;
USE_ERROR     : exception;
STATUS_ERROR  : exception;
DATA_ERROR    : exception;
DEVICE_ERROR  : exception;
END_ERROR     : exception;

private
  -- declaration of the file private types
end INPUT_OUTPUT;
```

```ada
package TEXT_IO is
  package CHARACTER_IO is new INPUT_OUTPUT (CHARACTER);

  type IN_FILE  is new CHARACTER_IO.IN_FILE;
  type OUT_FILE is new CHARACTER_IO.OUT_FILE;

  -- character Input-Output

  procedure GET (FILE : in IN_FILE;  ITEM : out CHARACTER);
  procedure GET (ITEM : out CHARACTER);
  procedure PUT (FILE : in OUT_FILE; ITEM : in CHARACTER);
  procedure PUT (ITEM : in CHARACTER);

  -- String Input-Output

  procedure GET (FILE : in  IN_FILE; ITEM : out STRING);
  procedure GET (ITEM : out STRING);
  procedure PUT (FILE : in  OUT_FILE; ITEM : in STRING);
  procedure PUT (ITEM : in  STRING);

  function GET_STRING(FILE  : in  IN_FILE) return STRING;
  function GET_STRING return STRING;

  function  GET_LINE (FILE : in IN_FILE) return STRING;
  function  GET_LINE return STRING;
  procedure PUT_LINE (FILE : in OUT_FILE, ITEM : in STRING);
  procedure PUT_LINE (ITEM : in STRING);

  -- Generic package for Integer Input-Output

  generic
    type NUM is range <>;
    with function IMAGE(X : NUM)    return STRING is NUM´IMAGE;
    with function VALUE(X : STRING) return NUM is NUM´VALUE;
  package INTEGER_IO is
    procedure GET(FILE  : in  IN_FILE; ITEM : out NUM);
    procedure GET(ITEM  : out NUM);
    procedure PUT(FILE  : in  OUT_FILE;
                  ITEM  : in  NUM;
                  WIDTH : in  INTEGER := 0;
                  BASE  : in  INTEGER range 2 .. 16 := 10);
    procedure PUT(ITEM  : in  NUM;
                  WIDTH : in  INTEGER :=0;
                  BASE  : in  INTEGER range 2 .. 16 := 10);
  end INTEGER_IO;

  -- Generic package for Floating Point Input-Output
```

```
generic
  type NUM is digits <>;
  with function IMAGE(X : NUM)   return STRING is NUM'IMAGE;
  with function VALUE(X : STRING) return NUM is NUM'VALUE;
package FLOAT_IO is
  procedure GET(FILE : in IN_FILE ; ITEM: out NUM);
  procedure GET(ITEM : out NUM);

  procedure PUT(FILE     : in OUT_FILE;
                ITEM     : in NUM;
                WIDTH    : in INTEGER := 0;
                MANTISSA : in INTEGER := NUM'DIGITS;
                EXPONENT : in INTEGER := 2);

  procedure PUT(ITEM     : in NUM;
                WIDTH    : in INTEGER := 0;
                MANTISSA : in INTEGER := NUM'DIGITS;
                EXPONENT : in INTEGER := 2);
end FLOAT_IO;


-- Generic package for Fixed Point Input-Output

generic
  type NUM is delta <>;
  with function IMAGE(X : NUM)   return STRING is NUM'IMAGE;
  with function VALUE(X : STRING) return NUM is NUM'VALUE;
package FIXED_IO is
  DELTA_IMAGE        : constant STRING
                     := IMAGE(NUM'DELTA - INTEGER(NUM('DELTA));
  DEFAULT_DECIMALS : constant INTEGER
                     := DELTA_IMAGE'LENGTH - 2;

  procedure GET(FILE : in  IN_FILE; ITEM : out NUM);
  procedure GET(ITEM : out NUM);

  procedure PUT(FILE  : in  OUT_FILE;
                ITEM  : in  NUM;
                WIDTH : in  INTEGER := 0;
                FRACT : in  INTEGER := DEFAULT_DECIMALS);

  procedure PUT(ITEM  : in  NUM;
                WIDTH : in  INTEGER := 0;
                FRACT : in  INTEGER := DEFAULT_DECIMALS);
end FIXED_IO;

-- Input-Output for Boolean
```

```
   procedure GET(FILE        : in  IN_FILE   ;
                 ITEM : out BOOLEAN);
   procedure GET(ITEM        : out BOOLEAN);

   procedure PUT(FILE        : in OUT_FILE ;
                 ITEM        : in BOOLEAN;
                 WIDTH       : in INTEGER := 0;
                 LOWER_CASE : in BOOLEAN := FALSE);

   procedure PUT(ITEM        : in BOOLEAN;
                 WIDTH       : in INTEGER := 0;
                 LOWER_CASE : in BOOLEAN := FALSE);

-- Generic package for Enumeration Types

generic
  type ENUM is (<>);
  with function IMAGE(X : ENUM)
                return STRING is ENUM´IMAGE;
  with function VALUE(X : STRING) return ENUM is ENUM´VALUE;
package ENUMERATION_IO is
  procedure GET(FILE        : in IN_FILE; ITEM : out ENUM);
  procedure GET(ITEM        : out ENUM);

  procedure PUT(FILE        : in OUT_FILE ;
                ITEM        : in ENUM;
                WIDTH       : in INTEGER := 0;
                LOWER_CASE : in BOOLEAN := FALSE);

  procedure PUT(ITEM        : in ENUM;
                WIDTH       : in INTEGER := 0;
                LOWER_CASE : in BOOLEAN := FALSE);
end ENUMERATION_IO;

-- Layout control

function LINE(FILE : in IN_FILE)  return NATURAL;
function LINE(FILE : in OUT_FILE) return NATURAL;
function LINE return NATURAL;        -- for default output file

function COL(FILE  : in IN_FILE)  return NATURAL;
function COL(FILE  : in OUT_FILE) return NATURAL;
function COL return NATURAL;         -- for default output file

procedure SET_COL(FILE : in IN_FILE;   TO : in NATURAL);
procedure SET_COL(FILE : in OUT_FILE;  TO : in NATURAL);
procedure SET_COL(TO : in NATURAL);-- for default output file
```

```
procedure NEW_LINE(FILE : in OUT_FILE; in NATURAL := 1);
procedure NEW_LINE(N : in NATURAL := 1);

procedure SKIP_LINE(FILE : in IN_FILE; N : in NATURAL :=1);
procedure SKIP_LINE(N : in NATURAL := 1);

function END_OF_LINE(FILE : in IN_FILE) return BOOLEAN;
function END_OF_LINE return BOOLEAN;

procedure SET_LINE_LENGTH(FILE  : in IN_FILE;
                          N : in INTEGER);
procedure SET_LINE_LENGTH(FILE  : in OUT_FILE;
                          N : in INTEGER);
procedure SET_LINE_LENGTH(N : in INTEGER);
                    -- for default output file

function LINE_LENGTH(FILE : in IN_FILE)   return INTEGER;
function LINE_LENGTH(FILE : in OUT_FILE)  return INTEGER;
function LINE_LENGTH return INTEGER;
                    -- for default output file

-- Default input and output file manipulation

function STANDARD_INPUT  return IN_FILE;
function STANDARD_OUTPUT return OUT_FILE;

function CURRENT_INPUT  return IN_FILE;
function CURRENT_OUTPUT return OUT_FILE;

procedure SET_INPUT  (FILE : in IN_FILE );
procedure SET_OUTPUT (FILE : in OUT_FILE);


-- Exceptions


NAME_ERROR   : exception renames CHARACTER_IO.NAME_ERROR;
USE_ERROR    : exception renames CHARACTER_IO.USE_ERROR;
STATUS_ERROR : exception renames CHARACTER_IO.STATUS_ERROR;
DATA_ERROR   : exception renames CHARACTER_IO.DATA_ERROR;
DEVICE_ERROR : exception renames CHARACTER_IO.DEVICE_ERROR;
END_ERROR    : exception renames CHARACTER_IO.END_ERROR;
LAYOUT_ERROR : exception;
end TEXT_IO;
```

```ada
package LOW_LEVEL_IO is
 type DEVICE_TYPE is {implementation_defined};
 type DATA_TYPE   is {implementation_defined};
 -- declarations of overloaded procedures for these types:
 procedure SEND_CONTROL     (DEVICE : DEVICE_TYPE;
                             DATA : in out DATA_TYPE);
 procedure RECEIVE_CONTROL (DEVICE : DEVICE_TYPE;
                             DATA : in out DATA_TYPE);
end LOW_LEVEL_IO;

package CALENDAR is
  type TIME is
    record
       YEAR   : INTEGER range 1901 .. 2099;
       MONTH  : INTEGER range 1 .. 12;
       DAY    : INTEGER range 1 .. 31;
       SECOND : DURATION;
    end record;

  function CLOCK return TIME;

  function "+" (A : TIME;     B : DURATION) return TIME;
  function "+" (A : DURATION; B : TIME)     return TIME;
  function "-" (A : TIME;     B : DURATION) return TIME;
  function "-" (A : TIME;     B : TIME)     return DURATION;
end CALENDAR;

generic
  type SHARED is limited private;
procedure SHARED_VARIABLE_UPDATE(X : in out SHARED);

generic
 type OBJECT is limited private;
 type NAME   is access OBJECT;
procedure UNCHECKED_DEALLOCATION(X : in out NAME);


generic
 type SOURCE is limited private;
 type TARGET is limited private;
function UNCHECKED_CONVERSION(S : SOURCE) return TARGET;
```

APPENDIX B

Notes for Fortran Programmers

There are several aspects of Ada which the exprienced FORTRAN programmer will find strange, however he will soon learn that the new features in the language actually help to minimise problems, and catch many errors at compile-time. It is evident that the Ada text is longer than the corresponding Fortran. The extra information that has to be given is used for checking. This reflects the fact that Ada is designed to be easier to <u>read</u>, accepting the price that it is not so quick to write.

The most fundamental difference between the languages is in the area of data types. Fortran has only a few data types (INTEGER, REAL, LOGICAL, DOUBLE PRECISION, COMPLEX and now CHARACTER), and although consistency checks are applied within each subprogram, there are many ways of breaking the rules (e.g. with COMMON, EQUIVALENCE and subroutine parameters), to work with data of one type as though it were another. Experience has shown that this area of Fortran is the most frequent source of serious errors. These are difficult to detect, particularly when a program is modified by someone else after the original designer is no longer available. For this reason the Fortran programmer should view the Ada typing rules as a way of preventing logical mistakes from getting into the running program. The opportunities in Fortran to save space by the techniques are avoided by the different visibility rules in Ada.

The following are detailed differences between the languages:

1. You must get used to using the semicolon and assignment symbols. Remember that the semicolon is needed at the end of almost every line; broadly speaking, those which do <u>not</u> have a semicolon are those ending with

   is loop select begin then else of record

or of course where the statement is too long to fit on one line.

The assignment symbol := is used in assignment statements. It is a good idea to think of the colon-equals combination as the `becomes´ symbol, and to read it as `becomes´ when you see it.

2. You must declare every variable you use (except loop indexes). There are a number of points to bear in mind about this. You do of course in Fortran have to declare any arrays you need, or any variables with initial letters inconsistent with their type, or anything in COMMON or EQUIVALENCE. In Fortran you collect the information of the same kind together (DIMENSION, REAL, LOGICAL etc.) so that the details of any particular array or variable are spread over several declarations. In Ada, all the information about a particular variable comes together, and there is a natural place to put any comment about it.

3. The treatment of COMMON is easier with Ada: you do not have to repeat the COMMON declarations in every subprogram. Use a package for each block of COMMON (which can include initial values, instead of a separate BLOCK DATA). As an illustration of this, some of the package given in section 7.1 corresponds to the following in Fortran:

```
        BLOCK DATA
        COMMON /STORE/ SCALE, K, JUMP, A, SM,
      1   INPUT, IFM, ALAT, ALONG, EORW, NORS,
      2   CHANGE, FRACT, SIG, VAL, LEG
        INTEGER EORW
        COMMON /FORMAT/ FMT
        REAL * 8  FMT(10)
        COMMON  /NSEW/  N, S, E, W
        INTEGER N, S, E, W
        DATA N, S, E, W/´N´, ´S´, ´E´, ´W´/
        DATA FRACT, SIG, CHANGE/3 * .FALSE./
        DATA JUMP /11/
        DATA FMT/ ´(2(F9.0,´, ´A1),´, ´T1,F5.0)´, 7*´ ´ /
        END
```

Notice that with a little more work the package NSEW could have been changed into an enumeration type, probably leading to a slightly more compact program.

4. There is nothing in Ada quite like EQUIVALENCE, but most of the occasions where you have to use it in Fortran can be dealt with using other facilities in Ada, such as application specific types and **rename** declarations. Fortran programmers who are using

EQUIVALENCE to give the same storage area more than one type (say REAL and LOGICAL) should rearrange the program so that the parts dealing with the different variables are in separate blocks — the storage will then be allocated properly without the danger of misuse.

5. Numerical constants need not distinguish the precision:

   1.0E+3

   can serve as a literal for SHORT_FLOAT, FLOAT or LONG_FLOAT (if available).The Fortran programmer can forget all about the D exponent number form. Similarly there is no need to use DSQRT etc.

6. Ada input/output is very different from that in Fortran, but the official package INPUT_OUTPUT is not mandatory, and facilities like those of FORTRAN are likely to be developed as library packages.

APPENDIX C

Notes for Pascal Programmers

Not surprisingly, in view of its ancestry, Ada contains a subset which is very close to Pascal. For this reason a Pascal programmer should have little difficulty in converting to Ada. However there are a number of detailed differences which must be appreciated by the Pascal programmer when writing in Ada.

1. Ada uses terminating keywords where Pascal uses a compound statement. Thus the Pascal compound statement

```
    IF x > y THEN
        BEGIN
            x := y;
            r := s
        END;
```

    is replaced in Ada by

```
    if X > Y then
        X := Y;
        R := S;
    end if;
```

    with no BEGIN, but the end marked as a terminator for the if statement. Similar considerations arise in Pascal wherever a statement can be replaced by one or more statements between BEGIN and END. The corresponding Ada structure always has an explicit closing keyword. This change makes it much easier to amend a program when you have to add an extra statement into a loop or conditional statement.

2. The semicolon is used in Ada to <u>terminate</u> statements, instead of for

232

statement separation. This is most strikingly illustrated by the Pascal statement

```
    IF p > q THEN
        x := 0        (* N.B.  No semicolon *)
    ELSE
        y := 0;
```

whose Ada equivalent has a semicolon before the **else**:

```
    if P > Q then
        X := 0;      -- semicolon needed here
    else
        Y := 0;
    end if;
```

3. For array indexes, Ada uses round brackets.

4. Ada expressions have more precedence levels than Pascal. This makes it easier to combine relations such as:

```
    X < Y and P = Q
```

which must be written as subexpressions in Pascal.

5. In a type declaration, where Pascal uses an equals sign, Ada uses the word **is**. Similarly, in a procedure declaration, where Pascal separates the specification from the body with a semicolon, Ada connects them with the word **is**.

6. Pointers in Pascal and access variables in Ada are very similar. The main difference is that no pointer symbol is used in Ada.

7. There is no special mechanism for sets in Ada. An array of BOOLEAN objects is used to represent a set, but there are no special notations for set-types, set-values or set-operations. In this respect, the features of Ada are not so convenient as those in Pascal.

8. Ada contains no equivalent to the more complicated forms of "read" and "write" statements in Pascal, where they take several actual parameters. A sequence of calls must be written.

9. Several irritating restrictions in Pascal are removed in Ada:

   Enumeration literals can be overloaded.

Procedure parameters may be arrays with variable bounds.

The order of declarations in Ada is less rigid. (No LABEL, CONST, TYPE, VAR ordering imposed.)

Compile-time constants may be given as expressions. For example, Ada allows:

```
PI    : constant  := 3.14159265;
TWOPI : constant  := 2.0 * PI;  -- impossible in Pascal
```

APPENDIX D

Pragmas

Pragmas concern details not affecting the logic of the program. A pragma may have arguments which may be identifiers, strings or numbers; they are written in parentheses after the pragma name. The following pragmas are predefined in Ada.

CONTROLLED   Takes an access type name as argument. It must appear in the same declarative part as the access type definition. It specifies that automatic storage reclamation should not be performed for objects of the access type except upon leaving the scope of the access type definition.

INCLUDE   Takes a string as argument, which is the name of a text file. This pragma can appear anywhere a pragma is allowed. It specifies that the text file is to be included where the pragma is given.

INLINE   Takes a list of subprogram names as arguments. It must appear in the same declarative part as the named subprograms. It specifies that the subprogram bodies should be expanded inline at each call.

INTERFACE   Takes a language name and subprogram name as arguments. It must appear after the subprogram specification in the same declarative part or in the same package specification. It specifies that the body of the subprogram is written in the given other language, whose calling conventions are to be observed.

LIST   Takes ON or OFF as argument. This pragma can appear
    anywhere. It specifies that listing of the program unit is to be
    continued or suspended until a LIST pragma is given with the
    opposite argument.

MEMORY_SIZE   Takes an integer number as argument. This pragma can
    only appear before a library unit. It establishes the required
    number of storage units in memory.

OPTIMIZE   Takes TIME or SPACE as argument. This pragma can only
    appear in a declarative part and it applies to the block or body
    enclosing the declarative part. It specifies whether time or space
    is the primary optimization criterion.

PACK   Takes a record or array type name as argument. The position
    of the pragma is governed by the same rules as for a representation
    specification. It specifies that storage minimization should be
    the main criterion when selecting the representation of the given
    type.

PRIORITY   Takes a static expression as argument. It must appear in
    a task (type) specification or the outermost declarative part of a
    main program. It specifies the priority of the task (or tasks of
    the task type) or the main program.

STORAGE_UNIT   Takes an integer number as argument. This pragma can
    only appear before a library unit. It establishes the number of
    bits per storage unit.

SUPPRESS   Takes a check name and optionally also either an object
    name or a type name as arguments. It must appear in the
    declarative part of a unit (block or body). It specifies that the
    designated check is to be suppressed in the unit. In the absence
    of the optional name, the pragma applies to all operations within
    the unit. Otherwise its effect is restricted to operations on the
    named object or to operations on objects of the named type.

SYSTEM   Takes a name as argument. This pragma can only appear
    before a library unit. It establishes the name of the object
    machine.

APPENDIX E

Attributes

The following attributes are predefined in Ada, for various kinds of entity. Write the name of the entity followed by a prime, then the identifier of the attribute, which must be appropriate to the entity. For attributes denoting a data value, we show the type of that value as in an object declaration, with some special (conceptual) types. These indicate values which are implicitly converted to the appropriate type when used in an expression.

Attribute of any object or subprogram X

ADDRESS : predefined_integer;

    A number corresponding to the first storage unit occupied by X.

Attribute of any data type or subtype T (not a task type)

BASE   -- type

    Applied to a subtype, yields the base type; applied to a type, yields the type itself. This attribute may be used only to obtain further attributes of a type, e.g. T´BASE´FIRST.

Attribute of any data type or subtype ,or any object thereof (not a task type)

SIZE : INTEGER;

   The maximum number of bits required to hold an object of that type.

Attributes of any scalar type or subtype T

FIRST : T;

   The minimum value in T.

LAST : T;

   The maximum value in T.

IMAGE   -- function (X : T) return STRING;

   If X is a value of type T, T´IMAGE(X) is a string representing the
   value in a standard display form.

   For an enumeration type, the values are represented, in minimum
   width, as either the corresponding enumeration literal, in upper
   case, or as the corresponding character literal, within quotes.

   For an integer type, the values are represented as decimal numbers
   of minimum width.   For a fixed point type, the values are
   represented as decimal fractions of minimum width, with sufficient
   decimal places just to accommodate the declared accuracy.   For a
   floating point type, the values are represented in exponential
   notation with one significant characteristic digit, sufficient
   mantissa digits just to accommodate the declared accuracy, and a
   signed three-digit exponent. The exponent letter is in upper case.
   For all numeric types, negative values are prefixed with a minus
   sign and positive values have no prefix.

VALUE   -- function (S : STRING) return T;

   If S is a string, T´VALUE(S) is the value in T that can be
   represented in display form by the string S. If the string does
   not denote any possible value, the exception DATA_ERROR is raised;
   if the value lies outside the range of $\overline{T}$, the exception

CONSTRAINT_ERROR is raised.   All legal   lexical   forms   are   legal
display forms.

Attributes of any discrete type or subtype T

POS   -- function (X : T) return universal_integer;

If X is a value of type T, T´POS(X) is the integer position of X in
the   ordered   sequence of values T´FIRST .. T´LAST; the position of
T´FIRST being itself for integer types   and   zero   for   enumeration
types.

VAL   -- function (J : universal_integer) return T;

If J is an integer, T´VAL(J) is the value   of   enumeration   type   T
whose   POS   is   J.   If   no   such   value   exists,   the   exception
CONSTRAINT_ERROR is raised.

PRED   -- function (X : T) return T;

If X is a value of type T, T´PRED(X) is the preceding value.   The
exception CONSTRAINT_ERROR is raised if X = T´FIRST.

SUCC   -- function (X : T) return T;

If X is a value of type T, T´SUCC(X) is the succeeding value.   The
exception CONSTRAINT_ERROR is raised if X = T´LAST.

Attributes of any fixed point type or subtype T

DELTA : universal_real;

The delta specified in the declaration of T.

ACTUAL_DELTA : universal_real;

The delta of the model numbers used to represent T.

BITS : universal_integer;

   The number of bits required to represent the model numbers of T.

LARGE : universal_real;

   The largest model number of T.

MACHINE_ROUNDS : BOOLEAN;

   True if the machine rounds to the nearest even value when computing
   values of type T.

Attributes of any floating point type or subtype T

DIGITS : universal_integer;

   The number of digits specified in the declaration of T.

MANTISSA : universal_integer;

   The number of bits in the mantissa of the representation of model
   numbers of T.

EMAX : universal_integer;

   The largest exponent value of the representation of model number of
   T.   The smallest exponent value is − EMAX.

SMALL : universal_real;

   The smallest positive model number of T.

LARGE : universal_real;

   The largest model number of T.

EPSILON : universal_real;

The difference between unity and the smallest model number of T greater than unity. Both unity and T´EPSILON are model numbers of T.

MACHINE_RADIX : universal_integer;

The radix of the exponent of the underlying machine representation of T.

MACHINE_MANTISSA : universal_integer;

The number of bits in the mantissa of the underlying machine representation of T.

MACHINE_EMAX : universal_integer;

The largest exponent value of the underlying machine representation of T.

MACHINE_EMIN : universal_integer;

The smallest exponent value of the underlying machine representation of T.

MACHINE_ROUNDS : BOOLEAN;

True if the machine rounds to the nearest even value when computing values of type T.

MACHINE_OVERFLOWS : BOOLEAN;

True if, when a computed value is too large to be represented correctly by the underlying machine representation of T, the exception NUMERIC_ERROR is raised.

Attributes of any constrained array type or subtype, or object thereof, A

FIRST : A´RANGE;

The lower bound of the first index.

FIRST(J) : A´RANGE(J);

The lower bound of the J´th index, where J must be a static integer expression.

LAST : A´RANGE;

The upper bound of the first index.

LAST(J) : A´RANGE(J);

The upper bound of the J´th index, where J must be a static integer expression.

LENGTH : universal_integer;

The number of elements in the first dimension of A.

LENGTH(J) : universal_integer;

The number of elements in the J´th dimension, where J must be a static expression.

RANGE   -- subtype

The subtype A´FIRST .. A´LAST, whose base type is the first index type of A.

RANGE(J)   -- subtype

The subtype A´FIRST(J) .. A´LAST(J), whose base type is the J´th index type of A, and where J must be a static integer expression.

Attribute of an object R of any record type with discriminants, or of any subtype thereof

CONSTRAINED : BOOLEAN;

    True if and only if the discriminant values of R cannot be modified.

Attributes of any record component C

POSITION : INTEGER;

    The offset within the record, in storage units, of the first unit of storage occupied by C.

FIRST_BIT : INTEGER;

    The offset, from the start of C´POSITION, of the first bit used to hold the value of C.

LAST_BIT : INTEGER;

    The offset, from the start of C´POSITION, of the last bit used to hold the value of C. C´LAST_BIT need not lie within the same storage unit as C´FIRST_BIT.

Attribute of any access type P

STORAGE_SIZE : predefined_integer;

    The total number of storage units reserved for allocation for all objects of type P.

Attributes of any task, or object of a task type, T

TERMINATED : BOOLEAN;

    True when T is terminated.

PRIORITY : universal_integer;

The (static) priority of T.

FAILURE : exception;

   The exception that may be raised by another task.

STORAGE_SIZE : predefined_integer;

   The number of storage units allocated for the execution of T.

Attribute of any entry E

COUNT : INTEGER;

   The number of calling tasks currently waiting on E.

APPENDIX F

Glossary

Access type, access value

An access type is a type in which the values denote dynamically created
objects. These objects are created by execution of an allocator. An
access value designates such an object.

Aggregate

An aggregate is a written form denoting a composite value. An array
aggregate denotes a value of an array type; a record aggregate denotes
a value of a record type. The components of an aggregate may be
specified using either positional or named association.

Allocator

An allocator creates a new object associated with an access type, and
returns an access value designating the created object.

Attribute

An attribute is a predefined characteristic of a named entity.

Body

A body is a program unit defining the implementation of a subprogram,

245

package or task. A <u>body</u> <u>stub</u> is a replacement for a body that is compiled separately.

Compilation Unit

A compilation unit is a <u>program</u> <u>unit</u> presented for compilation as an independent text, possibly preceded by a <u>context</u> <u>specification</u>, naming other compilation units on which it depends. A compilation unit may be a <u>library</u> <u>unit</u> or a <u>subunit</u>.

Component

A component denotes a part of a composite object. An <u>indexed</u> <u>component</u> names a component in an array or an entry in an entry family, by giving expressions denoting index values. A <u>selected</u> <u>component</u> names a component in a record, block or program unit, by giving its identifier.

Composite <u>type</u>, <u>composite</u> <u>value</u>

A value of a composite type comprises several components, which together form the corresponding value. In an <u>array</u> <u>type</u>, all the components are of the same type and subtype; individual components are selected by their <u>indices</u>. In a <u>record</u> <u>type</u>, the components may be of different types; individual components are selected by their identifiers.

Constraint

A constraint is a restriction on the set of possible values in a type. A <u>range</u> <u>constraint</u> specifies lower and upper bounds of the values in a scalar type. An <u>accuracy</u> <u>constraint</u> specifies the relative or absolute error bound of values in a real type. An <u>index</u> <u>constraint</u> specifies lower and upper bounds for an array index. A <u>discriminant</u> <u>constraint</u> specifies particular values of the discriminants in a record type.

Context <u>specification</u>

A context specification, prefixed to a compilation unit, defines the other compilation units upon which it depends.

Declarative <u>Part</u>

A declarative part is a sequence of declarations and related information (bodies and representation specifications) that apply over a region of a program text: their scope.

Derived Type

A derived type is a type whose operations and values are copies of those of an existing type.

Discrete Type

A discrete type has an ordered set of distinct scalar values. The discrete types are the enumeration and integer types. Discrete types may be used for indexing and iteration, and for choices in case statements and record variants.

Discriminant

A discriminant is a syntactically distinguished component of a record. The presence of some other record components may depend on the value of a discriminant.

Elaboration

Elaboration is the process by which a declaration achieves its effect. For example it can associate a name with a program entity or initialize a newly declared variable.

Entity

An entity is anything that can be named or denoted in a program. Objects, types, exceptions, subprograms and program units are all entities.

Entry

An entry is used for communication between tasks. Externally an entry is called in the same way as a subprogram; its internal behaviour is specified by one or more accept statements specifying the actions to be performed when the entry is called.

Enumeration type

An enumeration type is a discrete type whose values are given explicitly in the type definition. These values may be either identifiers or character literals.

Exception

An exception is a situation that prevents further normal program execution. Recognising that an exception has occurred is called raising the exception. An exception handler is a piece of program text specifying a response to the exception. An exception that has been raised is propagated through a program to discover the relevant handler.

Expression

An expression is a part of a program to compute a value.

Generic program unit

A generic program unit is a template for a subprogram or package. It may have parameters determined at compile time. A generic clause contains the declaration of generic parameters. Instances of the template can be obtained by generic instantiation. Such instantiated program units define subprograms and packages that can be used directly in a program. (There are no generic tasks; instead there are task types.)

Literal expression

A literal expression is an expression whose value can be explicitly calculated at compile-time. It must depend only on literal numbers or combinations of them using predefined operators or names of such literal expressions.

Lexical unit

A lexical unit is one of the basic syntactic elements making up a program. It may be an identifier, a number, a character literal, a string, a delimiter, or a comment.

Library unit

A library unit is a compilation unit that is at the outermost level in the whole program. A library unit may be the declaration or body of a subprogram or package.

Literal

A literal denotes an explicit value of a scalar type, for example a number, an enumeration value or a character.

Model number

A model number is an exactly representable value of a real numeric type. Operations of a real type are defined in terms of operations on the model numbers of the type. The properties of the model numbers and of the operations are the minimal properties preserved by all implementations of the real type.

Object

An object is a variable or a constant of a specified type. An object has a value of the appropriate type; if the object is a variable, its value may be changed during execution of the program.

Overloading

Overloading is the property that literals, identifiers, and operators may have several alternative meanings within the same scope. For example an overloaded enumeration literal is a literal appearing in two or more enumeration types; an overloaded subprogram is a subprogram whose designator can denote one of several subprograms, depending upon the kind of its parameters and returned value.

Package

A package is a program unit that defines a set of facilities for use by the rest of the program. It characteristically contains a number of related entities such as constants, variables, types and subprograms. The specification of a package contains all the information needed outside the package; the body of a package contains the implementations of the entities specified.

Parameter

A parameter is one of the named entities on which a subprogram, entry, or generic program unit may depend. A formal parameter is an identifier used to denote the named entity in the unit body. An actual parameter is an entity given in a subprogram call, entry call, or generic instantiation. A parameter mode specifies whether the parameter is used for input, output or input-output of data. A positional parameter is an actual parameter which matches the formal parameter in the same position. A named parameter is an actual parameter which matches the fomal parameter whose name is given.

Pragma

A pragma is an instruction to the compiler, which has no effect on the meaning of the program.

Private type

A private type is a type whose structure and set of values are not disclosed to the user of the type. A private type is known only by its name (possibly with discriminants) and by the set of operations defined for it. A private type and its applicable operations are defined in the visible part of a package. Assignment and comparison for equality or inequality are also defined for private types, unless the private type is marked as **limited**.

Program Unit

A program unit is a major structural unit; it may be a subprogram, package or task. Program units may be nested.

Range

A range is a contiguous set of values of a scalar type. A range is specified by giving the lower and upper bounds for the values.

Rendezvous

A rendezvous is the interaction that occurs between two parallel tasks when one task has called an entry of the other task, and a corresponding accept statement is being executed by the accepting task on behalf of the calling task.

Representation specification

Representation specifications specify the mapping between program entities and features of the underlying machine that executes a program.

Scalar types

A scalar type is a type whose values have no components. Scalar types comprise discrete types (that is, enumeration and integer types) and real types.

Scope

The scope of a declaration is the region of text over which the declaration has an effect.

Static expression

A static expression is an expression whose value may be calculated on entry to the enclosing scope. It must not depend on any locally computed values of variables.

Subprograms

A subprogram is a program unit whose execution is invoked explicitly. It may have parameters for communication between the subprogram and its caller. A subprogram declaration specifies the name of the subprogram and its parameters; a subprogram body specifies its execution. A subprogram may be a procedure, which performs an action, or a function which returns a result. Subprograms may be concurrently executed in several tasks.

Subtype

A subtype characterizes a set of values by constraining the set of possible values of a base type. The operations over a subtype are the same as those of the type on which the subtype is based.

Subunit

A subunit is a compilation unit that conceptually belongs inside another compilation unit, at a position indicated by a body stub. A subunit may be a subprogram specification or the body of a package or task.

Task

A task is a program unit that may be executed in parallel with other tasks. A task specification establishes the name of the task and the names and parameters of its entries; a task body defines its execution. A task type is a specification that permits the subsequent declaration of any number of similar tasks.

Type

A type characterizes a set of values and a set of operations applicable to those values. A type definition is a language construct introducing a type. A type declaration associates a name with a type introduced by a type definition.

Use clause

A use clause makes the declarations in the visible part of a package directly visible.

Variant

A record has variants if its components are at all optional. Components that are present or absent together constitute a variant. The collection of the several variants is called the variant part of the record. The selection of a variant is by the value of a discriminant.

Visibility

An identifier may be used at one point in a program text, with a meaning defined by a declaration given elsewhere. The declaration is said to be visible from the points where the declared entity is accessible. A declaration is directly visible from the points where the declared identifier may be used.

APPENDIX G

Ada syntax

The textual structure of an Ada program is shown in the following
diagrams. Each part of a program text is called a phrase, and is
illustrated by a diagram showing the phrases and atomic elements of
which it is composed. The lines in the diagrams show the order in which
the constituents of a phrase have to be written.

ident

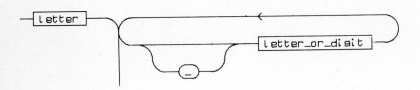

letter_or_digit

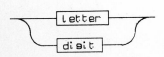

letter

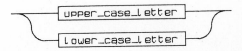

numeric_literal

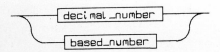

decimal_number

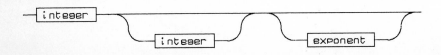

integer

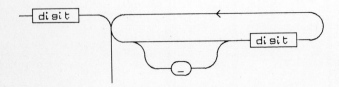

exponent

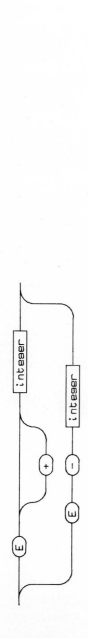

based_number

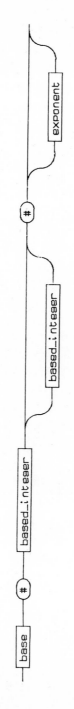

base

based_integer

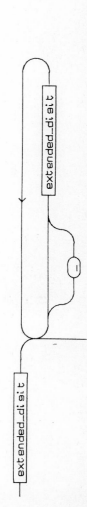

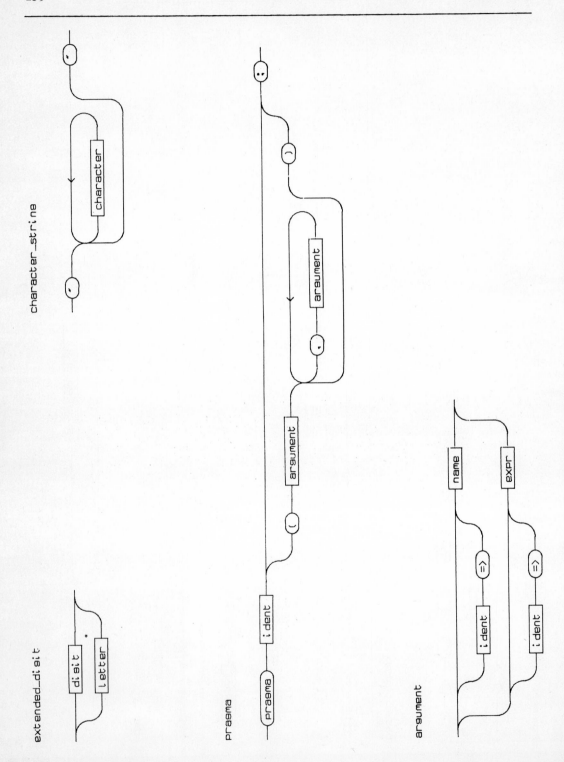

declaration

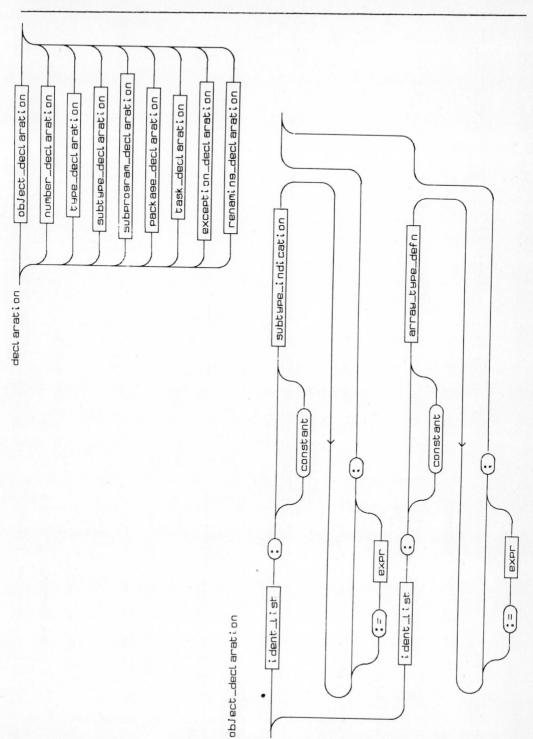

object_declaration

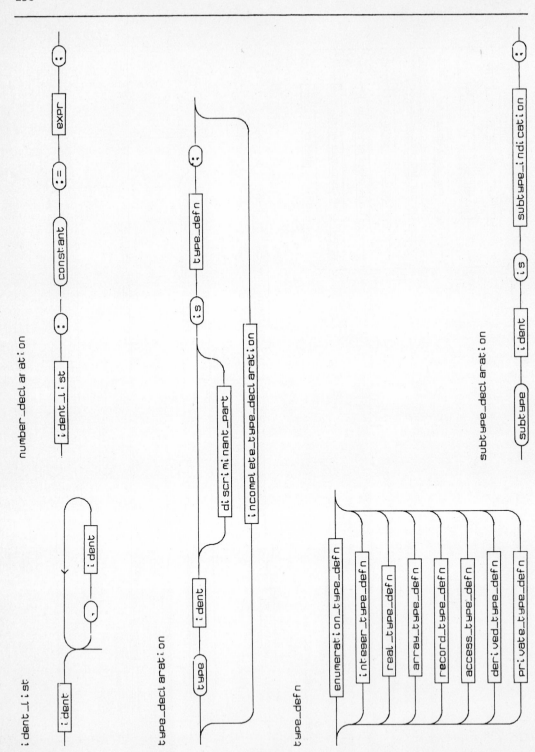

number_declaration

ident_list

type_declaration

type_defn

subtype_declaration

subtype_indication

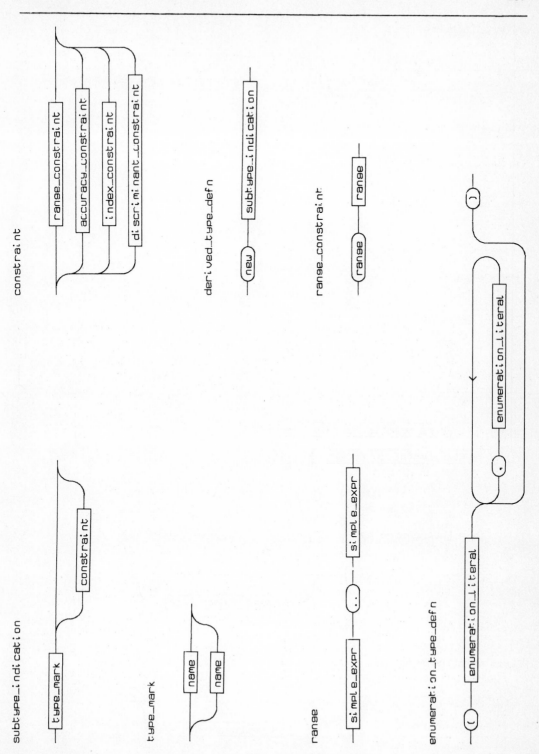

enumeration_literal

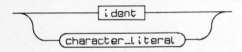

integer_type_defn

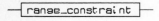

real_type_defn

accuracy_constraint

accuracy_constraint

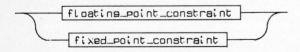

floating_point_constraint

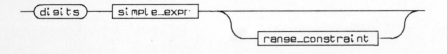

fixed_point_constraint

array_type_defn

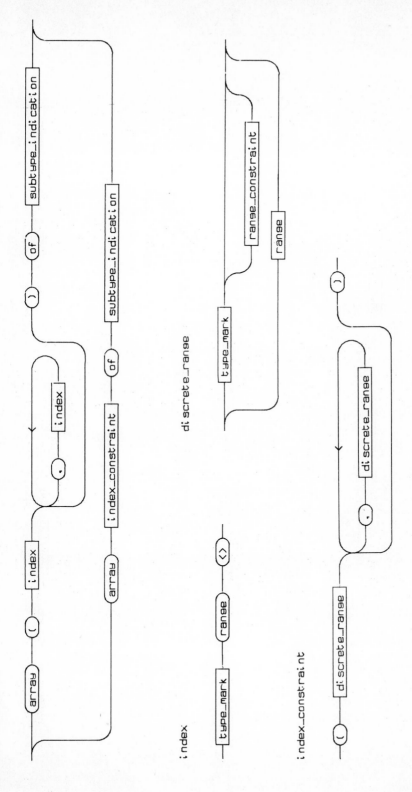

discrete_range

index

index_constraint

component_list

record_type_defn

component_declaration

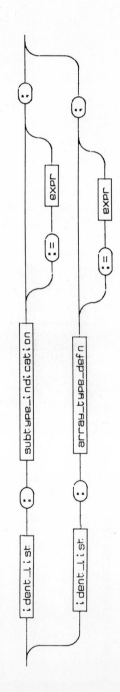

discriminant_part

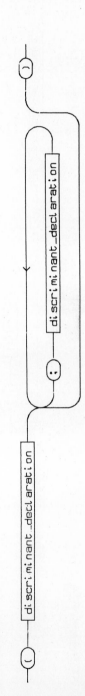

discriminant_declaration

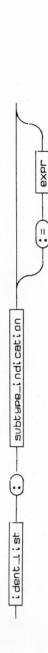

discriminant_constraint

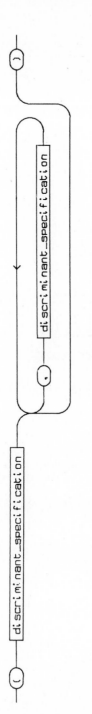

discriminant_specification

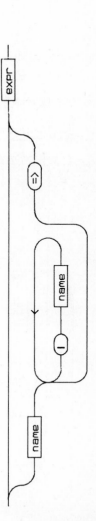

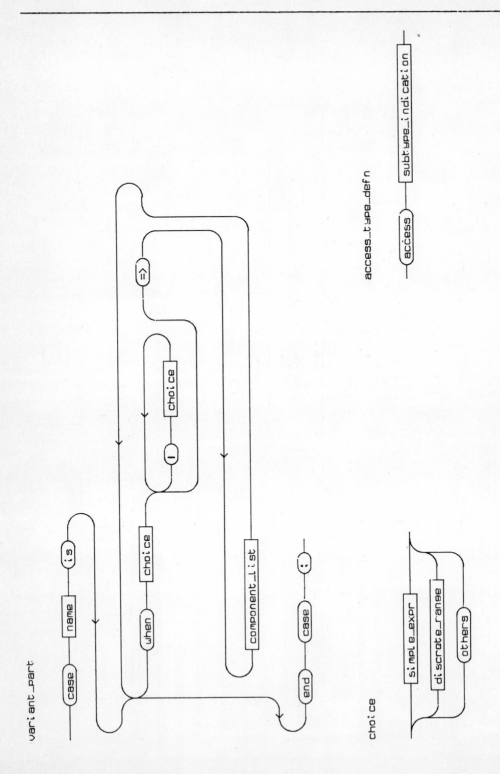

variant_part

access_type_defn

choice

declarative_item

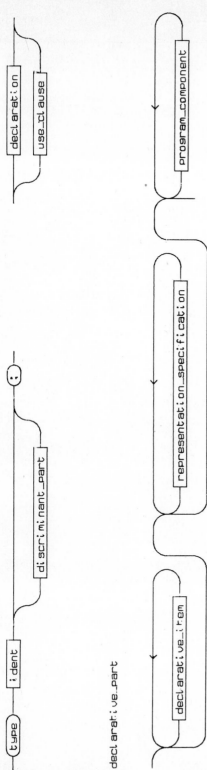

incomplete_type_declaration

declarative_part

program_component

body

name

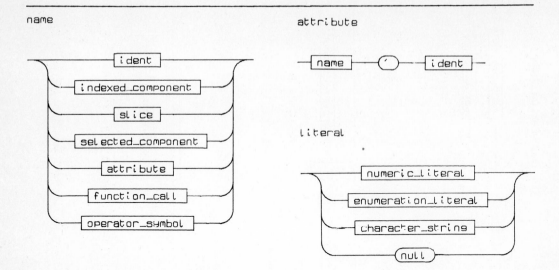

attribute

literal

indexed_component

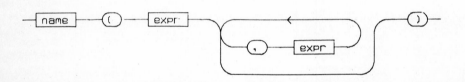

slice

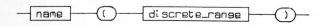

selected_component

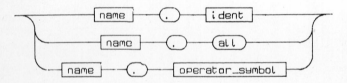

aggregate

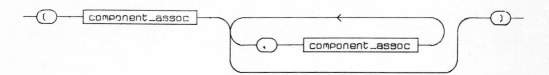

component_assoc

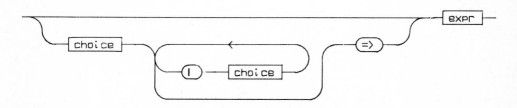

expr

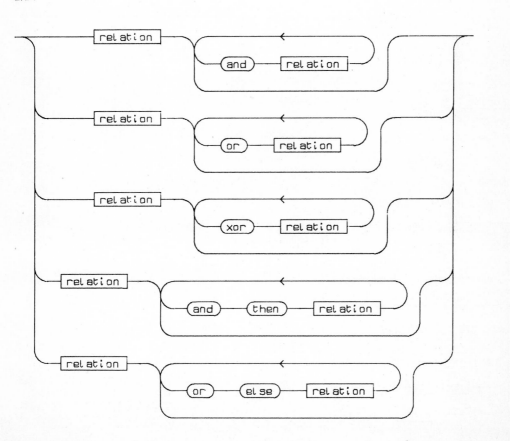

relation

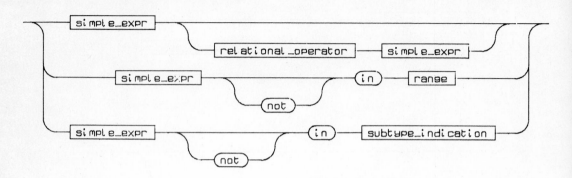

simple_expr

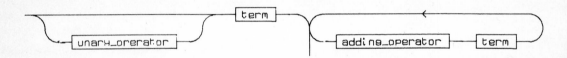

term

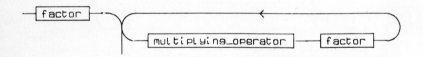

primary

factor

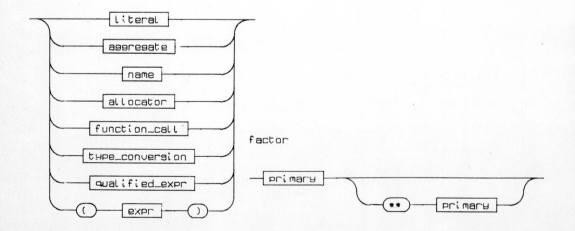

logical_operator

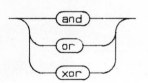

multiplying_operator

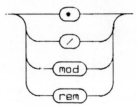

relational_operator

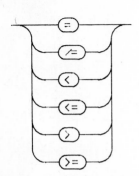

exponentiating_operator

adding_operator

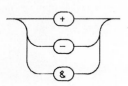

type_conversion

unary_operator

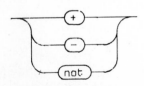

qualified_expr

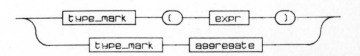

allocator

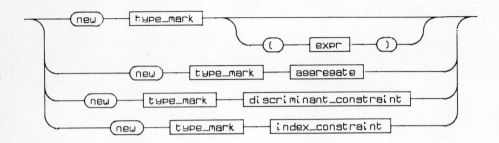

sequence_of_statements

statement

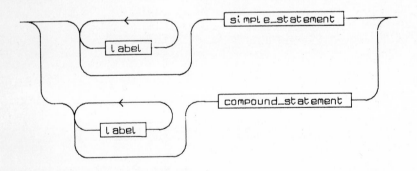

simple_statement

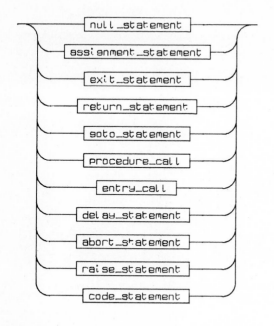

label

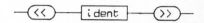

compound_statement

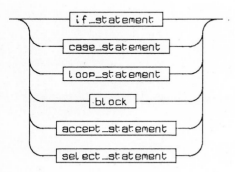

null_statement

assignment_statement

if_statement

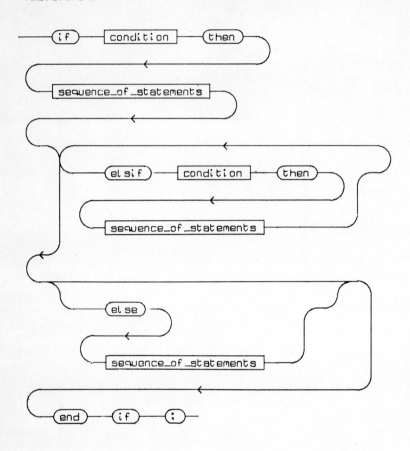

condition

loop_parameter

basic_loop

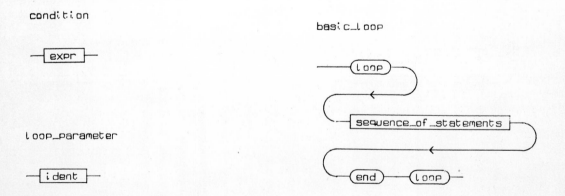

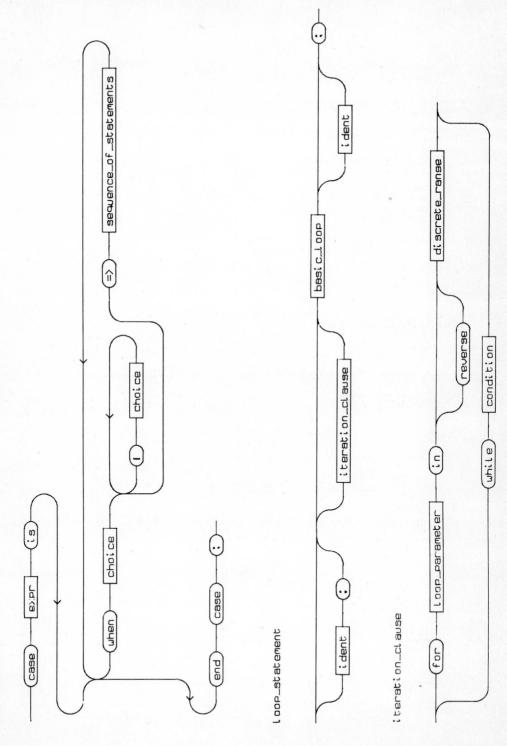

case_statement

loop_statement

iteration_clause

block

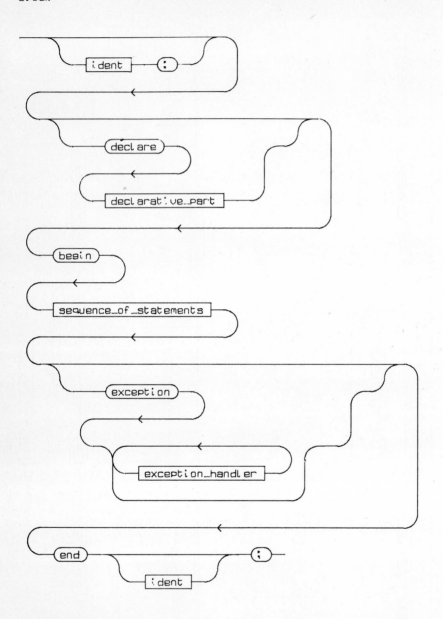

exit_statement

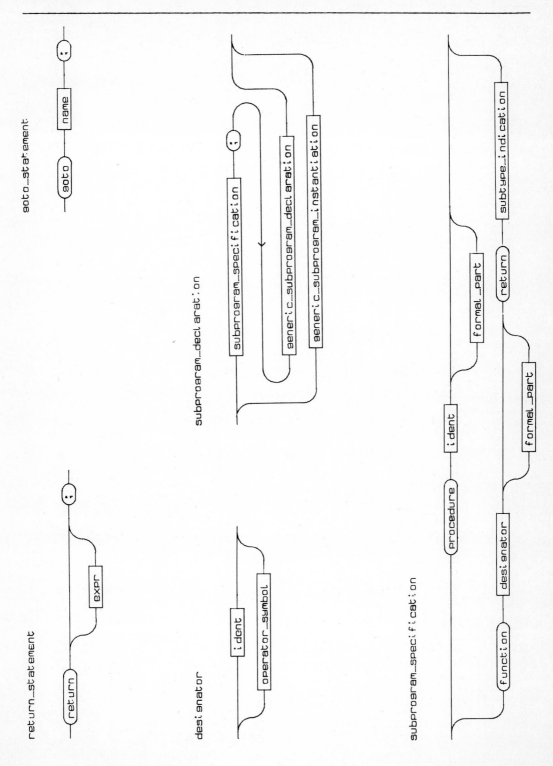

goto_statement

return_statement

subprogram_declaration

designator

subprogram_specification

operator_symbol

formal_part

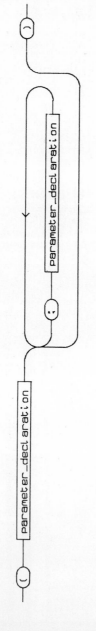

parameter_declaration

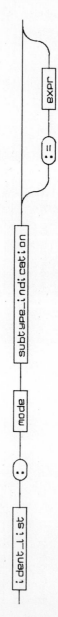

mode

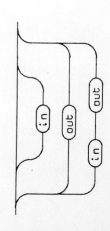

subprogram_body

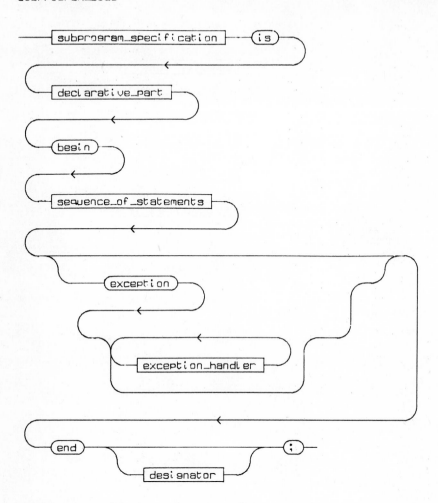

procedure_call

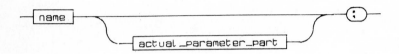

function_call

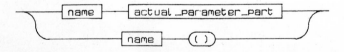

actual _parameter_part

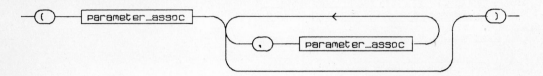

parameter_assoc

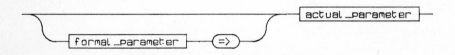

formal _parameter

actual _parameter

expr

package_declaration

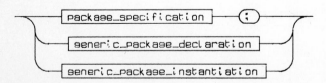

package_specification

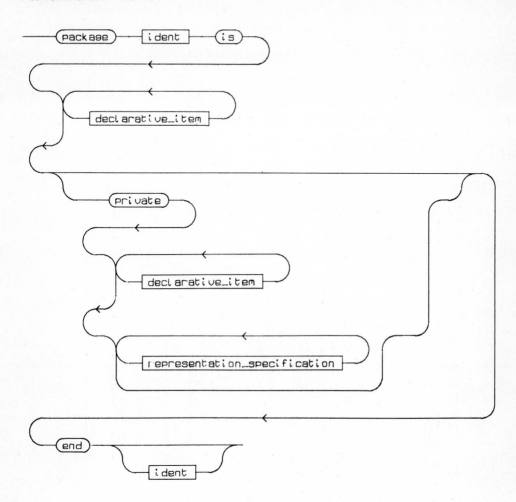

package_body

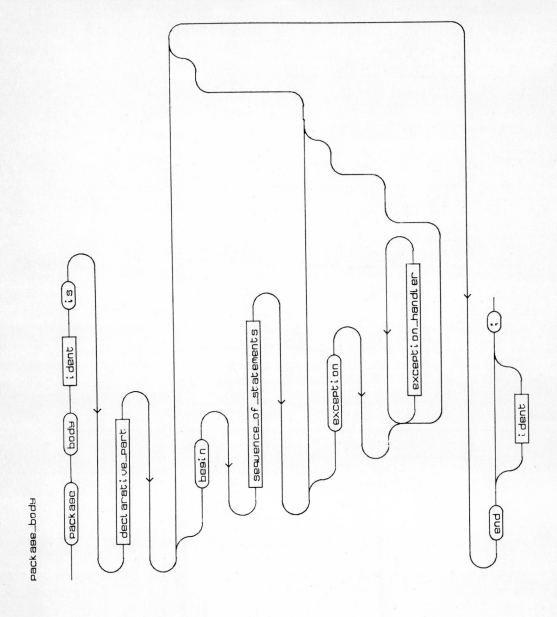

private_type_defn

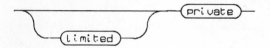

use_clause

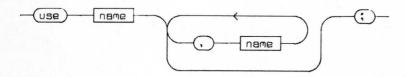

renaming_declaration

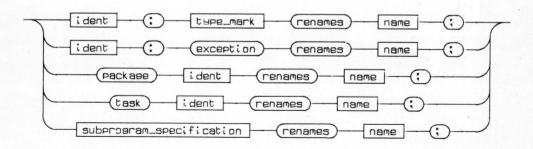

task_declaration

─┤ task_specification ├─

task_specification

task_body

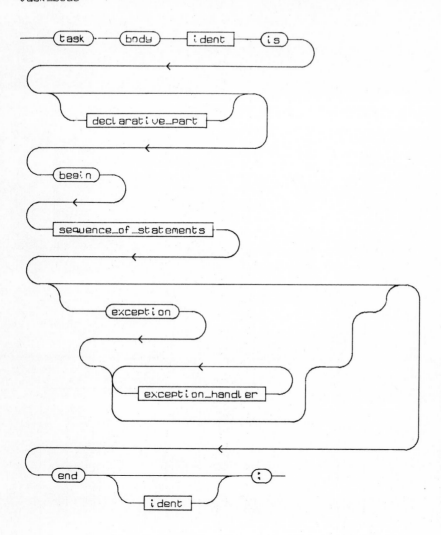

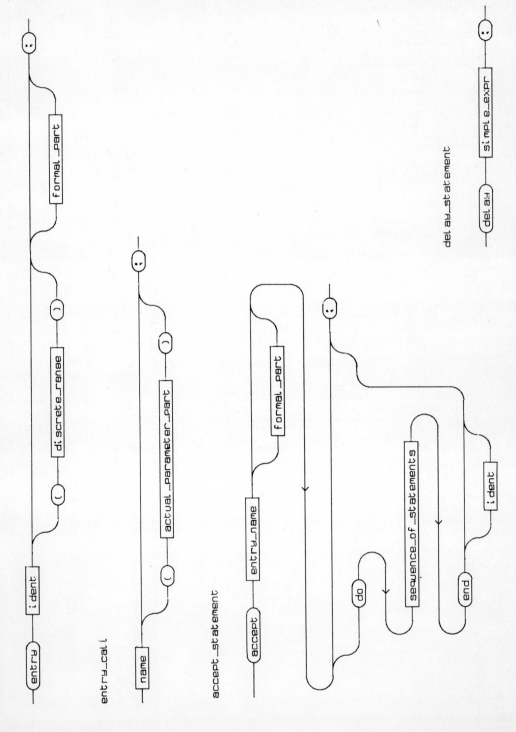

entry_declaration

entry_call

accept_statement

delay_statement

select_statement

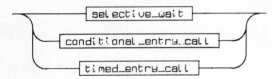

selective_wait

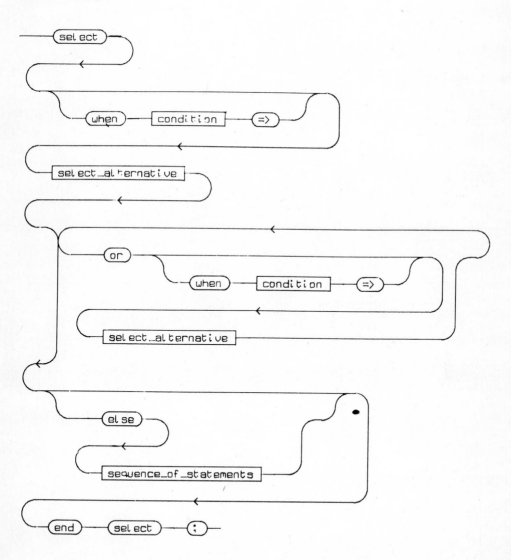

select_alternative

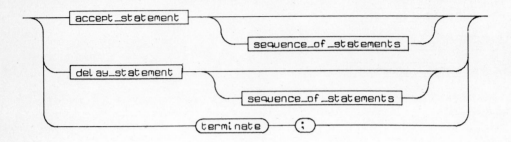

conditional_entry_call

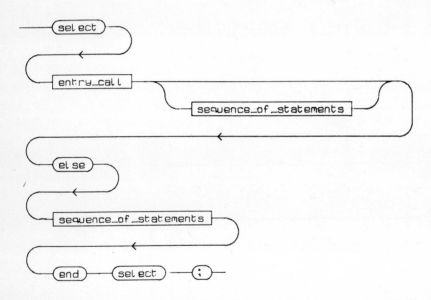

abort_statement

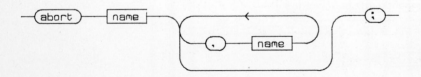

timed_entry_call

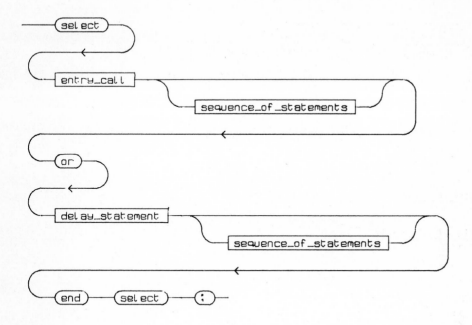

compilation

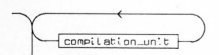

compilation_unit

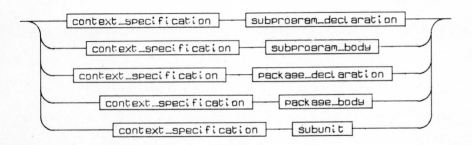

context_specification

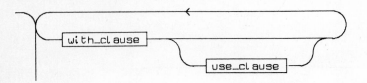

with_clause

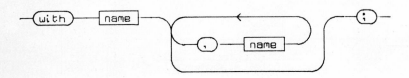

subunit

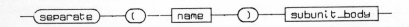

subunit_body

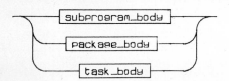

body_stub

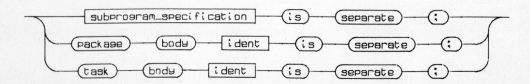

exception_choice

exception_declaration

exception_handler

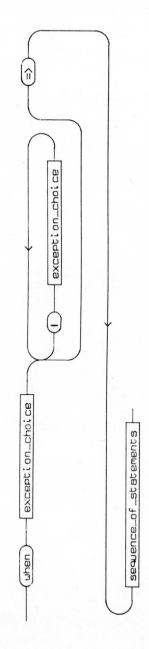

generic_subprogram_declaration

generic_package_declaration

raise_statement

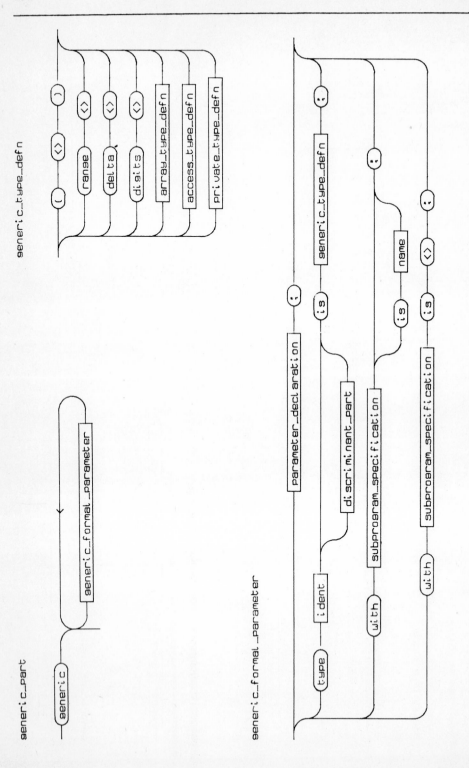

generic_type_defn

generic_part

generic_formal_parameter

generic_subprogram_instantiation

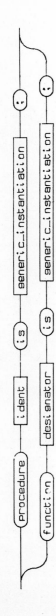

generic_package_instantiation

generic_instantiation

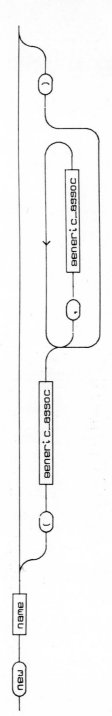

generic_assoc

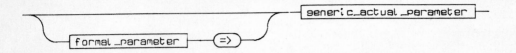

generic_actual_parameter

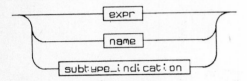

representation_specification

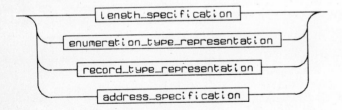

length_specification

enumeration_type_representation

record_type_representation

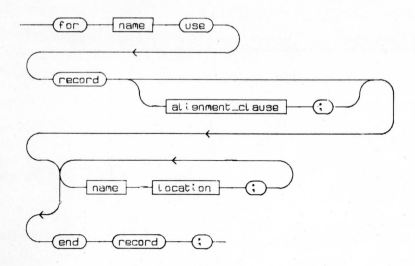

location

alignment_clause

address_specification

code_statement

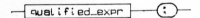

```
IN THE BYRON VAULT BELOW
    LIE THE REMAINS OF
       AUGUSTA ADA,
     ONLY DAUGHTER OF
   GEORGE GORDON NOEL,
      6TH LORD BYRON,
        AND WIFE OF
  WILLIAM EARL OF LOVELACE.

   BORN 10TH DEC  1815,
   DIED 27TH NOV  1852.

         R.I.P.
```

Inscription on a memorial tablet
in the parish church of Hucknall, England.
Courtesy of the rector, Canon D. Williams.